HAM

The Story of a Wiltshire Village

HAM

The Story of a Wiltshire Village

Robin Buchanan-Dunlop

PRIVATELY PRINTED

2011

First published in Great Britain in 2011 by

Robin Buchanan-Dunlop
Ham Greeen Cottage
Ham
Marlborough
Wiltshire SN8 3QR

A CIP catalogue record for this book is available
from the British Library

ISBN 978-0-9570510-0-3

Designed and typeset in Minion by Libanus Press, Marlborough
Printed and bound in Great Britain by MPG Biddles Limited

CONTENTS

Acknowledgements   6

Map of the Parish of Ham   7

1   Setting the Scene   9

2   Early Civilisation   12

3   The Saxon Charter of 931   20

4   Domesday Book   26

5   Beyond Domesday Book   31

6   The Land and its Dynastic Landowners   32

7   The Church in the Middle Ages   44

8   The Village and the Black Death   48

9   The Village in the 16th and 17th Centuries   57

10   The Reformation   60

11   The Civil War   62

12   The Village in the 18th Century   72

13   'Rule, Britannia!' and Hodge   90

14   Two World Wars   117

15   Sea Change   153

16   Coda   178

Illustration credits   181

Notes   182

Bibliography   186

Index   188

ACKNOWLEDGEMENTS

My first and very sincere thanks are due to Susie Eldridge whose idea it was to establish a Ham History Project. Without her initial inspiration and her constant encouragement this story would not have been written. My second thanks must be to the editors, past and present, of the *Victoria History* which contains in its history of Wiltshire a remarkably detailed account of Ham: it has been my lodestar. In foraging further I have spent a considerable time in the brilliant new premises of the Wiltshire and Swindon History Centre in Chippenham, and I owe a special debt of gratitude to its unfailingly helpful staff. My similar thanks are due to the Berkshire Record Office, the Hampshire Record Office and the National Monuments Record department of English Heritage in Swindon.

The oldest record relating to Ham is its Saxon boundary charter of 931 which is in the British Library. The central section in Old English defeated me until it was generously translated by Malcolm Godden, Professor of Anglo-Saxon at Oxford University. His translation now forms one of the keystones of Ham's story.

All researchers must dream of discovering a hitherto unknown source of material. In my case it was a suitcase of family papers about the Woodman family, which Polly Woodman, Henry Deacon Woodman's great-granddaughter, kindly allowed me to use. I am most grateful both to her and to Valerie Barker, Henry Deacon's granddaughter, for their help and permission to reproduce various photographs and documents.

Then there is a galaxy of current and former residents of Ham and its environs, who have helped me in various ways in writing this story, for which I shall always be grateful. They include Nicholas and Diana Baring, Jacki Barnwell, Pearl Best, Bill Bird, Andrew Blake, Gerald Boord, Belinda Coote, Mary Davenport, Charles Flower, Ron Forbes, Richard and Mary Gray, Anne Harris, Sue Hawley, the late Cecil Hoare and Ivy Hoare, Charlotte Lowsley-Williams, Michael Marriage, Andrew and Melanie Melsom, Doreen Miller, Michael and Richard Opperman, Tony Peace, Susie Philipps, Lilian Prateley, Norman Scutt, Melanie Shingles, Reg and Brenda Stevens, Robin Tubb and Quentin Webb.

Finally, I am indebted to Clive Priestley for his invaluable editorial assistance, to Anstace Gladstone for proof reading and to Michael Mitchell for his expert guidance in making this book publishable.

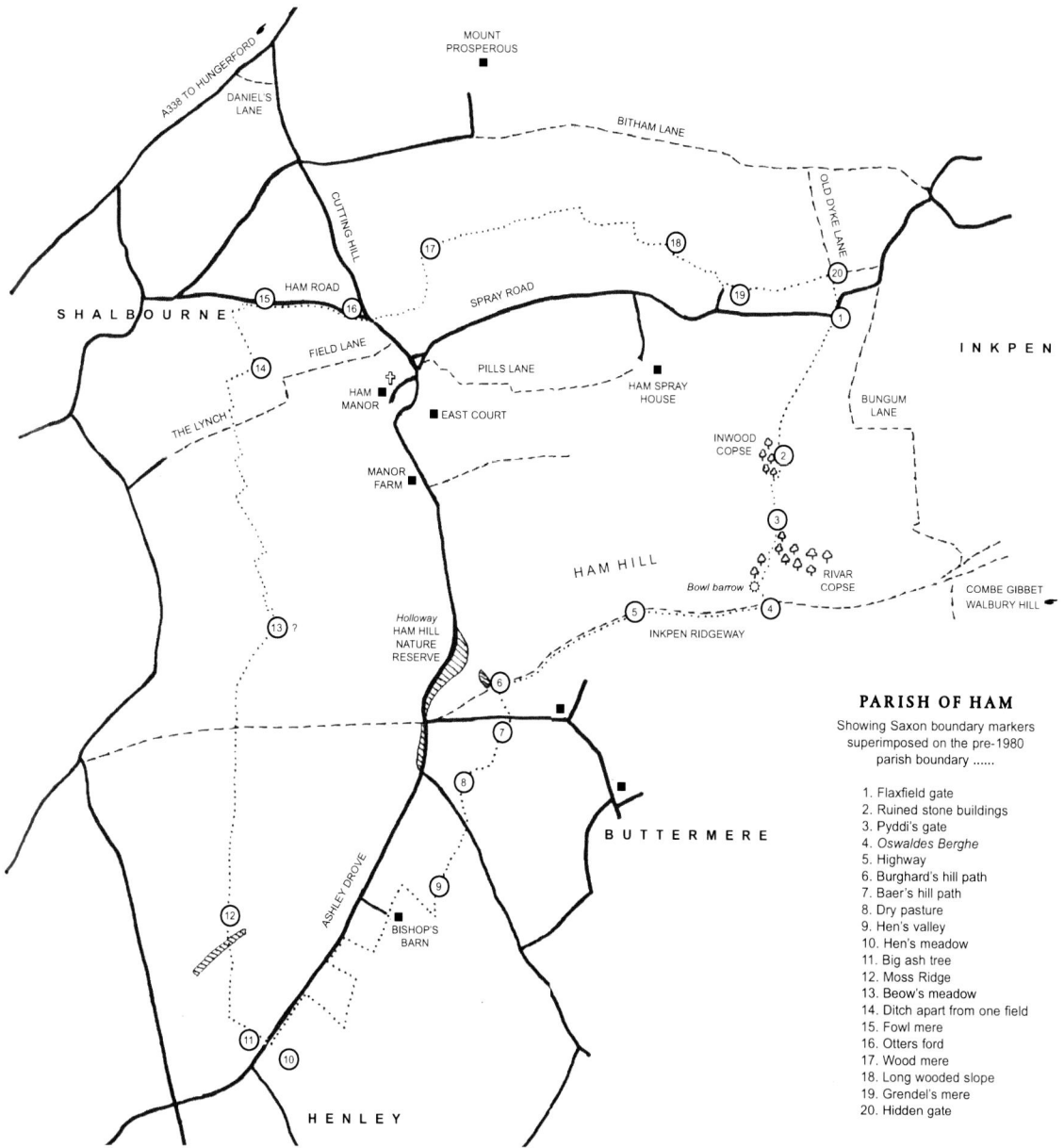

MOUNT PROSPEROUS

A338 TO HUNGERFORD

DANIEL'S LANE

BITHAM LANE

CUTTING HILL

OLD DYKE LANE

HAM ROAD

SPRAY ROAD

S H A L B O U R N E

I N K P E N

FIELD LANE

PILLS LANE

HAM SPRAY HOUSE

THE LYNCH

HAM MANOR

EAST COURT

BUNGUM LANE

MANOR FARM

INWOOD COPSE

HAM HILL

RIVAR COPSE

Bowl barrow

COMBE GIBBET WALBURY HILL

Holloway
HAM HILL NATURE RESERVE

INKPEN RIDGEWAY

B U T T E R M E R E

ASHLEY DROVE

BISHOP'S BARN

H E N L E Y

PARISH OF HAM

Showing Saxon boundary markers
superimposed on the pre-1980
parish boundary ......

1. Flaxfield gate
2. Ruined stone buildings
3. Pyddi's gate
4. *Oswaldes Berghe*
5. Highway
6. Burghard's hill path
7. Baer's hill path
8. Dry pasture
9. Hen's valley
10. Hen's meadow
11. Big ash tree
12. Moss Ridge
13. Beow's meadow
14. Ditch apart from one field
15. Fowl mere
16. Otters ford
17. Wood mere
18. Long wooded slope
19. Grendel's mere
20. Hidden gate

7

SETTING THE SCENE

*The pastures are clothed with flocks; the valleys also are
covered over with corn; they shout for joy, they also sing.*

Psalm 65

This is the story of a small Wiltshire village tucked away in a fold of the downs that has existed
for a thousand years. At the start of the previous millennium its population was probably not
more than 50. In succeeding centuries it never rose above 200, except for two surges of Victorian fecundity in the later part of the 19th century when it reached a peak of 255 in 1871 before
slipping back below 200 again. The story has several layers. Beyond the village is the land, the
manor or parish of Ham which King Æthelstan, the first king of all England, gave to his loyal
thane Wulfgar in 931. Binding village and land together are the men and women who worked
and fashioned the land, and over the centuries survived the vagaries of weather, plague,
economic fortune and war. It is also the story of the Church which after Wulfgar's death
owned the land until nearly the end of the next millennium, exerting a dominating influence
on the life of the village for much of that time.

The pattern of life in Ham changed in the 20th century. The land remained, but in the wake
of two world wars and advances in agricultural technology the farming community which had
been the heart of the village declined. In its place came a kaleidoscope of new arrivals, from
bankers to artists and writers. Amongst them were leading members of the Bloomsbury
Group, who between them made Ham their home for nearly four decades.

When the Ham Manor estate was sold in 1928, the sale brochure described Ham as an 'old-
world village'. Today the centre of the village still resonates with the echoes of earlier centuries.
It is not difficult to understand why. Around the village green stand a clutch of thatched
cottages and a public house, and then along a lane there is the manor house with on one side
an ancient church and on the other a former smithy. Between them these icons of rural life
conjure up an image of a typical West Country village through the ages. There were once
hundreds of such villages which together formed much of the warp and weft of England's
social history. As such Ham's story might be said to represent just another microcosm of

yeomanly southern England, but beneath the picture-postcard prettiness of the village and the beauty of the surrounding countryside lies a deeper, almost hidden history. Long centuries ago, at some time in the Dark Ages, the architects of Wansdyke – the 50-mile linear defensive earthwork arcing across the north of Wessex – selected the foot of Ham Hill as its eastern extremity and fulcrum. Later, the same accident of geography, the defile created by the Inkpen Beacon–Ham Hill escarpment, meant that throughout its earlier centuries the manor of Ham would lie close to the principal gateway to Wessex. So dig below the surface of Ham's story and much of the history of England suddenly unfolds. What part Ham played in that history must be mainly conjecture, but great events undoubtedly swirled around the manor throughout the centuries, and it is difficult to believe that they did not touch it, if only in some minor glancing way. And as if entwined with each other like a double helix, it is this rich sweep of the wider history of England which serves both to illuminate and to define Ham's own story.

Invasion, or the threat of invasion, has been a constant feature of England's history, and the scars of many of those events are still visible in the countryside surrounding Ham. Back in the early mists of time the Celts came and built great earthworks. Later the Romans came and then left, leaving behind the legacy of a remarkable network of roads. On their heels came the Saxons, possible builders of Wansdyke. The Danes then came and penetrated deep into Wessex before being forced back again by Alfred the Great. In 1066 the Normans, the last of the invaders, came and stayed, putting their stamp on the English way of life.

Five hundred years after the Norman Conquest the Spanish Armada sailed up the Channel, and perhaps a signal fire to warn of invasion was prepared on the escarpment above Ham to link up with the beacons on the south coast. Two centuries later Napoleon Bonaparte threatened Britain and men of Ham rallied to the colours. In 1940, Operation Sealion, Hitler's planned invasion of Britain, never reached fruition and the bells of All Saints' Church remained silent.[1] Men of Ham once again served in the armed forces and in the Home Guard. The dead from that war are remembered on the memorial in the church, and reminders of the threat of invasion can be seen in the pillboxes astride the Kennet and Avon Canal on the edge of Hungerford Common and elsewhere.

The threat of Soviet aggression during the Cold War that followed and lasted for most of the second half of the 20th century, though real enough, appeared sufficiently remote to most of the population of Britain who largely chose to ignore it, and it is doubtful whether any household in Ham kept a cache of tinned food, or a bucket of whitewash for painting on windowpanes, to ward against a nuclear attack. Events proved them right, but on the outskirts of Great Bedwyn there is a small underground bunker, its entrance now partly obscured by brambles. Until the dismantling of the Berlin Wall in 1989 and the subsequent break-up of the Warsaw Pact, it would have been manned by members of the Royal Observer Corps[2] in time of war to monitor the effects of chemical and nuclear missile strikes. It was one of a skein of such sites that covered the whole country, and its sphere of interest would have included Ham. Probably most if not all of Ham's inhabitants were blissfully ignorant of its existence, which is why it is easy to appreciate how such fragments of history can even in modern times drift into the twilight world between fact and folklore. This is a phenomenon that becomes increasingly dominant in the march back through time, and Ham seems to have more than its fair share of mysteries, riddles and lacunae in its past. But that merely adds to the fascination of its story.

2

EARLY CIVILISATION

Warner & Marten's *The Groundwork of British History*, that former bible of the schoolroom history lesson, begins with the sentence: 'The invasions of Julius Caesar are generally taken as a suitable point from which to begin the history of our land ....' It is doubtful whether Ham existed in any sense as a village in the Roman settlement that eventually followed, yet its history starts much earlier than that because long before there was a village as such men and women worked the surrounding land, and it was this land which in due course became the *raison d'être* for the village. Well over a million years ago the last of the Great Ice Ages began to sculpt and scour the terrain, creating the bones of the landscape of today. In the Vale of Ham this scouring breached the chalk uplands exposing the Upper Greensand, a distinction it shares with the wider Vale of Pewsey. Later vast stretches of woodland covered much of England, and later still Bronze Age man started the backbreaking task of clearing the woodlands for agriculture. He was no slouch and in time introduced spelt, an early form of wheat, and a hardy form of barley. As long ago as the 6th century BC the Greek writer Hecabeus noted that the people of Britain reaped two harvests in a single year. Before that a tall fair-skinned race had begun migrating northwards through Europe from the Upper Danube. They were the Celts and the first of them probably arrived in Britain in the 7th century BC. There seems to have been no specific military invasion as such. Instead colonisation based largely on trade was a gradual process over centuries, until by the 1st century BC Celtic culture was firmly established throughout Britain. The Celts brought with them the Iron Age.

Both Bronze Age man and the Celts possessed a shrewd awareness of the terrain. Although hillforts are usually associated with the Iron Age, long before the arrival of the Celts in any number Bronze Age Britons had identified dominating hills as natural focal points for tribal structure and religious rites. The hillforts they constructed as a result were not necessarily occupied. They were rallying points and symbols of power to create awe in the tribes around them. Bronze Age Britons must have roamed the steep escarpment above Ham, but the hillfort on Walbury Hill, just east of the parish boundary and the highest point on the North Wessex Downs, appears to be from the Iron Age and was possibly built around 600 BC. The bowl-barrow, formerly known as *Oswaldes Berghe*, at the eastern edge of the parish boundary, also comes from the Iron Age.[3] It is still visible just inside the southern edge of Rivar Copse. The two primary cremation burials found in it are characteristic of Gaulish burial rites, which ties in with the theory that the Celts who colonised Britain came from the sub-division known as the Belgae. There was another bowl-barrow on Further Down, the field flanked by the Buttermere and Vernham Dean roads on the parish's southern boundary, but it has been ploughed over and no trace of it now exists. However, other earthworks from the Iron Age period are still clearly visible on Ham Hill. One is just a shallow ditch slashed like a huge appendectomy scar across the flank of the field below the ridgeway and beside the footpath leading up from the Fosbury road. Another earthwork on the south-west parish boundary once apparently linked up with a ditch which ran north-east from Collingbourne Kingston.[4] Beside the crest of the Fosbury road as it breasts Ham Hill is a very prominent ditch, which man and weather subsequently developed into a holloway or sunken road, its steep ravine-like sides now forming the site of the Ham Hill nature reserve.

The exact purposes of these earthworks are not known, but these remarkable feats of engineering and manpower, the remnants of some grand design, are evidence of an active and well-organised civilisation, and one able to deploy a surprising amount of manpower. They are also evidence that Ham was once populated by the Celts, if only for the time it took to construct these earthworks.

Despite the elaborate fortifications of the Celts, when the Romans eventually came the hill-forts were swept aside with comparative ease. Julius Caesar's expeditions to England in 55 and 54 BC were little more than reconnaissances in force, and it was not until a century later in 43 AD that Claudius embarked on the real Roman conquest of Britain. By this time the population of England was divided into specific tribal groups, and the tribe which Claudius's legions would have encountered in Wiltshire was the Atrebates. There was no cohesion between the various tribes and this made the Roman subjugation of the country easier. The Atrebates quickly made their peace with the Romans, and the area escaped the various revolts against the Roman occupation which took place elsewhere.

To consolidate their conquests the Romans built an astonishing network of roads. They ran straight for miles and miles, only occasionally jinking round defiles, and were built with a paved and raised central section termed an *agger*. No Roman roads went through Ham but there were a number of roads within a few miles. The main Roman western trunk road from London forked at Silchester. One branch headed north-west through the Roman station at Speen (Spinae) near Newbury – when the road became known as Ermin Street – and then onwards to the legionary fortress at Gloucester. Beyond Speen it forked again, the westward branch running slightly north of the line of the A4 and passing through Mildenhall (Cunetio), another Roman station, to Bath. This was probably one of the earliest Roman roads built. Much later, in the Middle Ages, the road running along the same line of the A4 would become the most travelled road in England.

Another road advanced north from the Channel ports and then Winchester, passing close

to Tidcombe and on through Marten and Wilton to Mildenhall. It continued north until join-
ing Ermin Street at Wanborough. When the Saxons came they called these paved roads a *stræt*
or *streat* – the derivation of Ermin Street and other Roman roads where the word street has
been tacked onto the name. Unmade roads were called a *weg* or way, a description which
survives today in the byways and bridleways which criss-cross the countryside around Ham.
The *wegs* followed routes of ancient origin and where possible stuck to the uplands to avoid
damp low-lying clays which became impassable in winter.

The only known Roman site in the parish is that of a villa beside Inwood Copse on the eastern parish boundary, where possible Roman foundations are recorded. The site is listed in the
Victoria History where it is given a six-figure map reference.[5]   This would seem to imply solid
enough evidence, but in fact the attribution is based largely on clever academic detective work.
There is a reference to *Stan Ceastla* as a boundary marker for the manor of Ham in a Saxon charter of 931. Literally *Stan Ceastla* means stone buildings or stone castle in Old English. However,
Ceastla is derived from the Latin *castellum* meaning a small enclosure such as the walls around a
villa, and as the term appears in a number of Anglo-Saxon boundary charters it has been taken
to infer evidence of the ruins of a Roman villa. The map reference was initially arrived at by
dead reckoning from the positions of the adjacent boundary markers, but it is supported
by the information in the following footnote to an article in the *Archaeological Journal* of 1919:
'Mr O. G. S. Crawford of the Ordnance Survey has told me (the writer of the article) that the
farmer of this land turns up the remains of wall foundations at this point'.[6] Exactly when this
conversation took place, and who the farmer at Ham Spray was at that time, are not recorded.
There is now no visible sign of any remains in the area of the map reference, which is not
surprising as the ground must have been ploughed over almost annually since 1919. Fortunately, from crop shadows appearing on aerial photographs, it is possible to pinpoint the site
as a slight rise in the field known as Bunjum some 40 metres east of the southern tip of Inwood
Copse.[7] Using modern mapping this arguably places the villa just inside the parish of Inkpen in
Berkshire rather than on the parish boundary, but officially it is recorded as a Ham site.

At first sight this seems an odd place to build an isolated villa, apparently in the middle of
nowhere. There were, however, once hundreds of Roman villas similarly dotted about south-
ern England. Usually they were built within reasonable distance of a Roman road and near a
stream, as is the case in this instance; as well as the Roman roads to the north and west, Spray
Road a few hundred metres from the site is an ancient road probably of pre-Roman origin.
Other known Roman sites in the area include a bathhouse at Kintbury and villas at Castle
Copse in Great Bedwyn and at Littlecote. When the subsoil of the field to the east of Bungum
Lane, the eastern boundary of the field in which the site of the villa lies, was ploughed in the
1970s, shards of pottery and tiles were thrown up. This site has never been properly investi-
gated or recorded, but the earthenware fragments thrown up pose the question as to whether

there may have been other Roman buildings in the vicinity. However, Bungum is a corruption of *beaux gentilshommes*, a reference to the Knights Templar who were active in the Inkpen area, and the finds may therefore relate to this much later era. Another possible pointer to other buildings in the area is a field known as Upper Blacklands, which abuts on to the south side of Pills Lane midway between the village and Ham Spray. Blacklands is a common field name elsewhere and often denotes the site of former ancient buildings, but in Ham's case there is no record or local folklore to lend any substance to this connotation.

Many of the Roman villas were owned by native Romano-British aristocrats. Celtic Britons liked to keep up with the latest fashions and quickly copied the Roman lifestyle in matters of housing and dress. Latin was also adopted as the accepted language for business. So it is possible to imagine an early resident of the Ham countryside, having made a tidy fortune from grain or wool, then building a villa to put himself about a bit. What happened to the villa or its proud owner remains a mystery. That the villa should have been in ruins by the time of the charter is not remarkable, as even though it may well have had a later life as an early Saxon dwelling, at least 500 years would have elapsed since it was built.

By the end of the 3rd century the Roman administrative genius Diocletian had stamped his

Oswaldes Berghe: Iron Age bowl-barrow on the southern edge of Rivar Copse, Ham Hill (an elder bush is growing out of the central bowl)

Iron Age earthwork later developed into a holloway; it now forms part of the Ham Hill nature reserve

authority on Britain and divided it into four provinces. What became Wessex was part of the province known as Britannia Prima with its capital at Cirencester, but a little over a century later the Roman system of local government began to unravel. In 410 the Romans left Britain. It was a deliberate move. The barbarians were at the gates of Rome and even before 410 the legions had begun to be withdrawn. Hot on the heels of the Roman withdrawal came the Saxon invasion, and in 443 the Britons were appealing to Rome for help, but none came. The Saxon invasion was another gradual affair, and it was not until the end of the 5th century that the expansion of the Anglo-Saxon settlements reached Wiltshire. Britain was now entering the Dark Ages, an era from which few extensive written records survive giving it an aura of brooding mystery. Civilisation continued although by then the Roman way of life had disappeared, and even the great network of roads was disintegrating. The Saxons had little use for the roads as a strategic device and except for stretches they quickly fell into disrepair. Meanwhile the even older Celtic Britain was being absorbed by the new Anglo-Saxon order.

Now comes one of the great historical enigmas for Ham: who built Wansdyke and when, and where did it end. All that is known is that this defensive ditch was built in two sections, a western section which began west of Bath, and then an eastern section, and that the two sections were not necessarily contemporaneous. Some modern historians hold that the eastern section ended in what now remains of Savernake Forest. However, the earthworks running south across the Salisbury Road and along Daniel's Lane, then across the Hungerford road leading to Ham and over the field to Mount Prosperous – the course can be traced on Ordnance Survey maps – and finally running south again along Old Dyke Lane on the parish boundary to Spray Road, all seem to provide firm evidence that Wansdyke continued to the Ham Hill escarpment. Certainly this makes strategic sense, and crop shadows in aerial photographs show the line of Old Dyke Lane continuing for some 300 metres south of Spray Road. At the same time there is doubt about exactly where the ditch finally ended, because the shadows appear to peter out 500 metres short of the escarpment. It has been suggested that as the water table was much higher in Saxon times, the land at the foot of Ham Hill was a marsh and as a result the dyke did not need to extend the whole way to the escarpment. There are arguments for and against this. The woodlands either side of Spray Road at that point are even today notoriously boggy when heavy forestry work is attempted, and during the Second World War drillings above the site of the nature reserve on Ham Hill revealed a deep and substantial aquifer below the hill. In addition, the centre of the village is today still prone to flooding in wet weather, so it is quite possible that a much wider area immediately below Ham Hill was once marshy. On the other hand, the Saxon charter makes no mention of a marsh as such, and after a shallow valley the ground slopes upwards to Ham Hill. It also seems unlikely that a Roman villa would have been built with a marsh between the villa and Spray Road. An even more potent argument against the theory is the naming in the Saxon charter of Pyddi's Gate, which was sited somewhere at or near the foot of Ham Hill. While the specific purpose of Pyddi's Gate is not recorded, its name suggests that it was a gate or gap in the final stretch of Wansdyke which ran all the way to the scarp; it is believed that there was a series of gates or gaps in the dyke at regular intervals along its whole length.

When and why Wansdyke was built are equally problematical. One popular theory is that the Saxons built the dyke as a defensive fortification against the Danes. Wansdyke faces north which lends a veneer of support to this, but it can be quickly dismissed. Wansdyke is a corruption of Wodin's Dyke, and it is evident that the Saxons named it after one of their pagan gods from whom Wednesday (*Wodnesdaeg*) also takes its name. The cult of Wodin or Odin, the Norse god of heaven and earth, was widespread in pre-Christian Saxon England and the high ground above the Vale of Pewsey was a centre for its worship. Christianity reached Britain in the 3rd century and was widespread in Wessex by 630; according to *The Anglo-Saxon Chronicle*, Cynegilis who succeeded to the kingdom of Wessex in about 560 was the first king of Wessex to be baptised. So the dyke would have been built before then, and the Danes did not invade Wessex until the 9th century. Accordingly it must have been a defensive bastion against a much earlier threat. The kingdom of Mercia to the north is one possibility. Another plausible

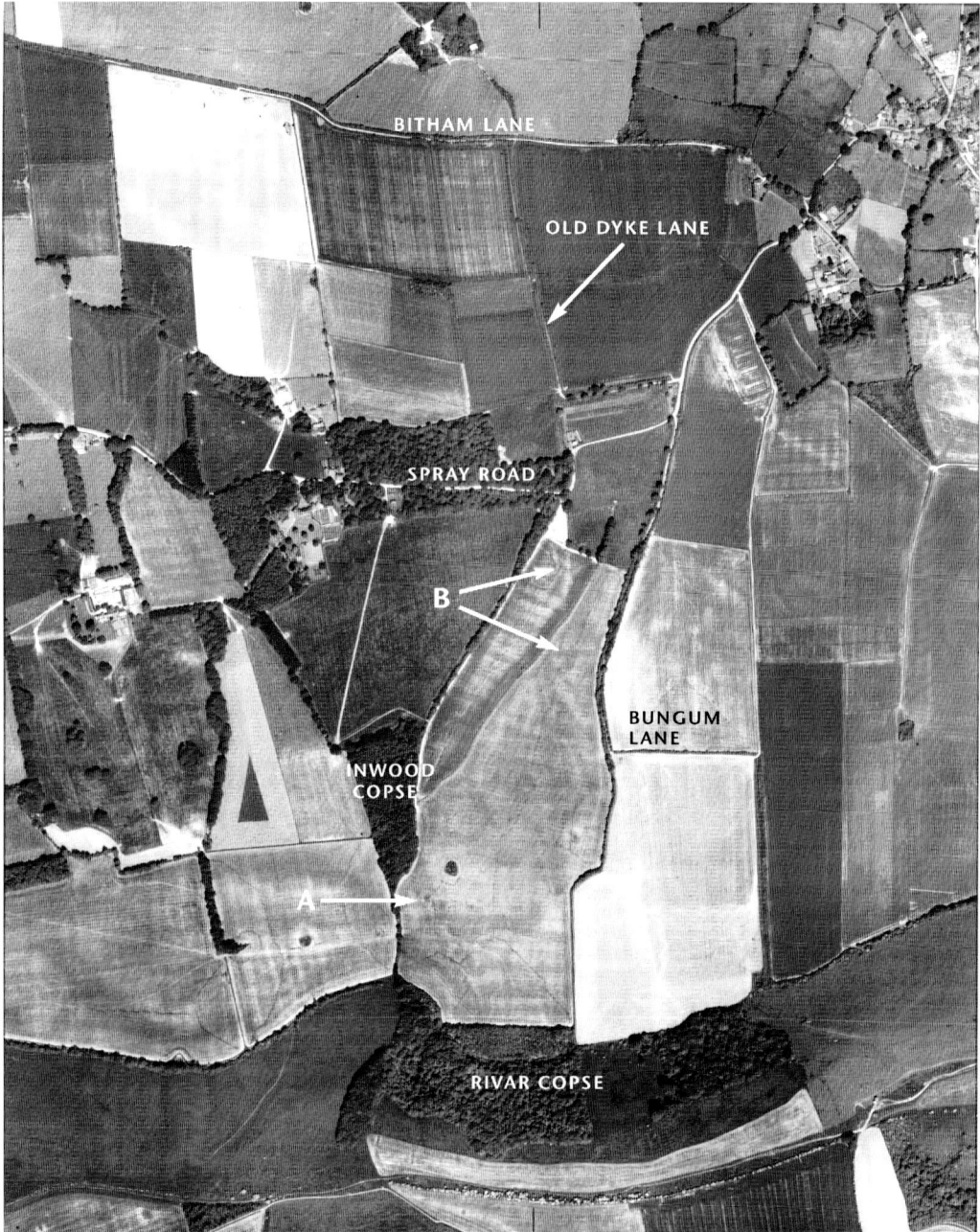

Aerial photograph June 1967. The crop shadows reveal, A: the site of a Roman villa, and B: the continuation of Wansdyke south of Spray Road

theory is that the dyke was built as a barrier against the invading Saxons by the Britons in the late 5th century or early 6th century, and was subsequently named Wodin's Dyke by the Saxons. Frustratingly *The Anglo-Saxon Chronicle* makes no reference to it, and so Wansdyke remains one of the enigmas of the Dark Ages.

The Danes came in force in the second half of the 9th century. In 871 having conquered the north and east of England, they advanced into Wessex and won battles at Marden, near Devizes, in which Ethelred was killed, and at Wilton, near Salisbury. Eventually Alfred, who had succeeded his elder brother Ethelred as king of Wessex, drove them out following the Battle of Ethandun, again near Devizes, in 878. Whether Ham had reached the status of a village by then seems doubtful, but men from the area would have been called up to fight in Alfred's *fyrds*. For the next 20 years the Danes continued to occupy the north and east of England but were content to leave the Saxons to control Wessex – the country of the West Saxons. The Danes then left, ushering in what has been termed the Golden Age of the Saxons, before returning almost a century later. Even at that point, with the Danish King Canute on the throne of England, Wessex was effectively governed by Godwin, a Saxon earl. Danish rule ended again in 1042, and in 1066 came the Norman Conquest.

3

THE SAXON CHARTER OF 931

To Beowulf was granted
Triumph in that fight; but to Grendel the flight;
In distress to death by the looming marshlands,
To his joyless home.

Beowulf (verse translation by Edwin Morgan, 1952)

It is impossible to pinpoint the origin of Ham as a village. Domesday Book suggests that it existed as a settlement of some 50 souls in the reign of Edward the Confessor who ruled from 1042–1066. There is, however, a specific reference to Ham a century earlier in a Saxon charter signed at a *Witangemot*, or council, at Luton on 12 November 931.[8] The charter records the granting of land at Ham to the ealdorman Wulfgar by King Æthelstan. There seems to have been no particular reason why Luton was chosen as the site for this *Witangemot*. It was then a town of several hundred people on the banks of the River Lea from which it would take its name. There were 101 signatories to the charter, including two archbishops and 17 bishops as well as Æthelstan and Wulfgar, and assuming each dignitary came with his own retinue the inhabitants of Luton must have felt that this particular act of royal patronage was a two-edged sword. An ambitious opportunist, Æthelstan strides through the annals of *The Anglo-Saxon Chronicle* with consummate panache and determination, and he would have brooked no dissent from the citizens of Luton. He was a grandson of Alfred the Great and ruled from 924–939 having succeeded his father, Edward the Elder, as king of Wessex. His aunt was married to the king of Mercia, and following the king's death he became king of Mercia too. He then married one of his sisters to the Viking king of Northumbria, and when the king died the following year Æthelstan invaded Northumbria and secured its throne. Having obtained recognition of his supremacy from the king of the Scots and the various Welsh kings, by the time of the signing of the Ham charter in 931 he 'governed all the kings that were in this island',[9] and he is named in the charter as *rex Anglorum*.

Six years after the signing of the charter Æthelstan defeated the king of Dublin and the king of the Picts and Scots at the battle of Brunanburh. In an heroic poem commemorating this feat of arms he is described as 'the King, ruler of earls and ring-giver to men',[10] and it is as a ring-giver – in this case the giving of land to his liegeman Wulfgar – that he touches Ham's story. Besides being an ealdorman or shire officer, Wulfgar, whose name meant 'wolf spear', was a *thegn* or thane. In principle a thane was a landowner who owed a fealty to a superior lord. As a royal thane Wulfgar was a nobleman in the upper echelons of this rank and owed an allegiance to fight for his king in war in return for a grant of lands. He lived in Inkpen and held land both there and at Buttermere, Denford, and Collingbourne, as well as the nine *cassati* (hides) he was granted at Ham. Today thanes might have slipped from the public consciousness were it not for Shakespeare's *Macbeth*. Shakespeare happily mixed fact with fiction, and although Macbeth existed as a king of Scotland and was killed in battle in 1057, he was never thane of Glamis or thane of Cawdor as Shakespeare dubbed him; thanes are not recorded in Scotland until the 12th century. By then thanes in England had disappeared with the Norman Conquest and its subsequent social upheaval.

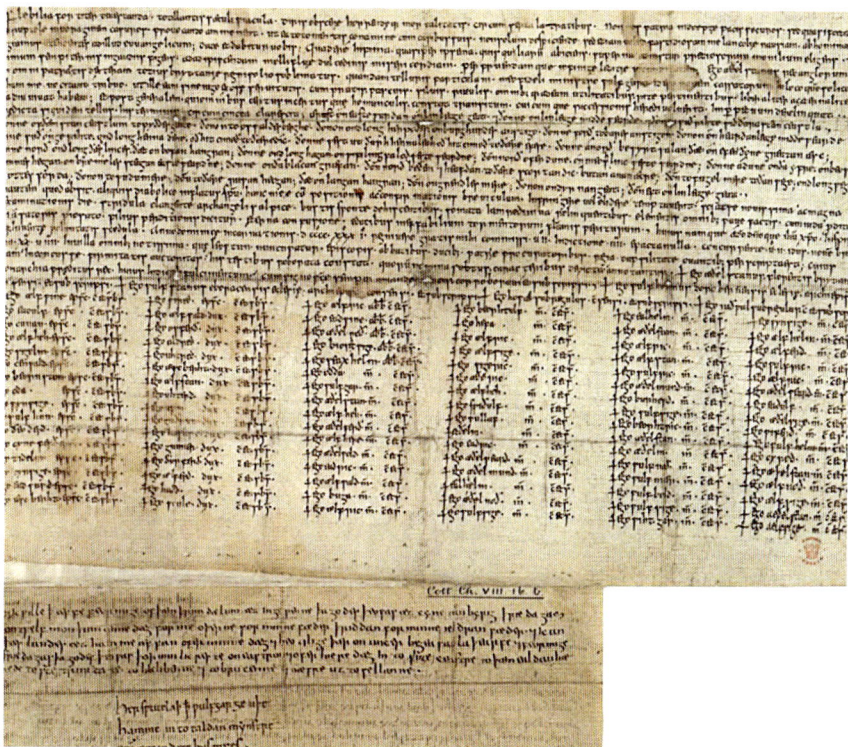

Saxon boundary charter of 931. The attachment at the bottom is Wulfgar's will leaving the manor of Ham to his wife Æffe and then to the church

The charter is written in medieval Latin but with the central section outlining the boundaries of Ham in Old English.[11] The clerks who drafted Æthelstan's charters were renowned for using a highly artificial language, and the clerk responsible for Ham's charter is known from his individual style as 'Æthelstan A'. As a result, boundary charters of this period are particularly notorious for their impenetrable language and the use of esoteric names for terrain features. Fortunately, Malcolm Godden, Professor of Anglo-Saxon at Oxford University, has circumvented these difficulties, and although the charter is essentially a legal document his translation below conjures up a marvellously vivid and almost lyrical picture of the country-side around Ham over a thousand years ago:

> Starting at the eastern end at the flaxfield gap/gate; then to the centre of the flaxfield; then south to the (ruined) stone buildings, then on from the stone buildings to the gap/gate of Pyddi, then on to Oswald's Hill, then along the highway to Burghard's hill path, and then on to Baer's hill path; then to the middle of the dry pasture, and then south and directly along the hens' valley, until it comes to the ditch/dike, then west out through the hens' meadow, until it comes to the edge/border, then keeping north along the wooded bank that is beside the big ash-tree; then north along the ridge/hill that is above the hanger. Then along the hedge to the west side of the fold/enclosure; then north over the hill to the west side of the moss-ridge; then down the slope to the hedge/enclosure of Beow's meadow to the east of the bramble wood; then to the dark thicket, then north along the heading to the short ditch/dike, apart from one field; from there to the Fowlmere as far as the road; along the road to the Ottersford(?); from there to Woodmere; then to the rough(?) hedge; then to the long wooded slope; then to Grendel's mere (or the gravelly lake); then to the hidden gap; then back to the flaxfield gap/gate.

The boundaries of the parish have remained largely unaltered since this charter, the only significant change being the extension of the boundary in the north-west corner in 1980 to reach up beyond Ham Road to Cutting Hill and Prosperous Road. So it is still possible to follow most of the original boundary markers across the countryside of today.

Starting at the eastern end at the flaxfield gap/gate: The charter's delineation of the boundaries begins where Spray Road intersects with what would have been a continuation of Old Dyke Lane, the surviving tail-end of Wansdyke, and then travels clockwise. Curiously Wansdyke is not mentioned despite a short stretch of the ditch forming part of the boundary. However, the eastern end of Wansdyke may have become substantially disintegrated by then, or more likely as various gates or gaps are mentioned as markers, the drafters of the charter considered that referring to Wansdyke itself was superfluous. The field adjacent to the parish boundary and immediately south of Spray Road, in the parish of Inkpen, is still called Flaxlea.

Then to the centre of the flaxfield; then south to the (ruined) stone buildings: The ruined stone build-ings are the remains of the Roman villa. *Then on from the stone buildings to the gap/gate of Pyddi:* Who or what Pyddi was is unknown, but the gap must have represented a prominent defile somewhere between the villa and the foot of the eastern flank of Ham Hill some 250 metres away. The angle of incline at the bottom of the escarpment at this point – the tip of the wood now known locally as the Bull's Tail – is very steep, about 65 degrees, which suggests that the gap was there. This could have been the final 'gate' in the tail-end of Wansdyke. The name of Pyddi has survived today in Pidget's Field, and in the 19th century the southern end of Inwood Copse was then known as Pidget Coppice and a small field immediately south of it was called Pidget Corner.

Oswaldes Berghe, or Oswald's Hill, refers to the prominent buttress on the eastern flank of Ham Hill with Rivar Copse on its northern face. The summit of the buttress is intersected by the ridgeway or highway which is the continuation of the boundary. However, the actual boundary marker is held to be the Celtic bowl-barrow some 50 metres below the summit. A mound or barrow is one of the translations of *berghe* and barrows were a common feature as markers in Saxon boundary charters. Today, half-hidden by brambles, nettles and elder on the edge of woodland, the bowl-barrow is barely recognisable, but 1,000 years ago it may well have been a much more prominent feature although by then already some 1,500 years old. Despite the apparent incongruity, the bowl-barrow was possibly named after Saint Oswald who was a 7th century king of Northumbria and overlord of much of Britain except for Mercia whose king, Penda, he was fighting when he was killed at the battle of Maserfeld in 642. Oswald would have been well known in Wessex folklore as he married the daughter of King Cynegilis of Wessex and stood as sponsor when Cynegilis was baptised. Whether or not this connection is correct, there is now no trace of Oswald as a local Ham place name.

Then along the highway to Burghard's hill path: The boundary then heads along the *herepath* or highway on the Ham Hill scarp, which was an ancient path and drove road long before the Saxons came, until it strikes Burghard's hill path. Burghard was a fairly common Saxon name and there may be a link with a 9th century ealdorman of that name. The hill path would have come from a northerly direction, but would have run slightly to the east of the current Ham-Fosbury road and may well have followed the line of the current footpath which runs up Ham Hill tangential to the nature reserve. *And then on to Baer's hill path:* This hill path is probably called after Baer, another Saxon name, although it could also be translated as the 'boar's path'. Its route would have run across the field west of Town Farm in Buttermere; there are several tracks running across this field on earlier Ordnance Survey maps.

Then to the middle of the dry pasture, and then south and directly along the hens' valley, until it comes to the ditch/dike, then west out through the hens' meadow until it comes to the border/edge: The dry pasture lies somewhere on the parish boundary at the head of the valley. It may well be the field now known as Further Down, where the soil would have contrasted with what would have been the much wetter fields at the foot of Ham Hill. Hens' valley runs along the parish southern boundary, and hens' meadow (*henna leah*) in due course gave its name to the village of Henley. Hens' meadow marks the south-west corner of the parish before the boundary turns north, and the border may refer to the edge of the wood forming part of the wooded bank.   *Then keeping north along the wooded bank that is beside the big ash-tree; then north along the ridge/hill that is above the hanger:* Lone prominent trees feature frequently as boundary markers in Saxon charters, and here the big ash-tree has given its name to Ashley Drove, the stretch of the Fosbury road leading south from the summit of Ham Hill, and to Lower Ashley Field and Ashley Coppice on the south-west boundary.

Then along the hedge to the west side of the fold/enclosure; then north over the hill to the west side of the moss-ridge; then down the slope to the hedge/enclosure of Beow's meadow to the east of the bramble wood: It is difficult to locate exactly where these various markers are today on the boundary as it swings 'north over the hill' – Rivar Hill – and 'down the slope'. The moss-ridge may refer to the Celtic earthwork which runs across the parish boundary at the southern end of Ashley Coppice. Beow's (short for Beowulf's) meadow would seem to be midway on the western edge of Great Field, where the fields now known as Manor Farm North and Manor Farm South join.

Then to the dark thicket, then north along the heading to the short ditch/dike, apart from one field; from there to Fowlmere as far as the road: It is possible to pick up the trail again at this point as 'the short ditch/dike, apart from one field' appears to be where a Shalbourne field juts into the Ham boundary just short of the old north-west corner of the parish,[12] the corner itself being marked by Fowlmere. In the 1839 enclosure map the fields in that corner are called Lashmoor, a corruption of the Old English *lacu*, a stream, and *mor*, a swamp or moor, so it was evidently a boggy patch. As a thousand years ago the water table was higher than it is now, the various meres or pools mentioned in the charter would have been distinctive features then and were probably linked by a stream.

Along the road to the Ottersford (?); from there to Woodmere: The boundary now heads east along the Ham Road from Shalbourne. A number of sources suggest that the early connecting track between the two villages was along Field Lane and the Lynch – a lynchet being a ridge formed by ploughing on a slope. However, the charter makes clear that Ham Road was also an established Saxon *weg*, part of the ancient way which later becomes Spray Road. The exact location of the Ottersford –or perhaps Ott's ford – is difficult to determine, but possibly it was at the dip in the road which is prone to flooding by Littlefield Cottage. Further on, Woodmere may have been where the footpath to Prosperous crosses the belt of trees in the valley where it also floods in winter and there is a man-made pond.

Then to the rough(?) hedge; then to the long wooded slope; then to Grendel's mere (or the gravelly lake); then to the hidden gap ; then back to the flaxfield gap/gate: The last pool is Grendel's mere. Although there is a field known as Pool Meadow which lies north of the Spray Road, roughly opposite Acorn Cottages and touching the parish boundary, the most likely site for this pool is Lower Spray where there is still a pond. This ties in with the reference to the long wooded slope preceding it to the west, and it is a comparatively short distance to the hidden gap which may have been where Old Dyke Lane now ends with a sharp right-angle turn to the east. Grendel is the monster in the epic Saxon poem *Beowulf* which was probably composed in the 7th or 8th

Cast-iron county boundary marker between Berkshire and Wiltshire on Spray Road. It also marks the site of the Flaxfield gate or gap in Wansdyke

century. It tells the story of how Beowulf, a leader of the Geats, a Swedish tribe, travels to Denmark to rid the king of the Danes and ruler of the Scyldings of Grendel whom he mortally wounds in single combat. Professor Godden comments that it is tempting to make a connection here with Beow's meadow, but the more prosaic translation may simply be 'gravelly lake'.[13] None of the surviving 19th century names of fields or woods in the vicinity sheds any light on which translation might be correct. A lease of land at Prosperous Farm in 1649 mentions a parcel of mixed ground of three acres called Grindells, but its location is not specified and the name has not survived. Another seductive clue is that on arrival in Denmark Beowulf is greeted by Wulfgar, a warrior and a prince of the Vandals, who ushers him in to the presence of Hrothgar, king of the Danes, but this has to be regarded as merely a literary coincidence.

On his death, by a will which survives as an endorsement to the Saxon charter of 931, Wulfgar left his estate to his wife Æffe for life and then to the Old Minster, Winchester. The land at Ham was evidently worked at that time but it does not necessarily mean that a village as such existed there. Nevertheless, from Domesday Book it is clear that a small hamlet was flourishing a century later, and it is from that point that the real history of the village starts to emerge.

4

DOMESDAY BOOK

Domesday Book is an extraordinary document, both in its scope as a national survey and for the wealth of information hidden behind the superficially terse entry for each manor. It was commissioned by King William at Christmas 1085 at his court in Gloucester, and the survey was carried out between 1086–7. However, it is not a precise snapshot of the country at that date. Although an army of commissioners was set to work to interview an even greater army of witnesses, Saxon records already existed and the findings of the survey are to a large extent based on those. Accordingly, in most cases Domesday entries begin with the acronym TRE, which stands for *Temporis Regis Edwardi*: in the time of King Edward. The snapshot, if it can be called that, is therefore mostly of a time at least 20 years earlier than the date of the survey. Often viewed as an early census of the population, Domesday Book is essentially a tax-roll. William wanted to know who owned what and the taxable value of that land, and as a result how much his kingdom was worth. Tax in the form of *geld* or *danegeld* had been exacted in Saxon times, although intermittently. It had ceased all together prior to the Norman Conquest, but William had reimposed it and at an apparently stiff rate. Accordingly, the questions in the survey – and there were probably about 18 of them – were all slanted towards finding the answers to the final two crucial questions: what was each manor (estate) worth in King Edward's time, and what was it worth in 1086–7.

Domesday Book is couched in a mixture of Old English, Medieval Latin and Norman French. A translation of the entry for Ham reads:

> The same bishop holds HAM. TRE it paid geld for 10½ hides and half a virgate of land. There is land for 7 ploughs. Of this land 5½ hides are in demesne, and there are 3 ploughs, with one slave. There are 9 villagers and 10 cottagers with 3 ploughs. There are 8 acres of meadow, pasture 3 furlongs long and 1 furlong broad, (and) woodland 6 furlongs long and 3 furlongs broad. Of the same land William holds 2 hides of the bishop. He who held them before him could not withdraw from the church. This manor was worth £6 when the bishop received it; now the demesne is worth £9; what William holds (is worth) £3.

The bishop who held the land was Walkelin, the first Norman bishop of Winchester. He had been a royal clerk to William and was enthroned in 1070. Winchester had been the capital of Wessex and at the time of the Norman Conquest was the capital of England. As such it was a powerful, rich and influential bishopric, and unsurprisingly Walkelin, a first-rate administrator, amassed a considerable portfolio of properties. Whilst most were in Hampshire, Ham was one of 12 properties held by him in Wiltshire and there were others scattered across the southern counties of England. By the time of Domesday Walkelin had assigned the profits of the manor of Ham to the monks of the priory in Winchester, St Swithun's Priory. The priory or monastery formed part of the cathedral, and in 1079 after Walkelin began the building of a new cathedral, the New Minster, the priory also became known as the Old Minster. Except for a brief period during the Commonwealth, the land at Ham remained in the ownership of the Church until 1914. Who the William was who held 2 hides from the bishop has to be an educated guess. It was a common Norman name and over 150 different Williams occur in Domesday Book, some as in Ham's case without a surname. The likely candidate is William Scudet (Shield) who held 3 hides from the Bishop of Winchester at Alton Priors and a further 4 ½ hides from the king at Westbury. He was King William's cook and in company with a number of other officials in the king's household he was granted lands – in his case for keeping the king's larder. Nothing is known about the previous owner of the 2 hides in Ham which were probably what later became known as East Court Farm.

A hide was notionally the amount of land which would support a *ceorl*, a free peasant, and his household; it was sub-divided into four virgates or yardlands. Hideage was the unit of measurement used for tax and local government. By the time of Domesday Book, England had been divided into shires or counties, and each shire was sub-divided into 'hundreds', a hundred being a grouping of manors with an assembly of village representatives which met regularly. Within Wiltshire, Ham was initially part of the Kinwardstone Hundred, a swath of adjacent manors. Sometime in the 15th century Ham was transferred to the Elstob and Everleigh Hundred, aptly named a 'ragged hundred' because its constituent parts were scattered throughout the shire. Everleigh was a manor near Collingbourne Ducis, and Elstob is simply a field at Enford, its name in Old English meaning 'trunk of elder'. The reason for this change appears to be because the various scattered manors in the Elstob and Everleigh Hundred all belonged to the Prior of St Swithun's Priory.

Trying to tie down the standard size of a hide is an elusive task. It is usually given as 60–120 acres. Even this wide range is open to question as there was considerable disparity in different parts of England. There is a view that hides in Wiltshire were as small as 40 acres, but a 14th century reference to virgates of 30 acres in Ham suggests that for Ham anyway a measurement of 120 acres was nearer the mark. However, if the pre-1980 acreage of Ham is divided by 10 ½ hides and half a virgate, the answer is close to 155 acres. It therefore makes sense to accept that hideage was principally a unit for administrative and tax purposes rather than an exact land measurement, and accordingly there might well have been at times an element of creative accounting involved. This may go partly towards explaining the unsolved discrepancy between the nine hides granted to Wulfgar and the 10½ hides recorded in Domesday.

A 'plough' was the arable capacity of a manor in terms of the number of eight-ox plough-teams needed to work it, so that too is a very broad measurement, and it is left to Saxon acreage to provide a much more accurate system of land measurement, though even that was far from precise. An *æcre* was a strip of land a *furh-lang*, furrow-long or furlong of 220 yards in length by 22 yards in width (writing at the end of the 19th century a Victorian historian commented that 22 yards was a measurement that every schoolboy knew, because it was the distance between the wickets in cricket!), but at the time of the Conquest there was no standard yard. This did not come until Richard 1's reign and was then designed primarily as a measurement of cloth rather than land. As a result an acre was measured in rods, a rod being the length of a pole needed to drive an eight-ox team. The length of a furlong was 40 rods and the width of an acre was four rods. In theory a rod equated to 5½ yards; in practice it could of course vary considerably.

Even if the measurements are imprecise, what Domesday Book does provide is a good insight into the nature of the land around Ham in the 11th century. There is a notion that England was still covered by vast forests at that time. In fact slash and burn had been going on for centuries, and although Ham was then still nominally part of Savernake Forest and subject to one of the forest eyres (courts), most of the land was under cultivation. Of that cultivation the majority was arable land, but this would not have been a patchwork of small fields and high hedges. The landscape would have looked much more like the farming landscape of northern Europe today: wide, open fields with strips of cultivation lacking hedges or manmade boundaries. Each strip tended to be long rather than wide, to avoid turning the plough-team too often. The eight acres of meadow, which were for mowing and therefore distinct from pasture, might however have been enclosed. The woodlands of nearly 400 acres were valuable as a source of fuel and building material, for pasturing swine for nuts and, perhaps surprisingly, for honey, a highly tradeable commodity which was culled from bees' nests in woodland clearings and banks.

The lonely slave, *servus* or serf, was a common feature of English life then. Some 25,000 slaves are recorded in Domesday Book; for comparison, Inkpen had 20 slaves and Shalbourne three. To be a slave was hereditary, or a man could be sold into slavery. In theory he could not own a house or land and was bound to work in the service of his lord. As a chattel of the lord he had a value but it was not much. If a slave were killed his kinsmen received 40 pence and his lord received *man-bot* (compensation or blood money) of 20 shillings, whereas if a villager were killed his kinsmen received £4 (or 200 Saxon shillings) and his lord received *man-bot* of 30 shillings.[14] Yet arguably he was not much more worse off than a Victorian agricultural labourer who was dependent on a local farmer for his livelihood and in hard times might end his days in the workhouse.

Villagers, also variously called *villani*, villeins or villains, were not freemen but could hold land in tenure which was not 'in demesne', that is land that was not in the sole ownership of the lord. Cottagers, *cotarii* or cottars, were a rung below villagers and probably worked on the villagers' land as well as their own smallholdings. From Domesday Book it is apparent that in Ham there were no freemen or *sokemen*, who were the two classes of non-noble landowners. The total working male population of Ham was 20, compared with 45 in Inkpen which had two manors and 30 in Shalbourne. Even if a figure for women and children were to be added, the population of Ham is unlikely to have been much above 50.

In those days the actual village of Ham probably comprised little more than four or five very rudimentary houses for the workers on the estate. As there was no river or significant stream, only a winterbourne – there are five wells in the village shown on the 1877 Ordnance Survey map, the settlement took shape around the crossway of the tracks leading north-south and east-west. This crossway is likely to have been in the area of where the manor house and church stand, the original hub of the village, rather than the village green as it is now. Whether the track running south was still the *anstig*, Burghard's hill path in the charter of 931, or whether it used the holloway parallel to the modern road which then debouched onto Ashley Drove, is unknown. Northwards was another track leading to Hungerford, which together with the *anstig* or its successor may have formed part of an ancient road leading from Hungerford to Andover. Westwards, as previously described, there were two roughly parallel tracks, one running along the line of the Lynch and the other along the route of Ham Road. Eastwards the latter joined with Spray Road.

In Old English *ham* means a village, hamlet, manor or estate. As a place name it was usually used as a suffix to a particular locality, as in Chippenham. Used on its own it may simply have reflected the smallness of the manor of Ham, but there is another much more likely derivation. *Hamm* means an enclosure. Often the term was used in the context of land enclosed by a bend in a river, but here it would mean land enclosed in a fold of the downs. In the charter of 931 and in later medieval documents the village is called *Hamme*, which supports the view that this is the correct derivation and it is the one now given in reference books. There are eight other villages called Ham scattered about southern England, and a multitude of ham manors, ham barns and ham roads, which can make research confusing.

The inhabitants of Ham would have spoken *Englisc*, or Old English, which was derived from West German. By the end of the next century Old English had largely died out. It is usual to think of these Wessex men as true blue Anglo-Saxon stock, but that is arguably a misnomer as their bloodlines may have run much deeper. In their veins could have coursed the blood of ancient Britons mixed with Celts from Gaul. The 400-year Roman occupation must have added something. In theory only officers in the Roman legions were allowed to marry, but no doubt nature took its normal course amongst the rank and file. The legions were largely recruited from Rome's conquered territories and were accordingly a rich European mix. Over-laying this was Saxon rather than Anglo-Saxon blood, as the Angles did not settle in Wessex. Possibly a dash of Scandinavian blood could be added. The Danish incursions into Wiltshire were relatively brief, but there would inevitably have been some rape and pillage, the age-old reward for the danger and privations of a warrior's life. It is this much more complex mixture of races and cultures that may provide a truer pedigree of the Ham residents in the 11th century.

5

BEYOND DOMESDAY BOOK

Over the next six centuries there are relatively few surviving historical records of Ham, and those that do exist are often little more than lists of names, wills or various financial accounts, all of which makes it difficult to set out a coherent evolution of the village during those centuries. Instead, a better idea of its development can be gained by looking at three inter-twined strands: the land which provided the staple employment for the village and the various landowners who farmed it, the church which was a principal fulcrum of its daily life, and the village as a community. Layered on top of these strands are three great national events, which in their turn must have had a profound impact on the village. The Black Death in the middle of the 14th century ravaged the whole of England and Ham would not have escaped. Not only did it inflict great misery, but it also created a social revolution that would have had a lasting influence on the future life of the village. Nearly two centuries later the Reformation broke the real power of the Church, and while it is perhaps difficult to understand today the extent of the shockwave, or series of shockwaves, that followed, it too would have brought a sea change to the lives of Ham's inhabitants. Then, after another century, the Civil War undoubtedly electrified the village. With the two battles of Newbury on its doorstep, the inhabitants could hardly have stood aloof from the divisions the war created throughout the country. Beyond the war itself, the Church was forced to relinquish its ownership of the manor of Ham during the period of the Commonwealth that followed.

6

THE LAND AND ITS DYNASTIC LANDOWNERS

Throughout the period from after Domesday to 1800 there were three main estates in the parish: Ham Manor, the original demesne estate; East Court, the land given to William Scudet; and Dove's Farm, although separate ownership of this farm cannot be traced until the 13th century. The Ham Spray estate did not emerge until the 19th century, and Wansdyke Farms into which it was later absorbed was a creation of the 20th century. In 1839 the respective acreages of the estates are given as Ham Manor comprising 384 acres of demesne land, a copyhold of 51 acres and a further holding of 482 acres formed from the various copyholds in the eastern part of the parish (Ham Spray), East Court with 279 acres, and Dove's Farm having only 77 acres.[15] These acreages were not constant in the preceding seven centuries due to various land exchanges, but they give a good indication of the relative sizes of the farms during this period. Throughout, the Church was the overall landlord of the entire manorial estate – what is now the Parish of Ham – but its influence over the development of the village and the land after the Middle Ages was muted. The real architects were the various families who in their turn oversaw the three farms.

View of Ham from the south. Manor Farm buildings are in the middle distance on the left

The Ham Manor estate was leased by the Hunt family dynasty for about two hundred years from the end of the 16th century until the mid 18th century. Surprisingly almost nothing is known of who farmed the estate prior to the 16th century. Two possible names emerge from the early 14th century, William Bunggy de Buttermere and John atte Righe, but there is no direct evidence of their involvement. Edmund Polhampton of the family associated with the East Court estate was the farmer there in 1502, and Thomas Faller[16] who appears in a tax list of 1545 farmed it from at least then until 1572. Even more surprisingly, considering that the Hunts were arguably Ham's most prominent family, very little is known about the family itself. The first Hunt was the John Hunt whose memorial is in All Saints' Church. He probably succeeded Thomas Faller towards the end of the 16th century and died in 1590 at the age of 90 leaving the estate to his wife Christian. On her death the lease appears to have passed to one of the Hunts of Ashampstead, Berkshire, and it is this branch of the family which farmed the land until some time in the 18th century.[16] All the eldest sons of the family were called John which makes it confusing in trying to distinguish one from another. Added to that the Hunts were a prolific family and it is therefore difficult to piece together a family tree from the parish records of baptisms and burials.

The line of John Hunts survived until well in to the 18th century, but by 1779 the lease of the Manor estate had passed to John Hunt Watts, the son of Richard and Mary Watts. The starting point of this change seems to have been a marriage settlement of 30 November 1676 when a John Hunt married Mary, daughter of John Watts of Speen, gentleman.[17] Under the marriage settlement a moiety (half share) of the remainder of the lease of the manor of Ham was assigned to his father and his mother Susannah, and a moiety was assigned to himself, John Hunt the younger. John the younger, who died in 1719, and Mary had a son John and also a daughter Elizabeth who married Richard Watts. However, Richard and Elizabeth Watts's only child was a daughter, also Elizabeth, who married Anthony Tassell, and so it is not clear how and why Richard and Mary Watts feature in the succession of the Ham Manor estate unless Mary was this Richard Watt's second wife.

Matters amongst the various John Hunts are equally obscure. Four John Hunts died between 1719 and 1754; three have tombs in the churchyard, dated 1719, 1733 and 1754, and a fourth death in 1749 is recorded in the parish burial register. After John Hunt the younger died in 1719, two John Hunts are signatories to an alehouse petition of 1720, presumably father and son. After the death of the next John Hunt in 1733, possibly the son of John Hunt the younger, a John Hunt, gentleman and freeholder, and a John Hunt, yeoman and copyholder, are mentioned in a list of potential jurors in 1736. Again it is easy to assume that they are father and son, but there is a catch. The first of these two John Hunts, who may be the John Hunt who died in 1749, was apparently the demesne landowner. If so, why did he not rate a tomb like the others? The second John Hunt, the copyholder, did not have a son and never inherited the demesne estate. His will of 1750 shows him to be a man of modest means. He left his brother Edward an annuity of two pounds ten shillings from the profits of his copyhold estate. He then left 20 pounds to his nephew Henry Hunt and the remainder of his estate to his other nephew Edward Hunt.[18] Nevertheless, when he died in 1754 he was given a tomb to match the other two Hunt tombs beside the church porch.

A further piece of this jigsaw is yet another John Hunt who appears as a signatory in the Poor Fund account book in 1795. He was the son of Edward Hunt who was probably the nephew of the John Hunt who died in 1750, and from whom he inherited the bulk of the latter's estate. His will of 1801 – he died in the same year as his father Edward – provides few clues except to establish that his elder son, also John Hunt, had already been 'provided handsomely for' by his grandfather Edward Hunt. By the time of the 1841 census, and probably some time before that, none of the original Hunt family was living in Ham.

Cutting through these riddles, what evidently happened is that at some time around the middle of the 18th century the Ham Manor estate slipped sideways to the Watts family via the distaff line, although the precise event that triggered it remains obscure. The earliest related record is a lease to John Hunt Watts from the Church dated 1779,[19] but adding further to the mystery the name of Richard Watts who died in 1775 has been scratched out on the lease and

Manor Farm House c. 1928. It was then a farm cottage with a carpenter's and wheelwright's shop attached

John Hunt Watts's name inserted. John Hunt Watts died in 1813 and was succeeded by his son, also John Hunt Watts, but the succession was not straightforward. The elder John Hunt Watts was a man of considerable means and in his will he carefully distributed his accumulated wealth to his four sons and daughter Mary. His eldest son John received the bulk of his estates in Ham, Buttermere and Vernham Dean. His second son Richard, a clergyman, was left a farm in Ogbourne St George plus £2,000; this was in addition to a previous gift of £5,000. His third son George received some freehold land in Ham which was let to John Poore – it is not clear where this land was, and his fourth son Francis Richens Watts who was 18 was to inherit Dove's Farm and £6,000 when he reached the age of 21. In the meantime Francis's mother Elizabeth would act as trustee for him. Elizabeth was left Dove's House in her own right, and almost quixotically in the midst of this division of property and money she also received her husband's chaise and four-wheeled carriage, with the instruction that her son John should provide her with a pair of horses which he might use when she did not need them. Finally, Mary was left the interest from an investment of £3,000, and the capital sum was to be divided equally between any children she had when they reached the age of 21. This bequest however stipulated that none of this was to go to her husband Thomas Cowderoy who later in the century would own East Court. This last condition seems strange as until the Married Women's Property Rights Act was passed in 1882, any property inherited by Mary would have automatically become the property of her husband.

When the younger John Hunt Watts died in 1829 he left his Ham Manor estate to his youngest brother Francis Richens Watts who already owned Dove's Farm, but there was a sting in the tail. Within 12 months of inheriting the estate, Francis was to raise £9,000 from it, a third of which was to go to his brother George and another third to his sister Mary. As in his father's will, the bequest to Mary contained the condition that it was to be given 'into her own hand for her own sole and separate use and benefit exclusive of her said husband'. Whether her father and brother were just protective of Mary, or whether there was some deeper unease about her husband, Thomas Cowderoy, is not known. Later and separately George would sue Francis and Mary and her husband over a land dispute, but it did not involve land at Ham. It was the matter of raising the £9,000 cash that would dog Francis for the rest of his life. It is unclear whether he was ever legally married, but when he died in 1867 that effectively ended the brief Hunt Watts dynasty.

By contrast, at what was later known as East Court, the estate which William the Conqueror gave to his cook William Scudet, it is possible to delve back into the 13th and 14th centuries. The estate name was a common one in the Middle Ages. There are for instance both a West Court and an East Court in Shalbourne, and a West Court in Inkpen, but none of these had any direct connection with Ham's East Court. For a hundred years after Scudet the trail goes cold. Then, William Marshall, Earl of Pembroke, appears to have held the overlordship of the estate at the beginning of the 13th century, although there is no substantive source to support this. Pembroke became Regent when Henry III succeeded to the throne in 1216 at the age of nine, and he may have held the estate on behalf of the boy king. Previously Pembroke had been one of the barons who had forced King John to sign Magna Carta. Ironically a year later, in 1216, he found himself having to expel a French force from Lincoln, which the barons had invited to England in their war with John at the end of his reign. He died three years later in 1219. At some point after that the overlordship may well have reverted to the crown, because a century and a half later there is a reference to Isabel, the daughter of Edward III, owning the land together with an estate in Hamstead Marshal.

However, well before that, back in 1249, the land at East Court is shown as being held by John of Ham who granted two hides in Ham to Adam of Portland and his wife Isabella. In return they conveyed a life interest in the capital messuage (the dwelling place) and half the estate to the same John of Ham for 10s yearly.[20] There are two records in the Wiltshire Feet of Fines which refer obliquely to this transaction: *Winton. Morrow of Purification, 33 Henry III. 1249. Adam de Portland &Isabella, quer. And John of Hamme, imped. Land in Hamme. Robert de Herotere puts in his claim*; and then the following year: *Westminster. Estate in 1 month. 34 Henry III. 1250. Robert de la Herotere, pet. And John de Hamme, ten. Lands in Hamme; And between same Robert and John, whom Adam de Portland & Isabella call to warrant. Lands in Hamme.* What happened to this claim is not clear. In 1287 it appears that William of Ham held the property which then included land at Spray and at Moordown in Buttermere. Today Moordown Farm lies just outside the south-western corner of the parish boundary. William granted a life estate in the property to Isabel of Ham the same year. Early in the next century the estate was held by Walter of Ham. He also appears as Walter atte Mulle in a tax list of 1332, but at some time before 1317 he had granted the estate to Richard de Polhampton and his wife Margaret.[21]

It is likely that Richard de Polhampton originated from the village of that name near Basingstoke which is mentioned in Domesday Book and now is home to one of the Queen's studs. It is uncertain whether he represented the main line of the Polhampton family but he was undoubtedly a man of prestige and influence. Richard de Polhampton was Sheriff of Cornwall from 1314–15 and Sheriff of Berkshire and Oxfordshire from 1315–17. He was evidently comparatively wealthy and held land in Crofton as well as in Ham. An inquisition, or formal inquiry, of 1317,[22] the year of his death, sets out his assets in detail:

> Richard de Polhampton held on the day that he died the moiety of the manor
> of Crofton for the term of the life of the said Richard and Margaret his wife, of
> the grant of Alan, the chief lord of the fee, the services therefore due and
> accustomed: it is held of William Kayngel, of Iattone Kayngel, by the service of
> the moiety of one knight's fee.

There is there a capital messuage with a garden, and it is worth per annum 12d. There are there 150 acres of land, the approvement whereof is worth per annum 16s 8d. Also 4 acres of meadow worth per annum 6s. Also 6 acres of wood, and the underwood is worth per annum 12d. Of rent of assize there is 40s per annum at the 4 principal terms. The services of customars are worth per annum 2s.

The said Richard de Polhampton held jointly with Margaret his wife in Hamme one messuage, and it is worth per annum 6d. There are there 70 acres of land, the approvement whereof is worth per annum 10s. Also 4 acres of meadow, worth per annum 4s. Of rent of assize there is per annum 14s at the 4 principal terms. The services of the customars are worth per annum 2s: to hold to the said Richard and Margaret his wife, and to Richard son of the said Richard de Polhampton, and to the heirs of the said Richard son of Richard for ever. The said messuage land, meadow rent, and services are held of the Earl of Norfolk and Suffolk by the service of 20s per annum and suit at court for all service.

Richard de Polhampton died 15th September in the said year (1317): Richard, son of the said Richard de Polhampton is his next heir, and is now six years.

Apparently Margaret moved swiftly after her husband's death to raise money. In 1320 she seems to have reconveyed the entire estate at Ham to Walter of Ham. In turn he retained about a third but regranted two-thirds and the reversion of two small estates of 16 acres and 40 acres to Margaret. In 1317, in addition to the lands at Crofton and Ham, Richard and Margaret had bought the manor of South Fawley near Shefford. It had been intended that this estate should go to their son, Richard, but he predeceased his mother who died in 1331. Instead it then went to his brother Thomas, and two years later to another brother Edmund who died in 1353 following wounds received in a quarrel at Enborne. Edmund was succeeded by his eldest son Richard who sold Fawley in 1364.[23] However, by 1362 the land at Ham was held by Geoffrey Polhampton and his wife Christian.[24] It is not clear how Geoffrey was related to the first Richard de Polhampton. Thereafter the trail at Ham grows cold again until a John Polhampton appears in a tax list of 1576 and again 30 years later in a subsidy list of 1606. Probably the same John Polhampton bequeathed the estate at Ham to his son John in or about 1619. The Polhamptons survived the Civil War and in 1666, the year of the Great Fire of London, a John Polhampton, possibly the son of the John Polhampton who had inherited in 1619, mortgaged the estate to Thomas Gunter of Gray's Inn:[25]

Between Bridgett Earls of Stratford under the castle of Old Sarum in the county of Wilts widdow of the one part and Thomas Gunter of Graios Inn in the county

East Court Farm House c.1928, still known locally as Cannings at that time

of Middx Esq of the other part. Whereas by Indenture bearing date of the sixth
day of this Instant month of October and made between John Polhampton of
Ham in the said county of Wilts of the one part and the sayd Bridgett Earls of the
other part and the said John Polhampton in consideration of the sum of four
hundred pounds of lawful money of England Did grant a lien bargaine off release
and confirm(ation) unto the said Bridgett Earls and her heyres in her actuall and
peaceable possession and soism then bring by virtue of an indenture of bargain
and sale for one yeare to her made by the said John Polhampton by Indenture
bearing date of fifth day of the same October All that Moity or halfe part of capi-
tall Messuage or Manor House of Ham in the said county of Wilts called East-
court and severall other lands tenements and hereditmonts therein mormoned
to have and to hold unto the said Bridgett Earls ....

Two years later in 1668, John Polhampton and his wife Anne, together with William and Adam
Polhampton, conveyed the property to Ferdinand Gunter. Some time afterwards the estate
passed to the Brotherton family through Thomas Gunter's eldest daughter Margaret, and in a
Land Tax assessment of 1780 William Browne Brotherton is shown as the owner. In 1820 it

appears to have been owned by William Brotherton's son, Thomas William Browne Brotherton, a lieutenant colonel in the 14th Light Dragoons stationed at Canterbury. The estate would then change hands rapidly with possession passing successively to Thomas Cowderoy in 1825, the Rev John Bushnell in 1839 and John Canning in 1843.[26] At some point later in the century Henry Deacon Woodman appears to have rented East Court from the John Canning Trustees, and it later formed part of the Ham Spray estate in the early 20th century.

The history of the title to Dove's Farm in the north-west corner of the parish is intermittent. The eponymous Daniel Dove did not own it until 1672, and long before that the Clarke family held it from the late 13th century or early 14th century to the late 16th century, or perhaps even longer.[27]

A John le Clerke was possibly the tenant in the early 14th century. A John Clarke was certainly the freeholder in 1525, and there are references to a Richard Clarke in 1576 and 1578. Later, the Watts family arrived on the scene in the early 18th century, and there is a beam taken from stabling in the old Dove's farmstead, known in earlier times as Dove's Yard, and now in the kitchen of the modern Ham Green Cottage on the same site, with the inscription *I WATTS SEN. I WATTS JUN. TOS WATTS 1739*. Curiously a Watts does not appear in the Land Tax assessment of 1780, and from that assessment it appears that John Bushell temporarily owned the property. However, by 1828 it was owned by Francis Richens Watts, who was born in 1795 and was the brother of John Hunt Watts, the owner of the Ham Manor estate.

The earliest elements of the two farmhouses, East Court and Dove's Farm (now Ham Cross), are believed to date from the 17th century. Manor Farm House, originally a modest estate cottage with a wheelwright's and carpenter's shop attached, was not built until the mid-18th century. Parts of the manor house itself go back to the late 16th century, but nothing is known of any farm buildings before that time. Similarly there are no early records of how the land itself was shaped and developed over the centuries. The earliest representative map of the village and its surrounding land appears to be the map of Berkshire by Jean Roque of 1761. Although the layout of the village depicted on the map is suspect – it shows the church as the westernmost building amongst other incorrect features – the general pattern of the series of large fields around the village ties in with the more detailed maps of the 19th century. The Andrews and Dury topographical map of Wiltshire of 1773 is much more general and consequently of little assistance. Instead it is necessary to go forward to the diocesan map of the manor of 1810 [28] and the enclosure maps of 1828 and 1839 [29] to get an accurate picture of how the pattern of the fields had developed since the time of Domesday Book.

Over the succeeding centuries the open field system with its strips of cultivation was transformed into fields surrounded by hedges and coppices. Enclosures began in the 13th century, mainly for grazing sheep. Ham was near one of the centres of the woollen cloth trade and there must have been a series of enclosures on the Ham farms from that time onwards – there is a

Plan of the Manor of Ham made for the Dean and Chapter of Winchester in 1810

reference to a common in Ham being enclosed in the 17th century[30] – but there is no detailed documentary evidence of this until the 1828 enclosure map. By 1828, except for a few remaining large fields such as The Down, Great Field, Little Field and Pidget's Field, the land had become subdivided into a patchwork of much smaller fields. There were also allotments or small copyhold fields – that is sub-tenanted from estate land, some of which were lumped together in fields known as 'severalls', which in the southern end of the parish became corrupted into 'seullards'. One of the older meanings of the word 'several' is land pertaining to each of the tenants of an estate. There was a series of fields on the north side of the Spray Road beyond the track running up beside Field House named variously The Severalls, Cowleaze Severalls, Middles Severalls and Further Severalls, from which the row of semi-detached houses along the road now takes its name.

From both the map of 1810 and the enclosure map of 1839 together with its accompanying documents and later tithe rolls, the various names of the fields and woods emerge. When most of them originated is impossible to determine, but from very early times the inhabitants of Ham must have needed the names of landmarks both for their work and simply to find their way around the parish. Some clearly date from Saxon times. As mentioned earlier, Pidget's Field and Ashley Drove are both derived from place names in the charter of 931. The road, fields and woods in the north-east corner of the parish called Spray are named after *spræg* meaning brushwood. Breach Meadow, south of Spray Road, comes from *bræc*, a strip of untilled land. As also mentioned earlier, the various Lashmoor fields south of Ham Road are a corruption of *lacu*, a stream, and *mor*, a swamp or moor. Culvers or Culvert Meadow, behind the Crown & Anchor, derives from *culfre*, a culver or wood pigeon. The curiously named Cocks Balls field, north of Spray Road, has a simple derivation: *cocc* is a male bird and *balc* a bank or ridge.

Other fields took their names from their various owners in later centuries, such as Brights Meadow which was possibly named after Robert Bright whose handwriting, now in faded brown ink, appears on the fly leaf of the parish poor fund account book for 1683. However, it is easy to leap to conclusions. Cowley's Copse just to the west of Lower Spray is clearly marked as such on the Ordnance Survey map of 1877 and later OS maps, but less than 40 years earlier it is shown as Cow Leaze Coppice on the tithe roll. Presumably an eager young 19th century OS cartographer asked a local inhabitant for the name of the woodland and carefully wrote down the answer phonetically. Quite possibly other ancient names of fields and woodlands have become similarly corrupted with the advent of modern mapping. There is not much imagination in most of the names, and many of them are probably duplicated in field names in hundreds of other parishes. Not unnaturally a number of them relate to the type of husbandry with which they were once associated, for example Milking Ground, Haying Field, Hoglands, Cow Leaze – leaze is an old term for pasture, Rickyard Field and Grubbed Mead. As time went by and large fields became sub-divided, the new fields kept the name of the original field and were distinguished from each other by prefixes such as Great, Little, Upper, Lower, Middle, Hither and Further. At times a field needed more than one qualification, such as Little Further Lashmoor.

There are surviving accounts from the Ham Manor estate for the mowing of grasslands in 1732 and 1733,[31] and these provide an even earlier insight into some of the field names. Most of the larger fields are recognisable from the later 19th century lists. Other names have either disappeared or, as in most cases, refer to scraps of meadow, allotments and small copyhold fields. Sometimes there is half a clue, as in 'Landway in ye Several at Bowling-drove and…the mead at ye lower end', although the exact location of Bowling Drove is uncertain. Odmead, short for The Old Meadow, is the field between Church Road and Field Lane with the footpath

Ham Manor mowing account for 1733

running through it – the shortened form of the name evidently stuck as it is still known as Odmead today. Other names, such as Square Mead, How Mead and the enigmatic 'The mead next ye gate', are a complete mystery. Most of the names appear in both sets of accounts, except for the fields of clover which are different for each year. In 1732 there were 51 acres of grassland and 14 acres of clover to be mown, and in 1733 there were 39 acres of grassland and 16 acres of clover. The cost of the mowing was about 1s 5d per acre for grassland and 1s per acre for clover. Mowing was a skilled technique requiring not only physical effort and a harmonised rhythm of the swing of the scythe, but an age-old understanding of the land as well as the following description written a century and a half later makes clear.

> The first mower examines the field to see which way the grass lies, for it usually has a list to one direction or another. Wind causes it to lean, rain beats it down, and where very strong and thick it falls of its own weight and becomes a tangle. Stepping round the field, the mower selects the best place to begin, and soon opens a drift like a roadway into it. [33]

In 1733 the mowing was carried out by a team comprising John Aldridge, James Aldridge, John Brookes and Samuel Marchman. John and James Aldridge were father and son, and John Aldridge would later bequeath an 'estate called Pollhamptons' (sic) to his grandson John, James Aldridge's son, born that same year.[33] John Aldridge senior died in 1753, but the Pollhamptons land specified in the will cannot have been the main East Court farm once owned by the Polhampton family as it was by then owned by the Brotherton family. So it is likely that it referred to a copyhold field or allotment. The 1810 map shows a small field called Aldridge's Ground just beyond where the track to Wansdyke Farms above Pidget's Field turns sharply northwards. Alternatively the land could have been in Shalbourne as John Aldridge, labourer, purchased 14 acres of leasehold land in West Court, Shalbourne in 1762 for the sum of £91 14s, a sizeable amount in those days particularly as he would have also had to pay an annual rent to his landlord, Lord Bruce.[34] By 1845 the Aldridge landholding in Shalbourne, now in the name of James Aldridge, had been reduced to four acres of meadow called Radbourne & Aldridges which was situated on the north side of Ham Road at its western extremity. This James Aldridge, possibly the great-grandson of John Aldridge the mower, was a blacksmith and had the leasehold of a house in Shalbourne which is now known as Lynch Farm.[35] This brief account of one branch of the Aldridge family provides a good example of the often extensive layers of copyholds, or rented smallholdings, cottages, fields and allotments, which existed below the main tier of land ownerships. These tenancies were usually for the lifetime of the tenant and were registered at an appropriate manor court.

7

THE CHURCH IN THE MIDDLE AGES

All Saints' Church is the oldest surviving building in the village. The exact date of its origin is uncertain. It has been suggested that there may have been a church at Ham in Saxon times, perhaps a simple wooden structure. If so, it is likely to have been very late in the Saxon era because the size of the village would not have warranted a church much before the Norman Conquest. What is certain is that a church existed by 1171, because it is mentioned in an act of the Bishop of Winchester in that year as part of his final disposition to his monks: *Hee sunt ecclesie (scilicet de Portlanda, de Wika,) de Bledona, de Hinetuna, de Hamme ....*[36] The bishop was Henry of Blois, a grandson of William the Conqueror and a brother of King Stephen, and accordingly an immensely rich and powerful man. A year later in 1172 he confirmed the right of St Swithun's Priory to present rectors to All Saints. While All Saints cannot claim to be one of the earliest churches, it was undoubtedly earlier than most. Henry of Blois's act of 1171 mentions 18 churches. By the end of the next century there were 345 churches in the Winchester diocese.[37]

The 12th-century church would have been a very simple affair, and possibly survives as the core of the nave of the existing church. The tooling on some of the quoins in the nave would support this. It is possible that stone from *Stan Ceastla*, the ruins of the Roman villa, could have been incorporated in the church as part of the foundations. A long shot perhaps, but at some time after 931 the remains of the villa were removed and are not evident elsewhere, and there are instances in England of Roman stonework being incorporated in other early churches. Whatever happened, the main construction of the church did not take place until the 13th century. The walls are constructed of rubble with the dressing of the stonework, such as the surrounds of windows, being carved from coralline limestone which comes from a belt of limestone running from Faringdon to Calne. It would have been a prodigious undertaking to transport the stone from some 20 miles away. As there were no navigable waterways available, it has been suggested that the stone was dragged on sleds across the downs, and this might have taken place in the winter months when snow would have made the hauling easier. Equally it might have been laboriously transported on carts along the tracks of the old Roman roads. Either way it says much for the power and influence of both the Church and in particular the Bishop of Winchester at the time that the feat was accomplished. The church tower was built or extended in the 14th century, probably in 1349 in the immediate aftermath of the Black Death.

Priests from St Swithun's Priory are likely to have been the early rectors at Ham. In 1284 the right of presenting rectors reverted to the Bishop of Winchester, but the earliest record of a rector by name does not occur until 1302 when Williamus de Staunford was appointed. This reflects the pattern of early church life in England where monasteries provided vicars – the

All Saints' Church from a watercolour by John Buckler, 1806

Latin *vicarius* meaning a substitute – before incumbents became established in parishes. Coincidentally, the first rector appointed by name at St Michael's Church, Tidcombe also dates from 1302. Williamus de Staunford's rectorship was shortlived as he was superseded by Williamus de Bedewynd two years later. There were in fact no fewer than seven rectors in the first 20 years of the 14th century. There was a rectory in the village from at least the end of the 13th century, as it was assessed for taxation in 1291 at £6 13s 4d.[38] Where it stood is not known, but it was probably near the church rather than where the later rectory was built in the 17th century. It would have been a very simple affair, probably no better than a peasant's cottage with only a few pots and pans and bedding. The rector would have shared it with a curate, clerk or visiting clergy. A scullion boy or poor widow would have looked after him. In theory priests were celibate but most had live-in partners, and sometimes but rarely they were formally married. As their names imply the early Ham rectors were local men, and their stipends would have been derived mainly from tithes. These were draconically enforced. A tenth of every harvest, every mowing, every felling of a tree, of the progeny of every farmyard animal – or in kind where this was not practicable, and of every shearing went to the priest. There was also a further tribute to the church levied on tenant landowners, known as churchscot. In Ham it was paid in kind with wheat, beer or poultry. Being a priest could be a lucrative profession and undoubtedly some if not many were in the priesthood purely for the money. Others, particularly local men from humble backgrounds – which fits the likely profile of the early Ham priests – were more conscientious in their duties. They would have conducted three services on Sundays. Early morning Mass was probably the best attended, followed by Matins and finally Evensong. The last usually attracted the least attendance because as a Sunday was the only break in a week of harsh physical toil, the afternoon was largely given over to merry-making. At the same time, as the main meeting place in the village, the church would have been the hub of village life. The services would have been social occasions with gossip, repartee and even flirtation continuing while the priest intoned the rites.

In 1362 the fortunes of the rectors of Ham were improved with the grant of 20 acres of land by Geoffrey Polhampton and his wife Christian: [39]

> It would be of no damage to the King or any other to allow the said John (Vicar of Shaldebourne) and William (Radele) to grant a messuage, 20 acres of land, and a rood of meadow, in Hamme to Ralph, parson of Hamme, for the maintenance of a chaplain to celebrate in the parish church of Hamme every day for ever. The premises are held of Geoffrey Polhampton and Christian, his wife, they hold them with a messuage and caracate of land from the Lady Isabel, the King's daughter, as of her manor of Hamstede Marchal by the service of 20s; she holds of the Bishop of Winchester, of his manor of Wydehay, porcel of the temporalities of his see, by the service of 20s, and the Bishop holds of the King by knight's service. The premises to be granted and worth 6s 8d a year. [A caracate was the same as a plough-land, ie the amount of land which could be tilled in a year by an 8-ox team.]

Curiously Ralph does not feature in the list of rectors of Ham in All Saints' Church, and nor is it known whether he came from Ham or elsewhere, but for ease of reference he is called Ralph of Hamme. (The Register of St Swithun's Priory mentions a Ralph Hamme, a monk of the Blessed Mary of Abington, being appointed a monastic visitor in 1405. Could he have been the same priest? If so, he is likely to have been in his 80s by then.) The list shows Henricus de Forde being appointed rector in 1336, followed by Thomas Mulleward de Shereborne without a date of appointment, and then Nicholas Hadham in 1378. In fact, the register of William of Wyke-ham [40] shows Hadham being appointed in 1371 and Mulleward replacing him in 1378. There is some doubt, however, whether Hadham replaced Forde without other priests intervening. There is no reference to a rector being appointed to Ham in the register of William Edington who was Bishop of Winchester 1346–1366,[41] but his register does refer to a Henry de Forde who was appointed to Houghton in Hampshire in 1349, and then to Freshwater in the Isle of Wight in 1350 where he was said to be 'broken in health'. It is unlikely that the diocese had two priests both called Henry de Forde, and it is therefore possible that Henricus de Forde was replaced at Ham sometime before 1346 by Ralph of Hamme. This was a time of great turmoil in the Church – nearly half the priests in the Winchester diocese died in the Black Death – and some confusion over appointments is understandable.

Irrespective of who was rector in 1362, the rectors of Ham were now farmers – 20 acres would have been a significant acreage in Ham at that time – and in between services they would have kilted up their cassocks to feed the pigs and carry out other farmyard chores. The rectory itself would in time become a small farmyard with various outhouses, and beyond their 20 acres, which from later records appear to have been scattered around the parish, the rectors would have had the right to pasture their sheep and cattle on the common land. While designed to pay for a chaplain, the income from the land would have added substantially to the rector's income from tithes. Other income came from offerings from the parishioners. These were scarce and probably amounted to no more than a penny once or twice a year on principal feast days such as Candlemas or Easter. Candlemas was the feast of the Purification of the Blessed Virgin Mary which took place 40 days after Christmas, and the villagers would all have been involved in a procession, each villager carrying a blessed candle which would then have been presented to the rector together with a penny. Additionally, wealthier members of the village might leave bequests in their wills for chantries; these were masses to be said for their souls to hasten their journey through Purgatory. By the late medieval period religion, and in particular its association with death, held the laity in a vice-like grip, and this obsession with death developed into an elaborate cult. Meanwhile the atmosphere of church services hardened.   The comparative laxness of the earlier services ended. Gossip and lolling about were banned, and instead parishioners were expected to stand or kneel meekly in silence. Yet confession and communion would still have been rare events for most of the village, possibly not more than once a year in Lent. A sermon would have been equally rare. Writing at the end of the 14th century, Chaucer makes his poor parson: [42]

> . . . . *a learned man, a clerk,*
> *That Cristes gospel trewely wolde preche;*
> *His parisshens devoutly wolde he teche.*

But according to other sources he was an exception, and Ham's rectors and chaplains almost certainly lived less testing lives.

8

THE VILLAGE AND THE BLACK DEATH

One nugget of Ham's story is a small clutch of early 14th-century records, which provide a window on life in the village seven centuries ago. The starting point is a tax list for 1332: [43]

John atte Righe	£6/8s
John le Skynnere	16s
John le Clerke	£2
John Dasevyle	12s
Geoffrey Foreman	16s
William Norman	£2/8s
Roger Mortymer	£2
Henry Foghel	12s
Walter atte Mulle	£2/8s
Adam Godnynge	£2/9s
John Mortymer	14½s
John Stapeton	14¾s
John Chalff	12s
Thomas Covenant	16s
John Grym	£3/4s

On the surface it appears that not much can be gleaned from this list except for the rich, Chaucerian sounding names. They leap from the page and as much as anything else summon up a picture of the rude pageantry of rural life in the 14th century. John le Skynnere evidently described his occupation at that time. Foreman, meaning swineherd, and Foghel, bird-handler or falconer, were probably descended from men who had at one time held those occupations. Norman could have been descended from a Northman or Viking, or alternatively a forebear could have come across with the Norman Conquest – the Norman French took their name from the Northmen or Vikings who settled Normandy – as a forebear of Mortymer would have done, Mortymere being a place name in Seine-Maritime. The name Grym is derived from the Old Norse for a mask or helmet. Others such as Godnynge (Godney) and Stapeton (Stapleton) suggest that their owners, or their forebears, originated from those Somerset villages.

More importantly, however, among these taxpayers are the owners of the three principal farms – the Ham Manor demesne estate, East Court and Dove's Farm – and identifying them is a puzzle. It is tempting to tie the farms to those paying the most tax, but that would be unsafe, because the tax, known as 'fifteenths', was levied on moveable assets and not land, and is therefore a guide only. The tax could vary quite widely as this tax list adds up to £26 10¼ s, and only two years later Ham was assessed for tax at £35.[44] Complicating the matter further, there are no less than six taxpayers assessed for £2 or more. It is possible to identify Walter atte Mulle, or Walter of Ham, as the tenant of East Court, to whom Margaret de Polhampton had reconveyed the estate following her husband's death in 1317. Who the tenant of Dove's Farm was is not so straightforward. John le Clerke could be a member of the Clarke family which owned Dove's Farm from the late 13th or early 14th century, but he is taxed for only 16s which seems meagre for a man owning some 70 acres of land. Alternatively the name could stand for Johannes de Pondfeld who was the parson or clerk at All Saints' Church from 1319 to 1336.[45] Again this does not fit conclusively as the grant of a rectory and land to the parson at Ham did not occur until 1362, and on balance the former attribution seems to be the more likely. Finally, John atte Righe who paid tax of £6 8s would seem to be the obvious choice as the demesne estate landowner. However, the Custumal of St Swithun's Priory, a book of customs written at the end of the 13th century or beginning of the 14th century, records a William de la Rye as one of eight virgaters in Ham – a virgater was a tenant of approximately 30 acres. This William, who was probably not free, is likely to have been a direct forebear of John atte Righe, which poses the question of how within a generation or two did the latter become elevated to the ownership of the demesne estate. The matter is further complicated by a reference in the Custumal to a William Bunggy de Buttermere who was taxed at 60s at the beginning of the century. His name suggests that he was descended from one of the Knights Templar, the *beaux gentilshommes*, and although little is known about him he appears to have been the only freeman amongst the tenants at Ham at the beginning of the 14th century. As such he is the obvious candidate to have been the tenant at Ham Manor at that time, but by 1332 he had disappeared entirely from the scene and this may have provided John atte Righe with the opportunity to seize his chance. Overall, while it is not possible to fit all the pieces of the jigsaw neatly into their proper places, it is clear that by the early 14th century Ham possessed a number of men of some substance.

Below the top tier of landowners there were a number of other tenants whose status is described in the following extract from the *Victoria History*:

> In the early 14th century there were 7 virgaters, 12 ½-virgaters, 9 tenants with 10 cottage holdings, and 7 tenants who held messuages. Several tenants also held small plots of 'forripelond' [forest land that had been converted to arable land and for which a reduced rent was due]. The virgaters each held 30 acres for which they owed rents of 5s. yearly and corn-rents. Besides the usual agricultural duties

they gathered nuts and apples. The ½-virgaters each held 15 acres and owed half the virgaters' duties. They each had to provide two men to reap at autumn boon-work [extra work at harvest time], and from them were chosen the woodward and hayward [men responsible for overseeing the common woodland and pasture respectively]. The cottagers held 10 acres each for 2s. yearly. Their duties included threshing and reaping and their wives were bound to wash the sheep. From them were drawn the ploughman, shepherd, and swineherd. Those who held the messuages mostly held 5a. each for 1s. yearly and the duties of driving animals to Chilbolton [near Andover, a journey of almost 20 miles; Chilbolton was another manor owned by the Bishop of Winchester] and of hoeing and reaping. [46]

It is easy to imagine Ham as a remote and isolated village in those days. In fact the village lay at an intersection of two major drove roads. The one referred to in the extract above led from Hungerford to Andover. The other was one of the ancient Wessex ways; known as the Inkpen Ridgeway, it ran from Walbury Hill along the Ham Hill escarpment and then on through Oxenwood, Everleigh and Collingbourne Kingston to Upavon. Later, a more local drove road branched off the ridgeway to run along Ashley Drove. There is a story that Bishop's Barn – which lies on Ham's southern boundary adjacent to Ashley Drove – is the site of an ancient tithe barn which was used by the bishop of Winchester in the Middle Ages to levy a toll on cattle and sheep being driven along Ashley Drove, but there is no specific evidence to support it. The wider picture conjured up in this extract is of a well-ordered and almost benign way of life in Ham despite its underlying feudalism. The reality was that it was a highly regimented existence which tied each tenant ruthlessly not only to his own land but to his lord's as well.

At the beginning of the century each virgater in Ham was required to pay an annual rent of 5s for his 30 acres, tallage or land tax of 10s at the Feast of Purification and at the feast day of SS Philip and James (3 May), and churchscot of half of a quarter of wheat 'by new measure'. Beyond that he was required to perform a formidable list of services for his lord. If he had a complete plough team of eight oxen he was required to plough one acre in winter and one in Lent. He was also required to harrow those two acres, plus another acre in winter and one in Lent – the last was known as doustlond. He had to find one man for hoeing for one day 'until the ninth hour'. In summer, with others, he had to scythe grass, make hay and then cart it. At harvest time he had to find three men, cart corn with his own cart for one day and stack straw when necessary for half a day; in return for the carting he received his dinner or two sheaves in the evening. When it came to sheep, he was required with others to move the lord's fold from field to field, and to dip and shear the sheep and lambs. Then there was a raft of carting duties: carting firewood for Christmas, timber for building or for repairs at the court, wattle and brushwood for making walls, wool and cheese to Wynton (Andover), and a quarter of corn to neighbouring markets for which he received ½ d in return. He was also required to fetch the lord's dinner when necessary from neighbouring markets for which he received his own dinner or ¼ d. On top of that he was required to collect nuts until the ninth hour and apples for one day, and if he made cider he would receive a bowl of apples in the evening as a reward.

Half-virgaters were required to provide roughly half of these services, but they too had to pay the full amount of tallage. Cottagers had a range of minor duties to complete, and these would vary according to whether the cottager was a ploughman, shepherd or swineherd. The wife of a cottager was required to milk the lord's sheep and in return received her share of whey. Cattle do not feature prominently in the Custumal and milk in those days in Ham appears to have come mainly from sheep. Below the cottagers were a small number of men and women who rented dwellings and small plots of land for which they paid or provided services according to their varying abilities. Lucia, a widow, held a messuage and four acres but was required only to pay a life rent of 5d, while Matilda Locrix – it is not clear what her status was – had to pay an annual rent of 3d for her messuage and also churchscot of two hens, as well as finding one man for 'all works in common'. While there was common land, all tenants had to pay for pasturing pigs, known as pannage: one penny per pig over one year old and ½ d for a six-month old pig. For all other animals over 2½ years old there was a pasturing charge, herbagium, of ½ d at St Andrew's Day (30 November). There were other catch-alls of a different kind. A tenant could not sell a horse or an ox without a licence, nor marry a son or a daughter without redemption (the payment of a fine). [47]

There were a few, and only a few, small rewards in return. At Christmas each virgater would receive a meal of two dishes at the lord's court on the third day of Christmas. However, in the run-up to Christmas, virgaters had each been required to thresh five sheaves of wheat at the lord's court, and fetch beer for which they received a penny. Half-virgaters, ploughmen and shepherds received a meal on the second day of Christmas but had no special Christmas duties to perform. Outside Christmas, any ploughman guarding oxen by night in winter was entitled to a small truss of straw, and anyone guarding oxen after dinner time in summer could have one ox in the lord's pasture. Similarly, anyone scything the lord's meadow was entitled to a heap of grass and could also halter a horse in the lord's meadow while scything. [48]

Many of these duties and rewards seem minor and even trivial by today's standards, but in a life of unremitting toil they had a cumulative effect. The various taxes would have been vigorously audited by St Swithun's Priory. While it was customary in most manors for the bailiff and reeve to present the annual accounts, unusually in Ham it was the duty of the bailiff and the hayward. The latter was clearly a man of some stature in the village. His annual rent was discounted by 2s and he was allowed to have two cattle and two pigs free of herbagium and pannage. He had custody of the lord's pigs and received a piglet each year. He was also allowed one acre of the best wheat, although not manured, and another piece of land known as Swenestyche. From 1 August until Michaelmas, and during visits of the chamberlain, he was fed at the lord's court. He was, however, required to give the lord 100 eggs on Easter Eve. Whether this had any specific connection with the ancient tradition, widespread in Europe, of giving painted eggs at Easter is not known.

The Custumal records a total of 43 tenants in Ham. This is double the number in Domesday Book, but it had taken some two and a half centuries to achieve this growth. Ham was still a small village, and the lives of its inhabitants were strictly orchestrated by the long arm of St Swithun's Priory, the lord of the manor and his various officers, and, not least, the tight grip of the church in exercising its sway on religious observance. All this, however, was about to change.

Two and half centuries after Domesday Book the Black Death struck. The Black Death, or the Great Death as it was known before the 19th century, is the greatest catastrophe in recorded history to have overwhelmed Britain. Its progress is well chronicled, and while it was undoubtedly capricious in where and how it struck – and as a result some accounts of its impact may have been exaggerated – the modern consensus is that it killed almost half the population of England. The first wave of the plague hit England in 1348 and 1349. There were further sporadic outbreaks in 1361, 1369, 1374–9 and 1390–93, but it was the first wave that crippled the country. As early as the 1330s rumours had been travelling along the trade routes of flood, famine and pestilence in Cathay. The pestilence spread relentlessly westwards and in 1345–6 it struck a Tartar army besieging a Genoese trading post at Caffa in the Crimea on the Black Sea. In an early example of biological warfare the Tartars catapulted their dead into the besieged garrison. The garrison flung the bodies back, but the damage had been done and the garrison fled back to Genoa in their galleys taking the Black Death with them. By June 1348 it had reached Paris, and a couple of months later on 15 August it reached Bristol from where it spread west, south and east. It is not known when it reached Ham but it is likely to have done so early in 1349; it had reached Inkpen by March.[49]

The plague was believed by many to signal the end of the world and, as now, someone had to be blamed. On the continent of Europe the Jews were the usual suspects and an easy target. They were accused of poisoning the water supplies to wipe out the Christian faith. This myth was given life by so-called confessions obtained under torture, and widespread massacres of Jews took place in what are now Germany, Austria and Switzerland. In England it was deemed to be the wrath of God for the wanton behaviour of the population. Two features in particular were singled out for condemnation by the Church. One was lascivious behaviour at tournaments. These events were popular occasions and the bigger ones might be compared to the upper echelons of today's football league or a game fair as they lasted several days and attracted numerous sideshows. They were designed to be showcases of male prowess and they naturally attracted a female following, but this fan club was different – they were cross-dressers:

> troop(s) of ladies ... sometimes as many as forty or fifty of them, representing the showiest and most beautiful (but not the most virtuous) women in the realm. They were dressed in particoloured tunics with short hoods and liripipes [the tails of hoods] like strings wound around the head, and wore belts thickly studded with gold and silver slung across their hips, below the navel, with knives called daggers in pouches suspended from them.[50]

People travelled long distances to visit tournaments but, unless they were local, whether they attracted anyone from Ham seems doubtful.

The other condemnation was the new fashions for dress. Again it seems that these fetishist fashions would have passed by most if not all of the residents of Ham. Quite apart from expense, working on the land demanded simple robust, loose clothing which was as weather-proof as possible. Nevertheless, some of the village's wealthier inhabitants might have been tempted to cut a dash to keep in step with what contemporary chroniclers reported as a national craze,

> . . . the English have been madly following outlandish ways, changing their grotesque fashions of clothing yearly. They have abandoned the old, decent style of long, full garments for clothes which are short, tight, impractical, slashed, every part laced, strapped or buttoned up, with the sleeves of the gowns and tippets of the hoods hanging down to absurd lengths, so that, if the truth be told, their clothes and footwear make them look more like torturers or even demons than men. Clerics and other religious adopted the same fashions ... Women flowed with the tides of fashion in this and other things even more eagerly, wearing clothes so tight that they wore a fox tail hanging down inside their skirts at the back, to hide their arses. [51]

No doubt the priest at All Saints' Church, probably Ralph of Hamme, preached homilies on both subjects, and he certainly would have received a diocesan exhortation to hold the Sacrament for Penance. William of Edington, Bishop of Winchester at that time, was another powerful and wealthy man who chose to reside at his palace at Southwark, directly across the river from the City of London, the hub and power base of the country – the ruins of the Palace of Winchester can still be seen on the South Bank. From Southwark on 24 October 1348 he issued a 'mandate for prayers to avert the pestilence, addressed to the prior and chapter of the cathedral':

Lamentation at the distress. The clergy are to appeal to the faithful for acts of penance; for the recitation of the seven penitential psalms on Sundays; for processions through the city, reciting the litany'. On the same day he followed this up with a mandate to the archdeacon of Winchester 'to appeal to all grades of clergy and religious (sic), that on Sundays and Wednesdays and Fridays they meet in the churches for the same penitential exercises. [52]

Exactly how the Black Death affected Wiltshire is not clear. England had survived a famine in 1315–7 which was due to a series of poor harvests and hard winters that had caused 10–15 per cent of the population to die. By the time of the Black Death the population was back to its medieval peak but it was once again in danger of outstripping the food supply, so that the plague struck at a people weakened by malnutrition, by poor hygiene and by heavy toil – an agricultural labourer was old at 40. The countryside may have been marginally better off than the towns, but in most houses in Ham there would have been no separate bedchambers, no beds and no privacy. The occupants would have slept hugger-mugger on the floor, possibly alongside farmyard animals, and probably huddled together for warmth – all fertile ground for any pandemic. From the problems experienced elsewhere in southern England a high attrition rate might have been expected in Ham, but there are three clues which suggest that the reverse could have been true. The first comes from research carried out by Professor Elizabeth Levett into the Pipe Rolls, or accounts, of the Bishops of Winchester in the 14th century.[53] These Pipe Rolls, in particular an unbroken series from 1346–1356, provided her with an unparalleled opportunity to investigate manorial accounts over the period of the Black Death. Her research focused on rents, fines, heriots, labour and the vacancies of tenements (houses). Fines were the system of manorial taxes which covered such matters as sales of leases, inheritance of annual rents, and the marriage of daughters both within and without the manor. A heriot was the giving by law of a live beast, normally a horse, cow or sheep, to the lord of the manor on the death of a tenant. Labour was the various services due by tenants to the lord for threshing, ploughing, harrowing and harvesting. If a tenement became vacant and no one 'of the blood' claimed it, the tenement became the possession of the lord. Based on her findings, Professor Levett gained a strong impression that in the Winchester manors there was continuity in both the method and the prosperity of agriculture over the period of the Black Death, rather than the complete ruination mooted for the country as a whole, and that it was evident that 'a loss of one third of the population is an over-pessimistic estimate'. These conclusions have to be viewed against the facts that Winchester itself was devastated by the Black Death, to the extent that building works on the cathedral were halted for 20 years, and that 48 per cent of priests in the Winchester diocese died in the plague. Also, it is not possible to tie her findings directly to Ham. She only took a sample of the manors for her research and Ham was not amongst them.

The reason for this omission is straightforward. Although the manor of Ham was owned by the Bishop of Winchester, its profits had been assigned to the Priory of St Swithun and as a result Ham does not feature in the Winchester Pipe Rolls.[54] The nearest manor to Ham in her sample was Woodhay some three and a half miles away. Nevertheless, it is significant that the clutch of Berkshire and North Hampshire manors in the survey all returned to more or less normal within ten years, despite a year of horrendous weather in 1350–51 in the immediate aftermath of the plague when storms and floods washed away houses and mills and ruined the harvest.

The second clue is that in 1377, less than 30 years after the Black Death, the number of taxpayers in Ham was 119.[55] This is eight times the number of taxpayers in the list of 1332, and even if the two lists are not directly comparable this reflects an astonishing growth in the village in the intervening 45 years. Indeed, if other members of families are added to the figure of 119, the overall population of the village was then probably greater than it is today, which suggests a large and thriving community at Ham in the second half of the 14th century. Many of the taxpayers would have been children at the time of the Black Death and children generally fared better than adults in the plague, but even so this statistic would seem to support Professor Levett's findings.

The third is a stone mullion-joint of a window in the tower of All Saints' Church bearing the date 1349 which is now plastered over. This suggests that the building of the tower or an extension to the tower – it is a three-stage tower – had begun in that year as a thanksgiving for the village having suffered comparatively lightly from the plague.

None of these clues amounts to compelling evidence, but there is just enough between them to suggest that it is not mere surmise that the death rate in Ham was significantly less than the national average. By the end of 1349 the worst was over and in December the Archbishop of Canterbury ordered people to say prayers for their survival. Life seems to have bounced back remarkably quickly, yet the Black Death left its scars. Ironically in the wake of the Church railing against loose morals when the plague started to bite, there was a marked widespread decline in moral standards afterwards. This must have given Ralph of Hamme even more to fulminate about. Unsurprisingly labour was in short supply and the plague sent wages, particularly agricultural wages, soaring. In an early example of labour exercising its collective muscle, those who had survived demanded a renegotiation of their services and excessive wages. Nationally the immediate increase in wages was reckoned to be 50 per cent or more, while in the Winchester diocese Professor Levett calculated the figure to be between 25–33 per cent. The villagers in Ham must have relished this change in their fortunes, but the King was having none of it and as early as 18 June 1349 issued an Ordinance of Labourers:

… we have ordained that every man or woman in our realm of England, whether free or unfree, who is physically fit and below the age of sixty, not living by exercising a particular craft, and not having private means or land of their own upon which they need to work, and not working for someone else, shall, if offered employment consonant with their status, be obliged to accept the employment offered , and they should be paid only the fees, liveries, payments or salaries which were usually paid in the part of the country where they are working in the twentieth year of our reign (1346) …[56]

This classic reference to a national wage freeze must have dampened spirits in Ham once again, and nationally it was one of the causes that led to the Peasants' Revolt some 30 years later.

The ordinance also highlights the sharp division which still existed between those who were free and those who were not, and that despite low levels of life expectancy labourers were expected to work until they were 60. The Black Death would lead to an ending of the feudal system of serfdom, but so far as Ham was concerned this would continue for another century at least, as the following entry for 1478 in the records of St Swithun's Priory illustrates: 'Manumission granted by the prior and convent to John Harald junior, son of Lawrence Harald, nativus of their manor of Ham, Wilts. All his offspring both those living and those as yet unborn and all his goods and chattels are included.'[57]

9

THE VILLAGE IN THE 16TH AND 17TH CENTURIES

A dozen years after the Black Death the life of England was more or less back on an even keel, an amazing feat of resilience considering the scale of the disaster. The Hundred Years War would continue to rumble on until the middle of the 15th century, although it is unlikely that the daily life of Ham would have been affected by it. The Black Death effectively spelt the end of the Middle Ages, but it is not until the late Tudor period that it is possible to pick up the threads again of what was happening in the village. The first thread is enigmatic. The taxation list for 1545[58] includes the following entry:

Ham and Haxton	£	s	d
The parson ther (sic)		3	4
William Pontentyne		8	
Thomas Fawler paid		20	
Robert Ryve	3	6	8

Haxton was another manor in the Elstub and Everleigh Hundred, and both manors' taxations were lumped together because of their small size. Earlier in the century Ham had been similarly joined with Henley in the Kinwardstone Hundred for the poll tax. Thomas Fawler (or Faller) was the farmer at the demesne estate but none of the others except perhaps the parson appears to have come from Ham. It seems that in 1545 copyholders and small freeholders were spared taxation, and the owners of two of Ham's three farms are certainly absent from the list. The mesh was tighter some 30 years later in 1576, when the taxation list included a separate entry for Ham: [59]

Hamme (sic)	£	s	d	£	s	d
Thomas Boyler gentleman	5				8	4
Thomas Cannon	5				8	4
Thomas Martyn	4				6	8
William Martyn	3				5	
Katherine Lewdon	3				5	
Richard Clarke	20				2	8
John Hunt	40			3	6	8
John Polhampton	5				13	4

Richard Clarke, John Hunt and John Polhampton were the respective owners of Dove's Farm, the Ham Manor estate and East Court Farm, and the amounts of taxation they paid reflect the sizes of their properties. Who the first five named were is a mystery. They were obviously well-to-do and Thomas Boyler is given the description of gentleman. The other men by inference were classed as yeomen. In Tudor times, and in later centuries, there was a marked distinction in the social hierarchy between the respective ranks of gentleman and yeoman. The John Hunt who is commemorated in a memorial in the church in 1590 is described as a yeoman, and another later John Hunt is described in a deed of sale dated 1664 as yeoman, yet the latter, or perhaps a forebear, appears in a list of *Compositions, or Fines, of Wiltshire Gentlemen, for not taking the order of Knighthood at the Coronation of Charles 1, levied in 1630, 1631, 1632.*[60] Charles was selling knighthoods to anyone with land valued at over £40 a year to raise cash, and John Hunt amongst others declined to pay. He was not let off the hook and was fined £14 for each of those three years. Despite that the Hunt family might then have had a claim to be recognised as gentry, and in a list of potential jurors for Wiltshire in 1736 there is a John Hunt, gentleman and freeholder, and also a John Hunt, yeoman and copyholder. The Polhamptons are more difficult to pin down. As a sheriff not once but twice Richard de Polhampton merits the accolade of gentleman, but nearly 300 years later Thomas Polhampton's will of 1597 describes him as yeoman. It appears that either the later Polhamptons of Ham became an offshoot of the line established by Richard de Polhampton, or over the centuries their status simply diminished as their estates dwindled. Nothing is known about the status of the Clarke family.

By the time of a subsidy list for Wiltshire in 1608 [61], in the reign of James 1, Thomas Boyler and the Clarke family had left the scene:

Ham	£	s
John Blake	1	4
John Lewenden	1	3
John Polhampton	1	3
Thomas Canon	1	3
Edith Chaplin vid (sic)	1	3
John Hunt	1	8
Willm Hore	1	3

John Hunt and John Polhampton, or perhaps their sons, are still there, as is Thomas Canon. John Lewenden is presumably the heir of Katherine Lewdon – the spelling of names was casual. John Blake and Edith Chaplin are newcomers. Possibly John Blake was the successor to Richard Clarke at Dove's Farm.

COMPOSITIONS, OR FINES, OF

WILTSHIRE GENTLEMEN,

FOR NOT TAKING THE ORDER OF

KNIGHTHOOD,

AT THE CORONATION OF KING CHARLES, I.

levied in 1630, 1631, 1632.

❧ ◆ ❧

AUDITOR OF THE RECEIPT,

EDWARD, LORD GORGES, *Collector.*

Richd. Aldworth, *Swindon ?*	12 10 0	Henry Maskelin, *Purton ?*	10 0 0
Robt. Arch, (?Archer,) *Clacke?*	10 0 0	Edw. Meddlicott *Warminster*	16 0 0
Thos. Barker,	15 0 0	Wm. Messe,	10 0 0
Math. Bee,	12 10 0	Jno. Organ, *Lambourne ?*	15 0 0
Thos. Bennett, *Salthrop ?*	25 0 0	Ferdinando Parry. *Eston Grey?*	10 0 0
Jno. Bennett, *Pytthouse?*	17 10 0	Wm. Pawlett, *Cottles ?*	25 0 0
Hen. Blake, *Pinkills ?*	10 0 0	William Pyle, *Bubton ?*	10 0 0
Richd. Blake,	12 0 0	George Reynolds,	24 0 0
Wm. Bower, *Lavington?*	12 10 0	Ric. Richmond, *Lydiard* ⎱ *Mil ?* ⎰	10 0 0
Anthy. Browne *Winth. Basset?*	20 0 0	als Webb,	

		James Abbott, *New Sarum.*	10 0 0
		Chas. Aland *Langley Burell,*	10 0 0
		Ric. Aubrey, *Easton Percye,*	10 0 0
		Jereuny Barnaby, *Chitterne,*	10 0 0
		Jo. Banister, *Bramshaw,*	10 0 0
		Wm. Barnes, *Semley,*	10 0 0
		Edw. Barrett, *Titherton Lucas,*	14 10 0
		Edmd. Bathe, *Netherhaven,*	11 13 4
		Jno Bayley, *Lye,& Worthey?*	10 0 0
		Hen. Bayley, *Ch——*	?? 0 0

Edw. Brydges, *Highershutt,*	10	Richmond. al—
Robt. Hord, *Urchfont,*	10 0 0	
Edm. Hungerford, *Chisebery,*	16 6 8	
Jno. Hunt, *Ham,*	14 0 0	
Gabriell Huttofte, *N. Sarum*	16 6 8	
Hen. Hyde. *Purton,*	17 10 0	
Seston Jones, *Westbury,*	24 10 0	
Richd. Kent, *Boscumbe,*	10 0 0	
Robt. Keynton, *Westbury,*	15 10 0	
Wm. King, *Monkton Farley,*	32 6 8	
Edw Long, *Monkton,*	28 0 0	
Wm. Lord, *Chisleton,*	10 0 0	
Jno. Lowe, *Calne,*	10 0 0	
Wm. Lucas, *Fovant,*	16 6 8	
Tristram Lyghte *Hampworth,*	10 0 0	
Geo. Markes, *Steeple Ashton,*	11 13 4	
Jno. Markes *de eadem.*	11 13 4	
Hen. Martin, *de eadem,*	11 13 4	
Edw. Martin, *Uphaven,*	17 10 0	
Wm. Mathews, *Combe Bisett,*	10 0 0	
Geo. Mervyn, *Knowell Epi.*	10 0 0	
Augustine Mervyn, *Knowell Epi.*	10 0 0	
Geo. Miller, *Sheperidge parva,*	14 0 0	
Hen. Mills, *Maddington,*	10 0 0	
Edw. Mills, *Cholston,*	10 0 0	
Ric Morse, *Baubury,*	10 0 0	
Wm. Mountjoy, *Biddeston,*	17 10 0	
Jno. Natt? *New Saram*	10 0 0	
Robt. Nicholas, *All Cannings,*	25 13 4	
Jno. Norborne, *Studley.*	28 0 0	
John Paradise, *Chitway,*	14 0 0	
John Penney, *Stoke Verdon,*	11 13 4	
Edw. Perrey, *Hymdon.*	10 0 0	
Hen. Phillipps, *Wanborough.‡*	10 0 0	
Jno. Phipps, *Sheperidge parva.*	14 0 0	
Arthur Poore, *West Harnham,*	10 0 0	
Edw. Poore, *Durrington,*	17 10 0	
Zachary Power, *Rudlowe,*		

Jno. Flower, *Melksham, Gent.*	11 13 4
Thomas Kent, *Depthford, Gent.*	10 0 0
Jno. Lowe, *The Citie of New Sarum. Esq.*	25 0 0
Isaac Lyte, *Easton Percy, Gent.*	10 0 0
John Mills, *Trowbridge, Gent.*	10 0 0
Jno. Nicholas, *Winterburne Gunnor.*	11 13 4
Thos. Sadler, *The Close, New Sarum. Esq.*	12 0 0
Thos. Warneford, *Senington.*	24 10 0
Francis White, *Langley, (Burel.) Gent.*	10 0 0
Wm. Yorke, *Salthrop, Gent.*	11 13 4

175 li.

Sol. ultio. Novr. 1631.

Thos. Aubery, *Chadenwich,*	28 0 0
Jno. George, *Ridge,*	10 0 0
Ambrose Mortimer, *Stockley,*	10 0 0
Thos. Smith, *Charnham Streete,*	10 0 0
Wm. Thorneborough, *Chicksgrove,*	21 0 0

79 li.

Solut. quinto Junij. 1632.

In this Impression I have corrected in many places the cacography of the original MS.
For the Copy of the Original I am indebted to F. Carrington, Esq. of Ogborn.

T. Phillipps.

M. H. 20 Ap, 1855.

19th century facsimile of a 1632 list of Wiltshire gentlemen – including John Hunt – fined for not taking the order of Knighthood on the coronation of Charles 1

THE REFORMATION

Well before the start of the 16th century religion in Ham would have been an integral part of life, as well as of the ritual of dying. The Reformation in the middle of the century changed that. It was not a sudden phenomenon and spanned four monarchs' reigns. Two men in particular in Ham would have seen it from start to finish. Ricardus Halydaye was the rector of All Saints from 1510– 68, and John Hunt, yeoman and demesne farmer, was born in 1500 and nearly outlived the century, dying in 1590. Possibly the early elements of the Reformation – Luther's writings, Henry VIII's divorce from Katherine of Aragon and break from Rome, and the subsequent Act of Supremacy – made relatively little impact on Ham. The dissolution of the monasteries which ended St Swithun's Priory's tenure of Ham in 1541 then gave a foretaste of what was to come. The Priory had been embroiled in church politics and controversy since Walkelin's day. Its monks thought nothing of trekking out to Rome to plead their cause directly with the Pope, and in the early 13th century they curiously won the right to wear caps because of the cold. Later, in the same century, in a coup d'état a monk seized the mantle of Prior by force of arms. In the lengthy furore that followed Henry III directed that no monastery should give food or shelter to any monk from the Priory. Now St Swithun's was finally brought to heel, and the manor of Ham came effectively under the control of the Dean and Chapter of Winchester Cathedral.

However, it was not until Edward VI succeeded to the throne in 1547 with Somerset as Regent that the full weight of the Reformation would have hit Ham. The Mass was abolished and in one of the many injunctions the clergy and people were required to 'take away, utterly extinct and destroy all shrines, all tables, candlesticks, trindles or rolls of wax, pictures, paintings and all other monuments of feigned miracles, pilgrimages, idolatry, and superstition; so that there remain no memory of the same'.[62] When Mary came to the throne in 1553 she reintroduced the Catholic faith and caused the altars to be replaced in the churches, but her Counter-Reformation was shortlived. Six years later her half-sister Elizabeth 1 slammed the door shut with the religious settlement of 1559, and in many cases the altars were torn out once again.

Exactly how Ham and its church fared in all this can only be guessed at. It is known that in the wake of the 1547 injunction the King's commissioners took, in 1553, 2oz of church plate from All Saints but left 9oz which was probably later replaced.[63] This was a very modest confiscation, but if Ham mirrored what was happening in many other parishes, most of the church valuables would have been discreetly sold or otherwise disposed of before the arrival of the commissioners. Another source records that the windows in the nave and chancel were reported broken in 1553.[64] This could have just been poor maintenance, but there is other evidence of many churches being reglazed at that time, and what seems more likely is that the windows had contained images of saints which were stripped out along with the altar – the current altar table is believed to be 17th century. What is quite clear is that apart from the bare walls – and even these have been altered – there is not one vestige of the pre-Reformation church visible in All Saints today.

Drawing of the memorial to John Hunt, died 1590, and his wife Christian on the north wall of All Saints' Church above the manorial pew

John Hunt must have hated seeing the church stripped of all its familiar iconography and the Latin mass replaced by a new service in English, and that may have been one of the reasons that spurred him to leave his monument in the church. Although the current pews date from the 18th century, by the time he died there would have been pews in All Saints, and as was the custom of the day he would have directed that his monument should be placed above the pew where he and his wife Christian had sat, so that even in death they would still be part of the community. And so, indeed, they still are. He was a shrewd as well as a pious man, and although Purgatory had been formally abolished he was taking no chances and gave 'fortye pounds to the mariage of poore maydens', and also 'three houses for poore and impotent people', to speed his journey to Heaven. The three houses were in Thatcham where he probably originally came from. Such houses were the forerunners of almshouses, a traditional feature of many villages. There were at one time two 'parish cottages' in Ham but they were sold in 1882,[65] and later purchased by Henry Deacon Woodman in 1895; they were located south of Manor Farm roughly where Manor Farm Cottages now stand.

11

THE CIVIL WAR

The Civil War of 1642–46 was nasty, brutish and long. It was a war no one wanted, and it might not have happened had Charles 1 and his enemies in Parliament not left themselves with nowhere to go. Even when war became inevitable it was thought that it would be a short war, but in the initial stages both sides squandered opportunities to strike a decisive blow. The two battles of Newbury in September 1643 and October 1644 illustrate this well.

In the first battle a weakened Parliamentary army under the Earl of Essex was hurrying back from Gloucester to London. Essex was intent on getting his army back to London intact. The Royalists were equally determined to bring him to battle before he could do so. Essex, however, twice stole a march on the Royalist forces monitoring his advance towards Newbury, and this was compounded when Prince Rupert in charge of the Royalist cavalry failed to rout the Parliamentary army as it was strung out along the Aldbourne valley. Rupert in turn outflanked Essex by getting to Newbury first, where the King's army formed a blocking position at Wash Common. Then, in a daring coup de main manoeuvre at dawn, Essex seized the dominating high ground, Round Hill, under the noses of the Royalist army. It proved to be the vital ground of the battle, forcing the Royalists to fight a series of bloody engagements to try and dislodge the Parliamentary forces who were protected by the close *bocage* country around the hill. Eventually heavy losses and shortage of ammunition compelled the King to withdraw to Oxford, leaving the way clear for Essex to lead his army back to London. It has been described as the hinge battle of the war, and a year later the Parliamentary army had an opportunity to clinch matters.

On this occasion Charles was on his way back from Cornwall with a weakened force and found himself faced with a Parliamentary army twice his size. He took up a defensive position at Newbury, and the Parliamentary army decided to attack him from two flanks in a pincer movement. The inherent risk of this tactic was compounded when the attack was not launched until three o'clock in the afternoon, and then the eastern wing delayed its assault for an hour. In the failing light neither wing was able to press home its attack, allowing the Royalists to escape.

In the end Parliament's New Model Army won the war at Naseby in 1645. Charles surrendered in 1646 and following the so-called Second Civil War he was executed in January 1649 at the behest of the Army. But 11 years later the pendulum had swung back again: the monarchy was restored, the surviving regicides met painful deaths, and the old form of Anglican service was reinstated in churches. So why should the war have affected a small rural village like Ham? The answer is that between 1643 and 1646 Ham found itself in the major cockpit of a full-scale civil war, in which it is estimated that at least one in five men of military age bore arms at one stage or another. It would be quite wrong to attempt to translate a national statistic to one small village, but equally it seems unlikely that the inhabitants of Ham were disinterested bystanders – or could afford to be even if that was what they wanted. Trying to assess what happened, and in particular which side Ham supported, is like attempting to unravel a detective story in which there is plenty of background noise but few real clues.

It has been said that if a line were drawn from Hull to Southampton, west of that line was for the King and to the east was for Parliament. Of course this is a very crude division. Even so, it is perhaps pertinent that Ham falls just west of that line in what might be argued was no-man's land. Another crude barometer was that the nobility, the gentry and the church were for the King and the common man was for Parliament. Again it is an over-simplification; after all, it was a group of nobles which had forced Charles into a corner in 1640–41, and some of these – the Earls of Essex, Warwick, Bedford and Manchester – took up senior military commands on behalf of Parliament. Both divisions were riddled with contradictions and nowhere more so than in Wiltshire. Of the 34 MPs for the county 12 came out for the King and 22 for Parliament. Both of Bedwyn's MPs were for Parliament, and the two MPs for Marlborough were split one for each side. Five of the MPs who supported Parliament were knights of the shire. More generally, the south-west of Wiltshire declared initially for the King and the north-east for Parliament, with Marlborough putting up a spirited defence to repulse an attempt by the Royalists to take it in 1642. Ten miles to the east of Ham, Newbury, a cloth town, which had been bled white by Charles's taxes also initially declared for Parliament, only to find that having a Parliamentary garrison billeted on it was even worse. Hungerford was probably for Parliament too, but having soldiers from one side or the other billeted on it for most of the war, it wisely kept silent on its true allegiance and overtly blew pragmatically with the wind.

As the war ground on the Royalists tightened their grip on the whole of Wiltshire, while Oxfordshire and much of Berkshire also provided a loose cordon of garrisons around Charles's base at Oxford.   Often a leading figure in the local community would sway it one way or another, and John Hunt of the Ham Manor estate would have been the most prominent person then in Ham. He would have still been smarting from the fines levied on him by Charles a decade earlier for refusing to purchase a knighthood. To add insult to injury he would have also been paying Ship Money. This was a tax ostensibly to maintain the royal navy. Charles was not the first monarch to impose it, but he did so at a penal rate in 1634. Although it was assessed differently in each county, generally the main weight of the tax – which was on land – fell on the middle classes, and John Hunt and his fellow landowners in Ham would have felt its lash prior to the war. So was he for Parliament, and did the men and women of Ham follow his lead?

In those days armies lived off the land. Ham was possibly too small and too remote to have soldiers billeted on it, but the village would not have escaped either army's need for food and forage. Following a series of poor harvests in the late 1620s and early 1630s food was already in relatively short supply at the beginning of the war. The situation quickly became acute and prices rocketed. England was already in the grip of the Little Ice Age at the time, and winters were longer and harsher, exacerbating these difficulties. Cattle, sheep, grain and fodder were all ruthlessly requisitioned. Horses too were in great demand for the cavalries and logistic requirements of both armies. Each side raised money through taxes based on property holdings but neither side was inclined to pay for what it took, and in any case taxation often became a matter of seizing goods in kind as supplies for an army. Perhaps Parliament was more likely to pay than the Royalists, but either way local landowners were effectively hit twice. This attack on the rural economy must have bitten deep in Ham where some 25 copyholders as well as the three principal landowners would have been affected by it. When Essex and his army were sloshing through the driving rain to Hungerford two nights before the first battle of Newbury, his quartermasters found that the countryside for some miles around Hungerford had already been stripped bare by the Royalists – and this was shortly after the harvest and before a hard winter. Beyond what was officially requisitioned, soldiers foraged and pillaged on their own account. The situation became so desperate later in the war that in Somerset and Wiltshire farmers banded together to form a defensive force against these marauders, which became known as the Clubmen. At one stage it was estimated that there were as many as 20,000 Clubmen in Wiltshire although it is uncertain whether they ever reached as far as Ham, their main sphere of operation being astride the Somerset and Wiltshire border. By the later stages of the war the whole of Wiltshire was held by the Royalists, and it is likely that these continual depredations would have pushed Ham into the Parliamentary camp even it were not already there at the outset.

But did the men of Ham actually fight in the war? Before the war there was no standing army. Instead counties were required to raise and maintain levies known as Trained Bands. These were a form of territorial army and they were probably more evident on the paper of county rolls than they were in the flesh. Training as such was scant if at all. Nevertheless, they were better than nothing and when the war started both sides rushed to scoop them up. At the beginning of the war the Trained Bands in Wiltshire apparently numbered some 5,000, and it is quite possible that they included men from Ham. As well as the Trained Bands there were volunteers, and in due course both sides instituted conscription. There is, however, no documentary evidence of what happened in Ham. At first glance burial records appear to offer a possible clue. Significant numbers were killed in the war, but unless a person was eminent and wealthy the chances of being repatriated to one's village for burial was remote. An eyewitness account of the first battle of Newbury records the dead being stripped that night where they fell and the naked bodies being taken away in carts the next day to be buried in pits. Amongst those killed in the battle was the Royalist Viscount Falkland whose memorial stands at Wash Common. His body was found the day after stripped and mangled, and he was only recognised by a distinctive mole on his neck. And that seems to have been the general pattern in the other battles as well. Whilst there were surgeons attached to regiments, and a degree of chivalry was shown towards the wounded of both sides, to be wounded and survive was rare as in those days surgeons had few remedies for war wounds, especially those inflicted by gunshot. Beyond the battlefield typhus and sporadic outbreaks of the plague also took their toll.

Unfortunately the burial records of All Saints' Church for the 17th century are sketchy. In particular there is a gap between 1635 and 1666. It is tempting to read something into this, especially as there is no record of any of the 20 male children baptised at All Saints between 1604 (when the baptism records begin) and 1623 who would have been of prime military age during the war being buried in the churchyard. However, it has to be accepted that this gap is more likely to be due to either poor record keeping or the loss of those particular records, rather than a score of men from the village being buried in a 'foreign field'.

To add to this riddle, a rent roll of the village for the Dean and Chapter of Winchester Cathedral for 1644[66] survives and is shown below. The bald list of names and rents paid projects an image of unruffled normality far removed from any civil war. Men such as Robert Bright, Richard Dyer and Matthew Hunt all feature again in village life at the end of the century or the beginning of the next and would have been of military age in 1644. There are four widows amongst the leaseholders but there is no evidence to tie their husbands' deaths to the war.

	£	s	d
Mr Curle of Buttermere	3	0	0
Laurence Hunt	3	3	1
John Hunt	1	0	0
Widd. Smales		12	0
Mich. Bennet		14	0
Rob. Bright		15	6
Mich. Hodges	1	3	6
John Cooper		11	6
Wm. Elton		6	0
Rich. Dyer		6	5
Widd. Ann Bennet		6	1
Rob. Merriot		4	7
Widd. Batt		1	2

William Warrant	4	6
Edw. Rolph & Rob. Symes	1	3
Widd. Grace Bennet	1	11
Math. Hunt	2	0

The final factor in this search, as ever in those days, was religion. Prior to the war Archbishop Laud's highhanded, doctrinaire policies towards the liturgy and governance of the Church of England, fuelled by a popular fear of Roman Catholics that was exacerbated by Queen Henrietta Maria's overt Catholicism, drove many of the moderate Protestants in Parliament and throughout the country into the arms of the Puritans. Feelings in Scotland were even more intense, and Laud and the King, who firmly supported Laud's policies, made the fatal mistake of trying to impose a new Anglican prayer book on the Scots, which resulted in the First and Second Bishops' Wars in 1639 and 1640 and subsequent humiliation for the Crown. Laud would end his days on the scaffold in 1645, but before then the old Anglican form of worship was being steadily dismantled throughout the country. At the end of the war a new Directory of Worship replaced the Anglican Prayer Book, and England found itself in the grip

Rent roll for Ham for the Dean and Chapter of Winchester, 1644

of a radical form of Protestantism. In an echo of the Reformation a century earlier, the altar rails which Laud had required to be installed in churches were ripped out, stained glass windows were smashed, and some of the great stone crosses in public places were destroyed. Worse still for many ordinary parishioners, the great Christian festivals including Christmas were abolished. At parish level there was also sequestration, the removal of rectors from their benefices and their replacement by clergy amenable to the new regime. Eighty rectors were sequestered by the County Committee in Wiltshire and they included the Reverend Robert Newlin of Ham at sometime before May 1646;[67] he had been rector of All Saints since 1643. The reasons for sequestration were various and the County Committee relied heavily on evidence being provided by local villagers. It seems unlikely that this was the case in Ham, because Robert Newlin would return as rector in due course and anyway it was not hard to look for a reason for his falling foul of the County Committee. He was President of Corpus Christi College of Oxford University and Oxford had been the stronghold of the King. Robert Newlin would be a grand survivor in more ways than one. He returned to Ham on the Restoration in 1660 and remained in office there until his death in 1687. During his exile he married a rich widow, Jane, the daughter of Dr Daniel Collins, Canon of Windsor, and from 1660 he was also the sinecure rector for Wroughton.[68]

In Robert Newlin's place the Reverend Henry Newlin was 'intruded', to use the terminology of the day.[69] Henry Newlin does not appear to have been any relation to his predecessor and was evidently a zealous and ambitious man. In 1649 it was reported that:

> In Hamme there is a parsonage presentative in the guift formerly of the Deane and Cannons of Windsor nowe in the state of the value of Seaventy poundes per annum, Mr Henry Newlin is the present Incumbent supplies the Cure, and preacheth constantlie twice every Lordes day and receives the profittes. Witnesses William Cooper Nicholas Newlin.[70]

Again it is not clear whether Nicholas Newlin was any relation. While there is outwardly nothing wrong in holding matins and evensong every Sunday, it is possible to detect just a hint of a sharp edge in the comment about receiving the profits. In any event, whatever the leanings of Ham's parishioners were in their religious beliefs, Henry Newlin seems to have been an uncomfortable rector for a small country parish. It is not certain how long he remained at Ham as the Reverend Richard Willowes (1656) and Reverend John Wilmer are also recorded as having served at Ham, but they may have been curates.[71]

The rectory was also sequestered and let for a year by the County Committee at £40.[72] A few years later in 1650 it was worth £70 yearly. It is not known where the rectory was at this stage or of what it consisted. The core of what is now known as The Old Rectory is believed to have been built in the late 17th century, which would probably place it after this point. The first concrete evidence of it as a residence comes in 1677 when it is described as 'the parsonage house, barns, stables, orchard, garden, backside, etc., quarter acre of meadow ground, meadow called Parsonage Several two acres', plus a further 20 acres scattered about the parish.[73] This description puts it firmly in The Old Rectory's current location. So it is likely that The Old Rectory was built sometime soon after the Restoration.

There is a possible reference to this rectory in part of a letter which was apparently written by the Bishop of Winchester to the president of a university college. It is not dated but the handwriting is consistent with the end of the 17th century, and the letter is evidently a draft. [74]

> Reverend Mr President
>
> The business of the Parsonage at Ham, relating to the design'd Inclosures, hath been very particularly, & I hope truly represented to me. And as I am of the Opinion, that when you are assured that the doing of it will be no ways prejudiciall (sic) to you, w(hi)ch I doubt not you will be, when you have unexceptional security given you for as long as you live, for what Rights do duly belong to you; so I have reason to believe that it may be a means to make that Living most advantageous to succession.

There are several mysteries to the letter. The initial attribution by the Berkshire Record Office was that the letter was written to the President of Trinity College – probably Trinity College, Oxford – but from further research this is clearly wrong, and the consensus now is that it refers to the Reverend Robert Newlin as President of Corpus Christi. The next mystery is its reference to enclosures. The glebe land belonging to the rectory was not enclosed until 1828 and the handwriting is too early for that, and so the letter may refer either to an earlier abortive attempt at an enclosure or, if the rectory were in the process of being built at the time, to its new siting in the village. Whatever the exact circumstances surrounding the letter were, it is clear that there was a desire by both parties that the rectory should attract high calibre incumbents.

A bigger prize for the Commonwealth was the sequestration of the Ham Manor estate from the Church. In 1649 the parliamentary trustees granted the farm house and demesne of about 304 acres to Henry and Thomas Hunt and the remainder of the land together with the manorial rights to the Reverend Hugh Whistler, rector of Faccombe-cum-Combe.[75] Both grants seem strange. It is not clear where Henry and Thomas fitted in to the Hunt family tree. There was a John Hunt, if not two John Hunts, in existence at the time one of whom must surely have been the demesne farmer – a marriage settlement of the 13th year of Charles 1's reign (1638) by John Hunt senior refers to John Hunt younger marrying Katherine Brownjohn.[76] Perhaps there was a sideways move in the Hunt succession. In any case the Hunt family seems to have been in good odour with the Parliamentarians. Stranger still is the case of Hugh

Whistler. He had been rector at Faccombe, a few miles away, since the age of 24 in 1618 and was an avowed Royalist, but for some reason the Triers did not catch up with him until 1656 when he was sequestered from his parish and replaced by John Tabard.[77] The answer probably is that like many other families whose loyalties were split he remained very well connected with the other side, in his case the Parliamentarians. One brother was an MP in the Long Parliament and another was a captain in the Earl of Essex's Horse and fought alongside the young Oliver Cromwell. One of Hugh's seven sons, Henry, later received a commission in a regiment of foot, his commission being signed by Cromwell.[78] However, what made Hugh Whistler a suitable recipient for part of the Ham Manor estate is still a complete mystery. Perhaps he and the Hunt brothers simply purchased the estate between them. He died in 1661, although his entry in *Walker Revised* suggests he died shortly before the Restoration. In any case with the Restoration the lands were restored to the Church.

There is no neat denouement to the detective story of Ham's involvement in the war. It would be convenient to say that Ham sided with Parliament and that some of its sons probably fought for that cause, but there is no hard evidence to support that, and much of the evidence that does exist seems merely to add to the riddle. What is certain is that Ham was caught up in the war and its aftermath, even if its role were largely a passive one.

There is a curious postscript to the Civil War and Restoration era. When Charles II died he was succeeded by his brother James II in 1685. The Duke of Monmouth, Charles's illegitimate son, mounted a rebellion against him but was defeated at the battle of Sedgemoor in Somerset. In the Bloody Assizes presided over by Judge Jeffreys which followed, hundreds of rebels were hanged or transported for life. There is a story that a part of the Bloody Assizes was held in Ham Manor, the ceiling of the drawing room in the house being specifically raised so that the room could be used as a court room. While the ceiling of the room certainly appears to have been heightened at some stage, the rest of the story is fiction. The Western Circuit of the Bloody Assizes is well documented. It took Jeffreys to Winchester, Salisbury, Dorchester, Exeter, Taunton and Wells, all assize towns. There was never any need to set up a makeshift court, let alone in Ham. Nevertheless, Ham Manor subsequently earned a reputation as a haunted house. The Delevingnes who owned it in the 1960s are said to have sold the house as a result, and the Philipps family who were there in the 1970s and 1980s can also recall mysterious happenings.

A link that has survived is a cache dated to the mid 17th century, which was discovered in a recess in a chimney breast in Tudor Cottage after the Second World War. It comprises an embroidered pair of leather gloves, shoes, a glass pipe and other items, some of which are now in the museum in Newbury. From the fineness of the gloves they were evidently owned by a gentleman, and possibly a Royalist, but there is no clue as to whom precisely they belonged or why they were hidden. Adding to the mystery and intrigue, the shoes must have belonged

Reg Haines beside the fireplace in Tudor Cottage where the 17th-century cache was found

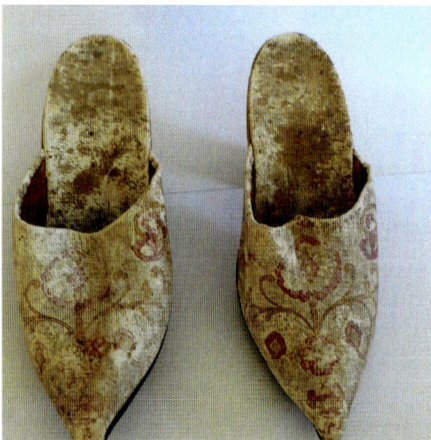

Part of 17th-century cache hidden in the chimney breast of Tudor Cottage: (from the top) a pair of green silk shoes which would have been fastened with buckles, a pair of embroidered gloves, and a pair of patterned leather mules

Tudor Cottage, one of two surviving dwellings in the village from the 16th century; the front door was originally in the gable end facing the road

to a gentlewoman. It is unlikely that the cache belonged to the owner of Tudor Cottage at that time, as the cottage was originally two semi-detached cottages and each cottage would have been too small for a gentleman's residence – by the 19th century they were two farm workers' cottages. Possibly the items belonged to a Royalist officer billeted in Tudor Cottage, who hid them prior to one of the battles of Newbury but did not survive to retrieve them. Equally they could have been loot from a baggage train of one of the armies, hidden until the war was forgotten but then themselves forgotten. Or perhaps they simply belonged to someone in the village who felt it best to hide them while the cool Puritan wind of war and Commonwealth was blowing, the secret dying with him.

18

THE VILLAGE IN THE 18TH CENTURY

> Rural England of the eighteenth century stands out as a unique and final
> exemplar of the qualities naturally bred in the soil. It maintained a type
> of existence which we do not see before that time in such untroubled
> perfection, and which have since been subjected to vicissitudes that have
> practically destroyed it altogether.

These are the opening sentences of *English Rural Life in the 18th Century* by the art historian William Gaunt, which was published in 1925. The book is illustrated with contemporary 18th-century work such as George Morland's charming rustic scenes and Thomas Rowlandson's jauntier episodes of rural life. Gaunt was writing for the *Connoisseur* series – what would now be described as coffee-table books – and the book was published not long after the First World War when Gaunt was 25, so his nostalgic and arguably rosy-tinted view of rural life in the 18th century is understandable. Yet he had a point. Domestically England was at peace after centuries of turmoil, and her foreign wars did not disturb rural life too deeply. Although there was still a marked hierarchy in rural village life – squire, yeoman farmer, copyholder and labourer – in which each notch of these strata was doubtless keenly felt and observed, the old feudal system was long gone. The middle decades of the century were bountiful in harvests, food was plentiful and prices were low. Surrounded by what by then had become known as 'sheep-corn country' Ham must have prospered.

There was, however, a seamier side to life. Justice could be arbitrary and by modern standards excessively harsh. There were nearly 200 offences for which a man or woman might be hanged. Other punishments ranged from transportation for life to imprisonment, flogging, whipping and branding. How the residents of Ham fared under this system is not clear. The only known instance of possible crime is a reference to a hand-out from the parish poor fund in 1788 to the wife of Joseph Hercomb while her husband was in prison. No trace of his crime and sentence can be found, and he may have been imprisoned for debt. Both Joseph Hercomb and his wife Mary died two years later in 1790. Their descendants would become blacksmiths in the village in the next century. Nationally, the scourge of the countryside as well as towns was drunkenness, proving perhaps that the problems of binge drinking are nothing new. The Crown & Anchor and the Cross Keys Inn, the latter situated on the site of Netherfield, roughly opposite the southerly junction of Ham Road and Cutting Hill, and which was later destroyed by fire, did not appear until the 19th century, but alehouses were popular in villages well before that time. In 1720 a Robert Shuttle applied to open an alehouse in Ham but the village was having none of it. The following petition was sent to the authorities:

> Wee ye Churchwardens and other ye Inhabitants of ye parish of Ham whose names are underwritten knowing it is ye design of one Rob. Shuttle to keep an Alehouse in our s(a)id parish doo humblely desire your Worships favour to discountenance ye same y(e)t wee may have no Alehouse in our parish aforesaid.[79]

Their plea was apparently effective because in a list of innkeepers licensed in Wiltshire in the 18th century there is none from Ham.[80]

It is not clear whether this blow for temperance was simply the village's natural aversion to the evils of drunkenness evident elsewhere, or whether it reflected a deeper Puritan streak in

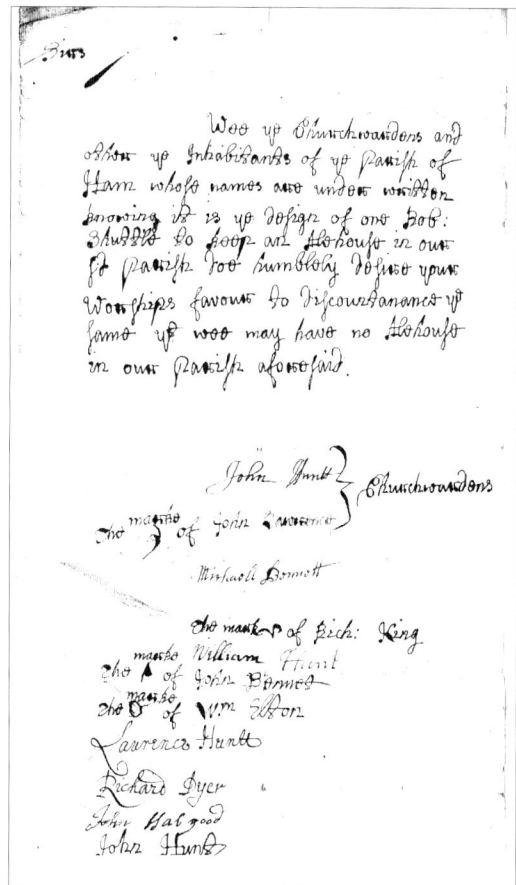

Petition by the village opposing the opening of an alehouse, 1720

the inhabitants' religious preferences. The latter seems unlikely because although there may well have been some who had welcomed the Commonwealth's new order of service, the return of Robert Newlin as rector with the Restoration, to be followed by Richard Gillingham who had just died and is discussed later, suggests a church and congregation well disposed to a traditional form of worship. There may have been other reasons why the village was opposed to Robert Shuttle, but whatever the cause any deep-seated inhibitions that might have been held were swept away in the 19th century with the arrival of not one but two public houses in the village.

Other contemporary artists and writers besides Morland and Rowlandson were keen to extol a romantic vision of the rural scene. Perhaps the best known was Thomas Gray whose *Elegy written in a country churchyard* enjoyed considerable popular acclaim at the time. Written in 1751, it was a hymn to the dignity and serenity of ordinary rural village life 'far from the madding crowd's ignoble strife'. Gray lived in Cambridgeshire but his churchyard could just as easily have been in Ham such are the local echoes in his verses. Ham's own memorial to this romance is in the epitaph carved on the gravestone of the village blacksmith, Alexander Shearman, who died in 1763:

> My Sledge and Hammer lies reclin'd
> My Bellows too have lost their Wind
> My fires extinct, my forge decay'd
> And in the dust my Vice is laid
> My Coals are spent my Irons gone
> My Nails are drove my work is done.

It would be nice to think that this was Ham's own iconic rhyme. In fact it was a popular epitaph for blacksmiths and appears in a number of other churchyards, some as far afield as Wales and the Midlands. It is attributed to a poet called Hayley and the earliest recorded examples date from 1743 and 1746.[81] Other craftsmen such as watchmakers, tailors, cobblers and even the blower of the bellows for a church organ (*No puffer he/ Though a capital blower/ He could fill double G/ And now lies a note lower*) also enjoyed the same kind of epitaph, and the gentle humour in the verses masked a genuine admiration for their particular skills. Alexander Shearman (the name is also spelt Sherman, Shermon, Shireman and Shirman) would have lived with his wife Susannah in Forge Cottage. The name does not appear in the records of the village in the previous century, but Alexander and Susannah had a large family and the Shearmans became well known locally: a Shearman was farming land at Inkpen in the late 20th century.

Trying to look beneath the veneer of romance which coloured the century is more difficult, although it is possible to shed some light on village life in Ham from three disparate sets of documents. The first is the will of Matthew Hunt who died in 1712.[82] It is perhaps more redolent of the late 17th than the 18th century, but it still gives an idea of the standard of living at the more privileged end of village society in the early part of the 18th century. It is not known when Matthew Hunt was born. It seems likely that he was a younger son of the John Hunt who was born in 1605. As such he would have been brought up in Ham Manor, after which he lived with his wife Mary elsewhere in the village. He did not own his house and paid an annual rent of 2s for it, and it is also evident that he shared the usual fate of younger sons and inherited no land. Whether he helped farm the family estate or held copyhold land is not known, but whatever he did he had little of real value to bequeath at the end of his life. Nevertheless, the catalogue of his possessions set out in his will below is fascinating both in its meticulous detail and in the importance attached to what today would be considered commonplace domestic furniture and utensils.

In the name of God amen. October the twelfth Annoq Dom: 1710. I Matthew Hunt Sen of Ham in the County of Wilts Yeoman being in Health but Weak of body but of Sound and perfect mind Memory & Understanding praised be the Lord therefore calling to mind the Mortality of my body and knowing that it is appointed for all men once to dye do thus make and Ordain my last Will and Testament in manner and forme following First and principally I give my Soule into the hands of God who gave it me and for my body I commend it to the Earth to be buried in Christian and devout manner at the Discretion of my Executrix hereafter nominated in the parish Churchyard of Ham aforesaid nothing doubting but at the generall Resurrection but I shall receive the same again by the mighty power of God and for the Worldly Estate wherewith it has pleased God to bless me with in this life I give devise dispose and bequeath in manner and forme following Imprimus I give and bequeath unto my well beloved son Henry Hunt one shilling and all the window shutters and benches belonging to my dwelling house and my best bedstead two Tubbs one Barrell and one pair of Hangills Item I give and bequeath unto my Son in Law William Oram one shilling and five years od yett to his son William my Grandson already past Item I give and bequeath unto my Son Matthew Hunt five pounds and all my Wearing Apparell and my Bible and the bedstead in the Hall Chamber Item I give and bequeath unto my Daughter Sarah Ward the sume of one shilling Item I give and bequeath unto my Daughter Mary Collins the sume of one shilling Item I give and bequeath unto my Grandson William Oram Son of my Daughter Elizabeth Doris these severall goods hereafter named to the only use and benefitt of the said William Oram the Younger after the Decease of Mary Hunt my now Wife. Six pewter porringers one pewter Tankard one pewter Candlestick two Tinn Candlesticks six pewter dishes six little pewter dishes one pewter Flagon One Cullonder two brass potts One Iron pot and pot hooks four Kettles two brass Skilletts and the Jack two Spitts and dripping pan the pair of great Andirons the little pair of Andirons Another pair of Andirons with brass heads One Iron Fender One brass warming pan One Iron fire one pair of beefe forks One Toasting Iron two pair of pothooks One Gridiron two Smoothing Irons two pair of Hangells One Cleaver and Trencher-Rack the great Cuppard standing in the Hall two pair of tongs One fire Shovell the great Brewing Tubb and Dough Civer One little Civer one Great Barrell One Side Cupboard one little Tableboard in the Parlour Chamber One truckle bedstead two fether beds three further bolsters two downe pillows one further pillow one fork bed one Red Rugg one pair of sheets One pair of pillow cases with the Curtains and Valens and Curtain Rodds in the Parlour Chamber four joynt sheets one Trunk one Coffer and White Chest One Tinn pudding pan one Bread Grater and my Will is that if my abovesaid Grandson William Oram the Younger shall happen to dye before he comes to the Age of one and twenty years that then the Abovesaid Goods shall be equally divided between my Son Matthew Hunt and my Daughter Mary Collins on their Exec-s and Assignes. Item and lastly after my debts and funeral charges be paid and disbursed my Will is that my said goods above bequeathed shall be used by my now wife Mary Hunt during her naturall life and All the Rest of my goods Chattels Moneys and personal Estate I give and bequeath unto my beloved wife Mary Hunt and do hereby Constitute and Appoint her Mary Hunt my now wife my full and Whole Executrix of this my Will and Testament And I do hereby desire Authorise and Impower my Son Henry Hunt and William Oram Sen to be trustees and supervisors of this my Will and Testament to taker care that the abovesaid Moneys and goods so bequeathed be applied to the uses hereby intended and that the same be not anyways wasted or imbeazeled ….

At the other end of the spectrum the accounts of the village poor fund [83] provide a marvellous glimpse of how another stratum of the village lived – and survived. The accounts book is a long slim volume, not unlike a modern accounts book in shape, with a year to each page. It is covered in a wrapper of vellum and fastened with a metal catch. It was begun by Robert Bright, overseer, and contains the detailed accounts of the disbursement of poor relief in the parish for the period 1683–1797. The system of poor relief in Ham emanated from the Elizabethan Poor Law of 1601, which placed the onus on parishes to care for the poor and provided for a poor relief rate to be levied on parishioners. There were two overseers each year who were men of standing in the parish. The names of the Hunt family figure frequently as overseers and towards the end of the 18th century the Watts family also features. The accounts were signed off each year by a number of other village inhabitants. To begin with the rector, Richard Gillingham, who died in 1719 and has a monument in the church, was a frequent signatory, but generally the signatories appear to have been selected democratically, and there are instances where a signatory makes his mark instead of signing his name. All the overseers and signatories were male. Occasionally a signatory later finds himself on hard times and becomes himself a recipient of charity. James Mackrell, also spelt Mackreill and Mackreil, was a churchwarden and signatory in 1775. Thirteen years later there is an entry: 'Bought for Js Mackrell 2 shirts and a pair of Britches 12s 6d'. The spelling of names throughout, as in most documents of that period, is haphazard. In 1696 Richard Dyers is listed as an overseer; in 1698 he signs himself as a signatory, Richard Dier, and a year later he signs himself as Richard Dyer.

Initially the names of the recipients are not mentioned, only the amounts handed out, but this quickly changes. In 1714, amongst others the following received payments: 'Rob.Bennet, Richardson's wife, Widd. Hopkins, Widd. Weston, Will. Hitchman'. In the same year there is 'A pair of shoes for Knight's girl 1s 6d', and 'A pair of breeches for John Weston 2s', who is presumably Widow Weston's son. Five years later there is an entry 'Rob.Bennet's coffin 8s'.

Death is dealt with kindly. In 1740 there is an entry for 'the woman that layd out Goody Simes 6s'. Goody, now remembered in the pantomime character Goody Two Shoes, was short for goodwife, a respectable form of address for a married woman of humble rank in those days. Women are variously referred to in the accounts book as Dame, Goody or Widow. By today's standards the differences in the costs of various items are sometimes surprising. In 1786/7 the overseers 'Paid Richd. Hobbs for thetching (sic) the Widow Randalls House and Spars 3s', to which is added 'Straw to thetch Randalls house 5s'. On the same page there are entries for 'Doctor Smith's Bill 6s, Wm Rose a pair of Britches 5s 6d' (more than twice the price of a pair of britches some 70 years earlier), and 'Expences for atending the Justis at Everly 10s 6d'(sic). The last entry seems strange for a poor fund but by the end of the century there are a number of more general entries. In 1788 the fund paid £20 for Parsonage Rates Uncollected and £15 6s for Parsonage Land Tax; seven years later the Parsonage Rates had risen to £32 10s but the Land Tax had not altered. However, the great majority of expenses throughout the century are payments to individuals, usually as an annual or, later on, monthly allowance. Wood for the poor is another frequent entry. Overall there seems to have been a true spirit of generosity, perhaps epitomised by two of the entries for 1788: 'Gave Herecomb's wife while he was in prison £1 12s' and 'John Rolfe Marriage etc ring etc £5 5s'. While most of the funds for disbursement would have come from the poor relief levy, occasionally other moneys were received. There is a receipt dated 25 April 1720 for a 'legacy of twenty pds from Mr John Hunt deceased for the use of the poor of this Parish'. It is signed by the Minister (sic) Philip Hayward and by William Elton, Churchwarden, who made his mark; they were the two overseers of the poor fund for that year. Disbursements from the poor fund increased from a total of £5 5s in 1683 to £178 2s 5d in 1795, but the latter was exceptional, the annual average being around £100 at the end of the 18th century. This still represented a very considerable figure for those times.

The third and arguably most informative document for Ham as an agricultural community is the surviving Ham Manor estate farm accounts for 1749–1759.[84] Although the accounts are now in a very dilapidated state, it is still possible to decipher most of the contents. Each double page sets out the income and expenditure for roughly a quarter of the year. They are all written in the same hand except for the final year, 1759, when a new hand begins. A John Hunt died in 1749, but whether these accounts were written by a Hunt or a Watts and who succeeded in 1759 for the moment remain mysteries. A particularly interesting feature of the accounts is that they not only cover a decade in what might be termed the years of plenty for harvests in the 18th century, but that particular decade is also viewed as the gateway to the Agricultural Revolution.

On 29 September 1754, midway through the accounts, a stocktaking sets out the assets of the estate. This would have been shortly after the harvest, and while it is not clear from the detailed workings in the accounts it is presumed that the values given to the cereals represent actual yields.

	£	s	d
Sheep – 3 rams			
84 weathers (sic)			
159 ewes			
123 lambs	128	14	0
Horses (7)	42	10	0
Pigs –1 sow			
9 little pigs			
4 stere (sic) hogs			
5 little steres	8	5	0
Husbandry tackle/ household goods			
(including a new wagon)	48	10	0
Old Cork Beans (1 barrel)	0	3	0
Wheat 47 acres	176	16	0
Barley 37½ acres	65	12	6
Oats 8 acres	14	0	0
Pease 15 acres	27	0	0
Beans 6 acres	14	5	0
Wool	12	0	0
Hay	55	0	0

Clover	28	11	0
Seed – lands ploughed	18	0	0
Dung – 30 loads above hill and 190 loads below	10	12	6
Turnips planted and clover to stand	5	8	0
Chaff	0	8	9
Poultry	2	0	0
Debtors and sundries	0	18	0
	659	9	9

Ham Manor Farm accounts for January–March 1754

That calendar year the turnover was £299 17s 2¾d with a deficit of £43 6s 7d. The main income came from wheat (£138), barley (£60), sheep (£21) and pigs (£16). Expenditure ranged from wages to killing rats and catching moles. The monthly wage bill was in the order of £4 7s. On top of that James Mackrell, the churchwarden who would fall on hard times some 30 years later, appears to have been employed as the foreman and paid £43 annually. There were additional expenses for the harvest in September (£27 9s 7½ d), haymaking, sowing, hedging, shearing and the cutting (castration) of lambs and pigs. The purchase of seed was also a major expenditure. Then there was the care of the horses and purchase of hay and bran for them. Harness was bought and Alexander Shearman the blacksmith's bill was a hefty £5 6s 5d. The names of the workhorses have a familiar, ageless ring: Dragon, Jolly, Duke, Grey, Captain, Whitefoot and Diamond. Six shillings were paid for the covering of the mare in July and again in September. Either the second payment was a success fee or it was a second attempt – the mare is referred to as the 'old mare' in the September accounts. The wheelwright also earned £5 16s 2d from the estate. The accounts do not reveal whether the wheelwright was a Ham man or whether he lived and worked elsewhere. There was certainly a wheelwright in the village by the middle of the next century, so it is just possible that Ham was largely self-sufficient at this time. Beyond purely agricultural expenses, land and window tax of £3 12s 10d was paid twice a year; the monthly contribution to the poor of Ham was 13s 4d; and further sums were paid twice yearly for the poor of Buttermere. The greatest expense, however, was £105 creamed off the farm revenues in cash. There is no explanation of how this was spent and it was presumably for the expenses of the family and the running of the manor house.

Although at one level all seems well ordered in the 18th century, Gaunt is arguably on shakier ground by inferring that it was untroubled perfection. Undoubtedly there were a cumulative number of events which bit deep into rural life in the first half of the 19th century. A surplus of labour was generated following the end of the Napoleonic wars. Both this and reforms of the poor laws, including a raft of workhouses built across the country in the 1830s (there were workhouses in Hungerford and Marlborough), led to low agricultural wages. In turn this was aggravated by the enclosure of common land and advances in the mechanisation of agriculture. The Corn Law of 1815 was designed to protect the British farmer but had the opposite effect for the common man by pushing up the price of bread. In 1830 the frustration of agricultural labourers exploded in the Captain Swing riots in which threshing machines were burnt. In its latter stages this movement spread along the Kennet valley; men of Kintbury and Shalbourne were involved, and at least three men from Ham appear to have taken part although two were acquitted. The riots were put down by troops and the punishments awarded by the courts were savage even by the standards of the times. The harsh conditions of rural life later in the century are immortalised in Thomas Hardy's Wessex novels. Yet the seeds of these problems were being sown long beforehand during the 18th century, and even in the 17th century.

It is generally held that the Agricultural Revolution lasted from 1750 to 1850, so that half of it – admittedly the more benign half – occurred in the 18th century. Some of the improvements were initially limited to the bigger landowners, but by the end of the century advances in agriculture were national in scope and Ham, with its sheep-corn economy, would have felt the benefits at yeoman level. The quality of cereal seed was steadily improving. This had started in the 17th century and cereal yields continued to improve throughout the 18th century, helped by the innovation of the seed drill. Jethro Tull had perfected his towed seed drill at Prosperous Farm just north of the parish boundary. It revolutionised the previous age-old, laborious and imperfect practice of broadcast sowing by hand that then had to be harrowed in. The 18th century was further bolstered by a long series of good harvests, particularly in the middle decades. Sheep breeds were improving too, and the sheep at Ham in the 18th century would probably have been Old Wiltshire, Berkshire Nott or Western – breeds known generically at Smithfield Market as Wiltshire Horned Sheep. Viscount 'Turnip' Townshend's introduction of a four-year crop rotation boosted both animal husbandry and arable yields. The value of crop rotation and the use of animal manure to fertilise the ground had been recognised since the Middle Ages but it had become trapped in a vicious circle. In theory the more animals the better the fertilisation and the bigger the yields, but in practice the size of herds was limited by the amount of fodder that could be grown to feed cattle and sheep in winter: the fodder gap. Townshend's fourth rotational year of clover or turnips as fodder bridged the gap. He died in 1738 so it is likely that his ideas had taken root in Ham by the middle of the century. From the Ham Manor stocktaking of 1754 it is possible to discern the importance both of clover and turnips and of manure to the estate; the 210 loads of manure are carefully shown as 30 'above hill' and 190 'below', giving a feel for the need to differentiate between the husbandry of land above Ham Hill and that below it in the mid-18th century.

Two other changes broke the agricultural mould in the 18th century. While the parish of Ham was divided into three main estates, like many other parishes it also contained numerous sub-tenanted copyhold estates and individual allotments. These had the effect of thwarting the best use of the land. It is estimated that there were some 25 copyholders in Ham in the mid 17th century. By 1780, as the Land Tax assessment list below shows, this number had reduced significantly, and by 1828 there were only six copyholders. [85]

An Assessment made in Pursuance of an Act of Parliament passed in the Twentieth Year of his present Majesty's Reign, for granting an Aid to his Majesty by a Land Tax to be raised in Great Britain, for the Service of the Year 1780.

Names of Proprietors	Names of Occupiers	Sums Assessed		
The Revd Mr Vanderplank	Mr John Hunt Watts	15	6	0
Mr John Hunt Watts	Mr John Hunt Watts	32	7	0
Wm Brotherton Esq	James Mackrill	14	7	4
John Bushell	Edith Stockwell	7	15	9
Ditto	Edward Hunt	0	3	7
Ditto	John Bushell	0	4	4
Edward Hunt	Edward Hunt	3	1	8
Ditto	Edward Hunt	2	14	5
Robert Bright	Edward Hunt	2	2	6
James Wheller	James Wheller	2	3	1
John Harding	John Harding	1	2	6
Francis Cooper	Francis Cooper	1	8	4
Ditto	Francis Cooper	0	13	2
John Torner	John Harding	1	2	6
William Mills	James Mackrill	0	9	1
Thomas Elson	Thomas Elson	1	8	4
Ditto for the Coppices	Thomas Elson	1	17	3
James Sutton	Francis Cooper	0	13	2
John Habgood	Francis Cooper	0	13	2
Richard Habgood	Richard Habgood	0	9	6

A number of other interesting points emerge from this list. The Reverend Israel Vanderplank is shown as being more heavily taxed than William Brotherton who owned East Court Farm. Vanderplank must have owned other land in addition to the 20 acres or so of glebe land unless his spacious rectory was also part of the tax assessment. As previously mentioned, it is curious that a Watts is not mentioned as owning Dove's Farm; by deduction the ownership seems to have passed temporarily to John Bushell, who was born in the parish in 1722. The Bushell family disappears from view in the 19th century, unless the Reverend John Bushnell who became the owner of East Court Farm by 1835 was a relation. There is a slight difference in the spelling of their surnames but in those days such differences were common. Lastly, from a social hierarchical point of view, it is interesting to note who is accorded a 'Mr' or 'Esq' to his name. There was obviously no pretence at subtlety.

The system of enclosures was another feature which led to better overall land management, although it must have simultaneously been a severe and bitter deprivation for those in the village who had relied on allotments and common grazing to supplement their incomes. Nevertheless, enclosures of common land ended the practice of permanent pasture and

Land tax list for the Parish of Ham
and Tithing of Henley, 1780

allowed crop rotation in its place. The formal enclosure acts were 19th-century creations, but long before that enclosures by private treaty had been taking place over previous decades if not centuries. Amongst the Winchester diocese manors there is evidence of enclosures in the 13th century. In Ham the regular pattern of the fields is testimony to a gradual process of land enclosure. *The Act for Inclosing Lands in the Parish of Ham, in the County of Wilts* [86] received Royal Assent on 21 March 1827. It provided both for the new enclosure of 639 acres and confirmed old enclosures of 975 acres; in other words 60 per cent of the parish was already enclosed by 1827. The enclosures included Great Field, Little Field, Pidgett (sic) Field, Several Mead and Home Meadow. Prior to its enclosure Great Field was common land, and the map of 1810 shows much of it divided up into strips of land or allotments for grazing and for growing hay and clover.

As well as the land, the inhabitants of the parish were changing too. There is perhaps a tendency to think of small rural villages in past centuries as having close, almost incestuous populations, but the truth is that there was a constant movement into and out of neighbouring villages, and sometimes much further afield, for marriage, work or the exchange of land. Looking at the surviving tax lists back over the centuries very few names survive for long. In Ham this movement accelerated in the 18th century. A search of the registers of baptisms and burials reveals 44 names in the village in the 17th century and 99 in the 18th century. There would of course have been others who did not appear in the registers, and as the registers for the 17th century are sketchy at times the apparent disparity in the numbers of families between the two centuries is probably exaggerated. A more reliable barometer of this movement is that only some 15 names from the 17th century survived into the 18th century, but even then this statistic is clouded by the various spellings of the names:

> Bennet, Bright/Brite, Coombs, Cumm/Cuming/Cummins/Commins/Commence, Goddard/Goden/Godon, Hapgood/Habgood/Hobgood, Hercomb, Hickman/Hitchman, Hunt, King, Long/Longe, Rolfe/Roffe, Romboule/Rombold/Rumbold, Smith, Tidcomb/Tittcumb.

Of the land owning dynasties only the Hunts are represented in this list. Another absentee is Ham's most prolific family, the Blundys, whose name does not appear in the 17th-century registers but occurs 37 times in the register of baptisms for the 18th century. The population of the village in 1801 was 188,[87] not far off the population at the beginning of the 21st century or the population in 1377, a generation after the Black Death, when the number of taxpayers was 119.

Whilst the pace of change amongst the inhabitants might have been accelerating, the bones of the village of today, in terms of the built architecture, were taking shape. Much of today's central mosaic of buildings was already in place. There was no village green, simply an open space at the junction of the three roads dismissed in a later tithe roll as waste ground. It would not become a village green as such until some time towards the end of the 19th century, and it would take a further 100 years or so before it was formally registered as a village green in 2010. Nevertheless, the notional centre of the village had drifted northwards from the manor house and church. The rectory marked the north-eastern extremity of the village. Built at the end of the 17th century, it was a relatively simple building and did not assume much of its present shape and appearance until the mid-19th century. In the field opposite the rectory there was a series of buildings which were presumably farm steadings. Beside the rectory was Dove's Farmhouse, now known as Ham Cross, surrounded by fields and outhouses. It also started life in the late 17th century but much of its present external character dates from the late 18th century. Opposite, The Old Malthouse had yet to be built but there was another building on its site in the 18th century. Beside it were Porch Cottages, at that stage three cottages and not the present two, and they would not get their upper storey until the 19th century. On the third side of the triangle was Dove's House, known later for a brief period as The Laurels, and also classified as the 'Dove's Farm homestead' when Dove's Farm was sold in 1908. Some of its interior dates back to the late 16th and 17th centuries, but in appearance it is essentially a Queen Anne house. In the 18th century it was the secondary residence in the village after the manor house. North of it was a block of three cottages and another pair of cottages which now form Dove's Farm Cottage, and to the south were two cottages, each with its own garden, which were transformed into one cottage in the 1940s and annexed to Dove's House.

Dove's House c.1928

Moving south through the village, Well Cottage had been built in the 17th century as a block of three cottages and at that time was known as Reprieve Cottages. Beyond it the Old School House had yet to be built, but there was already a building – or possibly two – on that site, perhaps the later home of the dame school which started life in the early 19th century. Opposite, the Crown & Anchor had yet to be built but again there were earlier buildings on its site. Then came the two major survivors of the late 16th century, Rose and Tudor Cottages, the latter being in fact two semi-detached cottages. Bridge Cottage, now Candlemas Cottage, and Manor Cottages had yet to be built. Down Church Road was Ham Manor. It too probably had late 16th century origins, but it is essentially a 17th- and 18th-century building partly remodelled in the 19th century. By the end of the 18th century it was an attractive and imposing house with its raised central clock tower, outbuildings and a dovecot with roosting niches for 344 pigeons.

Drawing of Ham Manor, 1787

Further south, East Court farmhouse had been built in the 17th century. On the other side of the road, Forge Cottage where Alexander Shearman plied his trade was also built in the same century. Where South House now stands was a cottage possibly dating from the late 16th century; a further cottage would be built in the 19th century. Manor Farm House, noted in the 1928 sale brochure of the estate as a 'picturesque thatched cottage' with a carpenter's and a wheelwright's shop attached, was built at some time in the 18th century. It is not clear whether Yew Tree Cottage had been built by then, but there was undoubtedly a building on that site. Beyond Manor Farm House there were buildings on either side of the road as far as the track running east to Ham Spray House, including a copyhold farmstead next to Little Field, but probably Little Field and opposite it Pond Cottage, which was pulled down in the 20th century, were built later on the sites of former cottages. Further along the Fosbury road where Hill House and Manor Farm Cottages now stand were two sets of cottages, one of which comprised the two parish cottages. These cottages were the equivalent of what became known later elsewhere as almshouses, but they fell into disuse as such at the end of the 19th century. The most southerly house in the parish, New Buildings on Ashley Drove, would not be built until the 19th century.

Of all the buildings in the village in the 18th century the oldest by far was All Saints'

Church, and like the land it had been a constant thread running through the life of the village for the previous six centuries. After the vicissitudes of those centuries the 18th century proved to be a particularly beneficial one for Ham's church. The first event was the presentation of a treble bell in 1712 by William Hunt and Michael Benet; the bell had been cast by William and Robert Cor of Aldbourne. It joined three other bells which had been presented in 1663 by William Hore and John Hunt, the two churchwardens at the time, and which were cast in Salisbury by Nathaniel Bolter and William Purdue II. Little is known about William Hore other than that he was born in 1605, the son of William Hore who is recorded in the Ham subsidy list for 1608, and later became a churchwarden. Elizabeth Hore who died in 1677 and has a memorial slab on the south side of the altar may have been his wife. There was nothing accidental about the date of 1663. Three years after the restoration of the monarchy it was still a time of national rejoicing. Charles II himself led the celebrations, spending between 1660 and 1663 a massive £30,420 14s 1½d on silver and gilt plate for the royal household to replace the plate melted down in the Civil War for cash. Ham's celebrations were more modest, but even if the village had leaned towards Parliament in the Civil War and some of its inhabitants were Puritan in their beliefs, it must have caught the national mood and, in particular, largely rejoiced in the restoration of the old order of service and the great church festivals. Certainly it must have been glad to see the back of the tiresome-sounding Henry Newlin 'who preacheth contantlie'. It is still possible to sense some of that rejoicing as the bells ring out today at All Saints on a Sunday.

The next benefit was a major refurbishment starting in 1733. The church would be refurbished again at the end of the century, then again in 1849 commemorated by the ciphers of Queen Victoria and Prince Albert incorporated in the tiling in the chancel below the altar step, and finally much later in the 20th century. The two earlier restorations would save it from the late Victorian passion for church makeovers, and more especially from the clutches of the senior Wiltshire church architect at that time, T. H. Wyatt, who would later become notorious for the banality of his restorations. The refurbishment in 1733 was extensive and included the rebuilding of the south chancel wall and the south side of the nave – although the windows were not inserted until the 1849 refurbishment – and the building of the porch and introduction of the raked gallery at the west end. Although two dates, 1733 and 1787, are given for the 18th century restorations, it seems more likely that there was a rolling programme from 1733 onwards, certainly continuing into the 1740s, in which among other things the present pews and altar rails were installed and the 17th century pulpit was lowered. The end of it in 1787 was marked by the replastering of the tower at considerable expense to the parish.

How all this was funded is unclear; there was no significant dedicated income for church repairs. In the 19th century, and evidently well before that, the very modest income from the Poor of Ham Freehold Allotment was used for this purpose, and this masks a small cameo of village life. In 1834 the Charity Commissioners ascertained that:

> There is a paddock of meadow land, situate in this parish, and containing half an
> acre, the rent of which is received by the churchwardens, and applied towards the
> repairs of the church. The land is let to William Elton, as yearly tenant, at the
> annual rent of £1, which is the full value. The land has been held from ancient
> time, and the rent been carried to the churchwardens' account, and applied to the
> repairs of the church. There are no deeds or writings relating to the land.[88]

The field was part of Culvers Meadow, behind the Crown & Anchor, and abutted onto Pills
Lane. It was recorded again in a Charity Commission Inquiry of 1905, and rent from the field at
the same rate of £1 appeared to continue until 1966 – the last recorded receipt in the church
accounts. The matter then blew up in 1978 when it was discovered that the field was being sold
as part of the sale of Mrs Marion Brown's house (now Brook House but then known as Blackbirds) and its adjoining land of five and a half acres. After some to-ing and fro-ing it seems to
have been accepted that as Pills Lane had been closed for some years and Mrs Brown owned
the fields on either side, the Poor Allotment had effectively become landlocked and was therefore not worth very much. An attempt was made to exact an increased rent, but in the end the
matter was resolved by the Poor Allotment being sold to Arthur Brown for £1,200 in 1987 with
the authority of the Charity Commissioners.

Even in its heyday the Poor Allotment income would not have made a significant dent in
the cost of the 18th century refurbishments. The popular theory is that these refurbishments,
or at least the first tranche in 1733, were funded jointly by the John Hunt who died in 1719 and
the Reverend Richard Gillingham, the rector since 1688 who also died that year. As well as
being contemporaries both men were friends. John Hunt's son John was the executor for
Gillingham's widow Mary's will, receiving a handsome silver tankard for his pains, and he may
have been Gillingham's executor too. John Hunt was a reasonably wealthy man for his time
and left £20 in his will for the poor of the village. It was 'to remain as a perpetual Stock to be for
ever employed….. for the most profit and Advantage that can be made thereof…' The charity
was discontinued at some point in the early 19th century,[89] but quite separately he might well
have put more aside for the church. Richard Gillingham's memorial in the church is a white
marble cartouche on the north wall of the chancel (the urn on top is curiously made of wood
and detachable). It is an elaborate memorial, and were it not for his munificence as a charitable
benefactor it might even seem overly grand for a country parson. The parish general register
for Ham (1720–1782) describes him as 'a gentleman of very excellent character and other
Christian virtues'. Of course, no less a testimony was to be expected for a man of the cloth,
but what could not be expected of him was the magnificent bequest in his will of £900 – in
excess of £1million by today's values – for whichever use his executors should judge was 'most

conducive to the honour of God'. This sum which was made up from an initial bequest of £500 and a further £400 being the value of his household goods, was subsequently given to what became the Corporation of the Sons of the Clergy, a charity that still exists today. He must, however, have also left money for his handsome memorial, and it seems likely that yet more money was left to All Saints' Church.

Nevertheless, these theories do raise questions. If the restoration of the church were being mooted at the time of the deaths of John Hunt and Richard Gillingham, it seems strange that neither of their wills made specific mention of it. The bequests could of course have been unexpected and therefore prompted the whole idea of the restoration. If so, it took an exceptionally long time for the churchwardens and the parish to plan and execute the programme of refurbishment. It may just have been a coincidence but

Communion cup of 1576

1733, the year in which the refurbishment started, also marked the death of another John Hunt, who was almost certainly the son of the John Hunt who died in 1719. So it is possible that the former's death may have resulted in a yet another bequest to the church which became the catalyst for the start of the project.

Somehow the funding was secured and the church has greatly benefited as a result. There is no mystery about the next gift to the church. In 1734 John Hunt, presumably the grandson of his forebear who died in 1719, made a gift of silver plate to the church. It comprised a communion cup and cover of 1576/7, with a maker's mark of a sun in full splendour, and a paten of 1719/20 by Humphrey Payne. The communion cup with its straight-sided bowl and simple flat-chased decoration is a wonderfully eloquent example of Elizabethan silversmithing. The 1560s and 1570s were good times for Elizabethan goldsmiths as scores of communion cups and flagons were being made to replace the small chalices, out of which only the priest would drink wine at communion, with cups which could be drunk out of by the whole congregation. The identity of the maker of the Ham cup is unknown; few makers' marks of that era, many of which were rebuses, can be traced to a particular goldsmith. Perhaps the sun in splendour stood for a goldsmith named Day or Bright, or alternatively it may have been a pun denoting a Dark or Night. Both the cup and the paten are still in use today.[90]

13

'RULE, BRITANNIA!' AND HODGE

Perhaps Gaunt was right in one sense. Perhaps the 18th century was the nearest Ham would get to the romanticists' rosy-tinted perception of life in the countryside as an Arcadian idyll. However, it is easy to be seduced by the 18th century, sometimes dubbed by historians the 'long 18th', and despite its ups and downs farming would continue to remain central to the village of Ham throughout the next century. The end of the 18th century and the beginning of the 19th were marked by change and revolution. The face of agriculture had already altered dramatically thanks to 'Turnip' Townshend's crop rotation, Jethro Tull's towed seed drill, and Robert Bakewell's and Thomas Coke's breeding methods for sheep and cattle. It would continue to change as the Agricultural Revolution bit deep into the 19th century. The Industrial Revolution had also started although it would leave Ham largely untouched, except perhaps in the fullness of time to entice some of its sons and daughters to seek better paid employment in the towns. The American Revolution had already taken place. The French Revolution had just ended but France under Bonaparte, its new First Consul, was on the rampage. In 1798 Horatio Nelson had won a stunning victory at the Battle of the Nile. Three years earlier the Ham parish poor fund gave two shillings to five sailors, possibly in a flush of patriotic fervour following Lord Howe's victory in the Atlantic on the Glorious First of June the previous year. Further afield, Arthur Wellesley, the future Duke of Wellington, was carving a name for himself in India.

To the residents of Ham the dovecot built by John Hunt Watts in 1794 would have ceased to be a novelty. Of much more concern to them the smell of invasion was once again in the air. The building of the Martello towers along the south coast would not start until 1804, but perhaps as the new century dawned anxious mothers in Ham were already warning their children to behave or else 'Boney would come and get them'. Meanwhile patriotic gentlemen were busy raising militia regiments. The Wiltshire Yeomanry had been formed in 1794 and quite possibly the young men of Ham were being encouraged to join it. Other men from the village would rally to the colours of the regular army and later fight in the Peninsular War and at the Battle of Waterloo. They included Daniel Sope of the 95th Foot, Benjamin Russell who served variously in the 103rd, 12th and 27th Foot, and Robert Blundy of the Royal Artillery.[91]

It is all too easy to label the later Victorian era as a series of stereotypes. Britain was building its huge empire and boasting, not without reason, that Britannia did indeed rule the waves in the words of the 18th century song. And there was sometimes more than a degree of truculence in its foreign policy epitomised by a later music-hall song that 'We don't want to fight, yet by jingo! if we do, We've got the ships, we've got the men, and got the money too'. The money had initially been gained on the back of the prosperity of the 18th century and was now fuelled by the Industrial Revolution, a revolution which translated the flowering of the arts and science and invention that had coloured the 18th century into product design, mass manufacture and great feats of engineering. Roads, railways, waterways, bridges, tunnels and public buildings were built both at home and abroad, many of them today still providing key parts of the infrastructures of Britain and its former empire. Mechanisation increasingly replaced centuries-old hand skills, including those used in farming. Many other craft skills would remain but these continued at a different level as triumphantly demonstrated by the Great Exhibition of 1851. In this new environment the middle class which had begun to emerge at the end of the 18th century flourished and expanded. Contemporary commentators poked fun at it for, in their eyes, aping assiduously the perceived lifestyle of the upper classes. In turn later commentators would foster an image of a Victorian upper class suffocating in its high moral tone, smug primness and sexual repression. Nearer the mark, it was still a world in which each man and woman was expected to know his or her station in life and observe it.

There were setbacks both at home and in the country's foreign policy, the latter inflicting stinging blows to national pride, but the overriding image throughout much of the century is of Britain in the ascendancy. However, that ascendancy excluded those at the bottom of the pack, the ordinary working man and woman. Much of the working class was surviving, just, at starvation level. The plight of the urban poor was at least recognised even if little was done about it. *Punch* which was first published in 1841 ran an article in October that year entitled 'Report on the Public Distress', which contained the following illustration:

> The family consisted of a husband and wife, four girls, eight boys, and an infant
> of three weeks, making in all fifteen individuals. They told me they were literally
> dying of hunger, and that they had appealed to the vestry, who had referred them
> to the guardians, who had referred them to the overseer, who had gone out of
> town, and would be back in a week or two.

No doubt journalistic licence was employed in this sketch, but the point was made. Because of the lower standard of wages and often appalling rural accommodation, conditions for the agricultural labourer were arguably worse. Yet despite the efforts of reformers such as William Cobbett, the misfortunes of the rural poor were largely ignored for most of the century. Partly this stemmed from a lack of understanding by an urban elite who christened the agricultural labourer 'Hodge'. It was a derogatory term. Hodge was viewed as illiterate and slow-witted and accordingly only capable of menial tasks; if he were paid more he would only drink it in the public house. Ham had its share of what society and the press dismissed as Hodges, and to understand what life was like in Ham in the 19th century, the records that have survived need to be viewed against the mirror of what was happening both to agriculture in general and to the agricultural labourer in particular at national level.

The fortunes of agriculture swirled like a giant sine wave throughout the century. The wars with France severely limited imports of grain from the continent and domestic prices spiralled creating profits for the landowners. The story for the labourer was quite different. In 1795, some ten miles from Ham, there was a meeting of magistrates at the Pelican Inn in Speen. From this the Speenhamland System emerged. Instead of parish relief based on the 1601 Elizabethan Poor Law, under the new system agricultural wages were to be topped up by the parish to a basic subsistence level based on the current price of bread. Doubtless well intentioned, it had the opposite effect by keeping wages low. Both landowner and labourer suffered following the peace in 1815, but the labourer suffered far worse. He was hit by a series of further hammer blows: the flood of cheap post-war labour, the Corn Law of 1815 and, later, enclosures and the increasing use of mechanisation in farming, including the threshing machine which had first been introduced in the 1780s. It is not difficult to understand why the frustration of the agricultural labourer should have spilled over in 1830 in the so-called Captain Swing riots. [92]

On the face of the records only three men from Ham were involved in the riots: John Willoughby and George Sheppard who were acquitted of destroying machinery at William Woodman's Ham Spray estate, and Charles Bowley aged 26. Bowley was rounded up with a number of Shalbourne men by the Wiltshire Militia and mounted constables together with local magistrates, and was subsequently convicted on 23 November 1830 at the Wiltshire Special Assizes for robbing William Barnes of one sovereign and other monies. He was part of a mob that had gone about attempting to levy money in the area. For this he was sentenced to be hanged. Fortunately for him a collective petition signed by 27 men from Ham was sent to the authorities pleading for clemency on the grounds that he was of previous good character, sober and industrious, it was his first offence and he had been led astray by others.[93] The Times reporter covering the trial commented that 'he got a most excellent character from the prosecutor and from the clergyman of his parish (the Reverend Sumner Smith)'.[94] As a result the judge, Mr Baron Vaughan, felt that 'it was his duty to recommend to the Crown for a considerable mitigation in sentence'. His sentence was later commuted to six months hard labour. Two men from Shalbourne and three from Kintbury were also condemned to death, but following similar petitions only one of them, a Kintbury man, was eventually hanged.

Appalled by the injustice of the sentences all three villages were clearly protective of their own, but it would be unfair to cast Mr Baron Vaughan as the villain of the piece. It was apparent that he had little option in passing a mandatory death sentence for robbery. Destroying a threshing machine was evidently a much lesser offence. At the same assizes a Charles Bowton was convicted of breaking a thrashing (sic) machine, and in passing sentence Mr Baron Vaughan said that 'as this was the prisoner's only offence, and was not accompanied with robbery, and as he had very low wages (7s a week), which probably might have been a cause why he was more easily led into his crime, for which however he should know that no rule of wages, however low, afforded an excuse, the Court considering also his previous good character, adjudged him 3 months hard labour'. [95] The judge's recommendation for clemency in the case of Bowley also suggests that he was not only fair-minded but properly indifferent to political pressure. A month before Bowley's trial, on Saturday, 30 October 1830, *The Times* ran an article commenting on a list of burnings in Kent, one of the starting points of the Captain Swing riots:

> This will be called by every body an unnatural and most frightful aspect of affairs, in an agricultural community like that of the county referred to. Frightful indeed it is, but not now unnatural, inasmuch as crime is the inevitable consequence of desperation – of that horrible feeling which has been produced amongst a large proportion of the labourers of England.

The following Tuesday the recently appointed Whig Prime Minister, Lord Grey, spoke in Parliament: 'He agreed that distress might have driven some of the labouring poor into great excesses, but nevertheless those excesses should be visited with great severity'.[96] The French Revolution was not yet a distant memory, and Grey's anxiety to nip these riots in the bud is understandable. Not surprisingly William Cobbett waded in on behalf of the rioters, but his appeals were blunted by the low esteem in which the establishment held him. *The Times* had reported in January the same year that 'with the most malicious feelings, (Cobbett) had used every means to excite the resentment of the working people against their employer'. [97] He would subsequently be tried for seditious libel in support of the riots, but having skilfully conducted his own defence the jury acquitted him.

The census of 1841 shows that a decade later Bowley was back in the fold at Ham as an agricultural labourer, together with his wife Hester (or Esther) and six children. They are shown as a single household so presumably were living in a rented cottage. In the 1840s he appears as a casual labourer for William Woodman and by 1861 he was a forester working with his son George. Towards the end of his life – he lived to be 85 – he was living in one of the two parish cottages south of Manor Farm. He is buried in All Saints' churchyard, and his descendants would continue to live in Ham throughout the 20th century. It is not known who employed him on his return from prison but the caring society that had existed in the village in the previous century clearly carried on into the next. Ham was a small community and the affairs and concerns of its inhabitants must have been well known to everyone including the landowners. In this Ham was fortunate in not suffering the fate of many other villages where there were absentee landlords represented by agents, both intent on maximising profits with little or no concern for the welfare of their employees.

Some time before the Ham Enclosure Act of 1828 a tectonic shift in the pattern of land and landowners had occurred in the parish, which would have significant repercussions through-out the century. In the run-up to the Ham Enclosure Act, an act of 1827 [98] appointed George Barnes and James Cowley, land surveyors, to determine the 'dividing, allotting, setting out and inclosing (of) the said open and common fields, meadows, pastures, commonable and waste grounds in the parish of Ham'. In determining their award the two land surveyors held a public meeting at the Bear Inn, Hungerford. Those entitled under the act were the Reverend William Gomm (25 acres of glebe land), Thomas Cowderoy (East Court), John Hunt Watts (Ham Manor estate) and Francis Richens Watts (Dove's Farm), together with 'several other Persons'. The Land Tax Assessment of 1829 shows the 'other Persons' to have included the Reverend Thomas Henry D'Avenant and Richard Flewell. The Reverend D'Avenant owned two severalls totalling about five acres which were quaintly named Simms and Jackass. He left them to his daughters and they were later purchased by Henry Deacon Woodman at auction in 1865. Richard Flewell was an even shadowier figure but a very important one. He appears to have lived in Ham towards the end of the 18th century as his four daughters were baptised at All Saints' Church between 1784 and 1796. According to a land tax assessment, by 1800 he was the copyhold owner or tenant of a new estate of 482 acres in the east of the parish, mainly at Ham Spray.[99] The accuracy of this assessment may be suspect as a Winchester terrier of 1810 shows him owning only a total of 224 acres made up of three copyholds known as Bushel's, Cooper's and Tidcomb's.[100] However, it is possible that he owned another 237 acres of downland which are not apportioned in the terrier. How Flewell built up such a large holding is not known, and to add further to the confusion his appearance in the tax assessment of 1829 is spurious as he was in fact dead and buried in 1820. If this seems careless, in the 1880 assessment, 60 years after his death, Flewell was still being shown as the proprietor of the Ham Spray estate, although by this time his name had been changed on the forms from Flewell to Kewell and then to Keevil, and John Hunt Watts was still being shown as the proprietor of the Ham Manor estate although he had been dead for 50 years. Presumably whoever were the current landowners at the time paid the taxes and the Board of Taxes, the forerunner of the Inland Revenue, was content. It has meant, however, that these annual tax assessments cannot be relied upon to chart land ownership in Ham in the 19th century accurately, and as a result it is necessary to draw on other sources to disentangle what is often a labyrinthine chain of landlords and tenants. Nevertheless, despite these disparities, it is apparent that Flewell was responsible for the genesis of what would become known in the next century as Wansdyke Farms.

The records of the Court of the Manor of Ham show that below the tier of principal

The village of Ham from the Enclosure Award map of 1828

landowners there was a steady stream of minor tenants still renting small copyholds and cottages, usually for the period of their lives, for some time after the enclosure act came into force. Even where the copyholds were reasonably substantial, in the region of 20–50 acres, they were invariably cobbled together from a miscellany of very small plots of one acre or less.

The ownerships and tenancies of the Ham Spray estate in the first half of the century are certainly confusing. Who owned the estate after Flewell's death in 1820 is not known, but the Ham Enclosure Award map of 1828 shows John Hunt Watts owning the copyhold of the majority of the various fields and woods in question, and it is evident from the engrossment of the award that Richard Flewell's title, which he shared with John and Harriet Flewell, was for his lifetime only. From the farm accounts of Ham Spray the following year it appears that the property was then owned by William Woodman, although he is more likely to have been the copyhold owner.[101]   However, ten years later the tithe awards of 1839 confirm Woodman as the owner of 485 acres. William Woodman was born in Combe, the son of Henry Woodman who later farmed at Stitchcombe near Mildenhall. By the time he arrived at Ham Spray Woodman was already a landowner on his own account. In 1826 William Cobbett visited his farm at Aldbourne Warren and commented in his book *Cobbett's Rural Rides*:

> We passed the homestead of a farmer Woodman, with sixteen banging wheat-ricks in the rick-yard (*banging* was a 19th century colloquialism for 'thumping'), two of which were old ones; and rick-yard, farm-yard, waste-yard, horse-paddock, and all round about, seemed to be swarming with fowls, ducks and turkeys, and on the whole of them not one feather but was white!

Yet, despite the tithe award of 1839, the land tax assessment of the same date shows Ham Spray tenanted by Francis Richens Watts [102] who had inherited the Ham Manor estate from his brother John Hunt Watts in 1829. As the land tax assessments have to be treated as suspect, this apparent mismatch of records may again simply reflect a complex series of superior leases and underleases. What is quite clear is that Woodman was farming Ham Spray in the 1840s. His wages bill for 1844 was:

	£	s	d
Rolfe's Boys	14	3	-
Richard Haines	20	5	-
Samuel Cummins	19	1	2½
William Waite	23	1	2
William Humphris	23	1	10
John Digweed	23	16	6
John Salt	21	11	-
Isaac Underwood	30	-	-

George Digweed	8	12	-
Thomas Willoby	15	10	-
Charles Walter	9	1	-
William Baker	4	12	6
George Clayton & Sons	42	8	3½
Henry Bowly	18	7	-
George Hoare	19	5	4½
The Woman's Labour	21	14	11
David Digweed	17	18	10½
For Extra Labour	29	1	6
For Odd Reaping	9	-	-
	390	11	2

The following year he employed two more men and the wages bill had risen to £430. In 1847 Ham Spray was enfranchised to Woodman [103] who by then was living in Ham according to the 1841 census. The census also shows Martha Deacon, a servant aged 30, living in his household. She was in fact his common law wife. They had a son in 1828 who does not appear in the 1841 census but features in legal documents as plain Henry Deacon. Little is known of what lay behind this misalliance, but it must have been awkward in a society which was becoming obsessed with moral propriety. William Woodman had been living with his mother and perhaps as a member of an upwardly mobile family she disapproved of Martha, forcing him to keep his affair with Martha and their son a secret. This may also explain why in an age of prolific families Woodman had only one child. In any event, possibly because Henry Deacon was about to attain his majority, William and Martha were married in 1848.[104] The 1851 census shows all three of them living in Dove's House, with Henry Deacon having assumed his father's name. Martha would continue to live in Dove's House after William Woodman's death.

While there may have been undercurrents, on

Extract from the Ham Spray farm accounts of 1845 showing extra labour costs which included threshing, chalking, mowing, dipping and shearing sheep, making sheep hurdles, and mole and rat catching the surface all was happy and normal domesticity at Dove's House in 1851 as the following letter in June that year to William Woodman from Henry Levick of West Woodhay shows:

My Dear Sir

I have sent my Boy with a Cart as agreed for the Plants, you was so kind as to promise. I have sent a double periwinkle and a couple of pansies which are the only things that I can at present see that are really worth my send-ing and which you have not.

Hoping Mrs Woodman & self are well I remain with many thanks

Yours very truly

Henry Levick

Meanwhile, probably at some time in the 1830s, Ham Spray House was built as a farm-house for the Ham Spray estate, although Woodman family tradition records Henry Deacon Woodman building it in 1850. What seems likely is that it started as a modest farm building in the 1830s, which was then enlarged in the 1850s when Henry Deacon Woodman set up home there with his first wife Mary whom he married in 1855.[105] By the end of the century the house had been enlarged again. In 1862, nine months before his death, William Woodman made over the Ham Spray estate to his son, but five years later Henry Deacon Woodman sold it to Charles Wright, a newcomer to Ham.[106]

William Blundy's invoice to William Woodman for thatching three cottages and elming (bundling straw for thatching), 14 February 1849

While on the face of it the sale of Ham Spray seems a strange decision following his father's efforts to obtain the freehold of the estate, closer examination reveals Henry Deacon Woodman at the age of 34 to be developing into a shrewd businessman as well as an able farmer, skills no doubt learnt from his father. The 1861 census shows him living in Ham Manor and farming 1,238 acres; his father had been renting the Ham Manor estate from at least 1846. The owner of Ham Manor was still Francis Richens Watts who was clearly under financial pressure as he took out at least two mortgages on the estate, one of which was not redeemed until his death in 1867.[107] These circumstances are not surprising as his brother's bequest of the Ham Manor estate to him in 1829 had required him to raise capital of £9,000. His own will instructed his executor to sell his estate so that the proceeds could be given to Jane Watts, otherwise called Jane Cripps, and to her children after her death. Jane Watts or Cripps seems to have been either his common law wife or his legal wife, or more probably both in turn, and in any case the children were undoubtedly his. Although baptised under their mother's name of Cripps, they would in due course bear his name; both Jane and all the children, even a child who died in infancy, are shown as Watts on the obelisk-shaped monument to the family of Francis Richens Watts in Ham churchyard. No record of the transaction between Watts and Woodman now exists, but it is evident that Woodman seized his chance and purchased the estate, selling Ham Spray to finance it. He would later buy back Ham Spray.

Important though these changes of land ownership were for Ham, other far-reaching changes were also taking place throughout England which would determine the pattern of life in the village for much of the century. The Speenhamland System ceased in 1834 with the introduction of the Poor Law Amendment Act which ended outdoor relief and set up workhouses. The act was designed to iron out inconsistencies in the implementation of relief, and to provide a uniform adoption of measures which would be overseen by poor law unions comprising groupings of various parishes. Again doubtlessly well intentioned, collectively the measures proved to be draconian in their scope: 'except in cases of sickness or accident, no relief is to be given in money to any able-bodied pauper, who is in employment, nor to any part of his family; if any able-bodied male pauper applies to be set to work by the parish, one half at least of the relief is to be in kind; (and) no relief is to be given by payment of house-rent, or by allowance towards the same'.

The following year Ham was included in the Hungerford Poor Law Union. A decade later in 1847 a workhouse for 344 inmates was built on the south side of Park Street, Hungerford. It would have a small but sad role in the life of Ham.

At the beginning of the 1840s the economy of the country as a whole was at a low ebb. Trade was depressed and a rapid increase in the population resulted in overflowing workhouses and starvation for many. Ham must have shared at least in a minor way in this misery. Fortunately the Repeal of the Corn Laws in 1846 signalled a revival of farming and some amelioration of the lot of the agricultural worker, although the price of corn dropped only slightly. The 1850s and 1860s would become known as the Golden Age of farming. The price of corn held up on the back of strong demand from a still growing population which in general was now better paid, and as a result between the 1830s and the 1860s the amount of land under corn and arable cultivation almost doubled nationally. Wiltshire was amongst the leading corn-producing counties and most of the land at Ham except the steep flanks of Ham Hill would have been under the plough. This marked a significant change in the economy of Wiltshire. Murray's *Encyclopaedia of Geography* published in 1834 describes Wiltshire unequivocally as a manufacturing county due to its woollen industry: 'The produce is of the finest description; superfine broadcloth, kerseymeres, and what are called fancy articles'. The encyclopaedia went on to say that only a fifth of the land was arable. Now, in the 1850s and 1860s, Wiltshire was part of an age of what was called high farming. There was investment in artificial fertilisers, better drainage, new farm buildings and the increasing use of machinery. Steam traction engines for threshing were being introduced from the 1840s and reaping machines from the 1850s. However, only the really big landowners could afford this level of investment and it is doubtful whether the landowners at Ham, even the Woodmans, could have competed in this league.

There is no reason to believe that Ham's landowners were not reasonably benevolent employers within the dictates of the prevailing financial climates. Nevertheless, despite the boom in farming the agricultural labourer was still only eking out an existence. Enclosures had ended the swaths of small allotments and common land which had previously enabled him to supplement his wages by growing his own vegetables and keeping a few farm animals. The average weekly wage for a labourer at Ham Spray in 1840 and again in 1850 was 8s which reflected average national rates,[108] and the going rate for piece-work for mowing was 2s an acre, scarcely double the rate paid in the Ham Manor estate in the 1730s. In 1860 the average national rate shot up to 9s 6d, and from 1870 to the end of the century the rate hovered around the 11s mark with a high point of 12s in 1882 and a low point of 10s a decade later.[109] What the corresponding rates were in Ham is not known, but it is doubtful whether Henry Deacon Woodman, the businessman, would have paid more than the prevailing local rate. Even these modest wages would have been bitten into by reductions for wet working days. The saving grace was the annual harvest when not only extra wages were paid but it involved women and children as well, and it was the harvest in these middle decades of the 19th century rather than Gaunt's vision of an 18th century Arcadia which for Ham was probably the last hurrah of traditional farming. Fortunately the farmer and the labourer needed each other, the farmer to get in his harvest as completely and as quickly as possible, and the labourer to draw extra wages to see him and his family through the lean winter. Great pride was taken in the traditional skills of reaping, stooking and the loading of wagons. Until the Education Act of 1870 it was customary for schools to have a holiday at harvest time so that the children could be employed, the younger boys driving horses or helping with the gleaning which was more generally the work of women and young girls.

According to various records there was a 'petty' school in Ham in 1808. By 1833 there was a school for 20 children paid for by their parents, and in 1858 this became a parochial school for 30–40 children taught by a mistress in a schoolroom.[110] Where the schoolroom was is unclear but it was probably on the site of the later school. The schoolmistress was initially Sophie Whale and then Mary Pithouse. Born in 1836 to an agricultural labourer in Ham, Mary Pithouse appears to have been amongst the fortunate fee-paying children in the earlier school. Her father John Pithouse must have scrimped and saved during difficult times to send her to school unless benevolence came from elsewhere, and perhaps as a result he is recorded as being 'on the parish' in his old age. In 1871 following the Education Act the number of children being taught reportedly leapt to 24 boys and 37 girls, but these numbers look suspect. The schoolhouse was built in 1874 and the highest attendance in 1875, its first year of operation, is recorded as 36.[111] It is also evident that despite the Education Act tradition still ruled in Ham. In the week of 13 August 1875 the schoolmaster reported, 'A short attendance (20). One half holiday, breaking up for the Harvest holidays. Five weeks'. Then on 24 September he recorded,

The Village School c.1910

'The first week after harvest. Very short attendance (20); the children are gleaning'. Nearly 20 years later in 1893 it was a very hot summer and the harvest was three weeks early. This resulted in earlier holidays and the following entries in the school log: '24–28 July. Very poor attendance on Monday and Tuesday owing to commencement of Harvest. Broke up for Harvest Holidays', and later, '28 August. Re-commenced after nearly 5 weeks holidays. Very fair attendance, the weather having been very good'.

The harvest was the high point of the year and ended with Harvest Home, a secular and not a religious celebration. It culminated in a harvest supper provided by the farmer, which usually ended in something of a bacchanalian revel. Songs were sung late into the night, many of them bawdy, and it is possible to imagine choruses such as the *Cuckoo's Nest* [112] being thumped out in Ham:

> It is known oh my darling it is no such thing
> Pay and commar sense may tell yar it is a great sin
> Yar maidenhead to lose and then to be abused
> And have no men a daisy with your cuckoo's nest.
> Some like a girl that is pretty in the face
> Some like a girl that is slender in the waist
> But give to me the girl that can wriggle and will twist
> And at the bottom of her belly is the cuckoo's nest.

Doubtless a few maidenheads were lost on these occasions, but from whichever side of the blanket they came, new arrivals continued to swell the population in Ham at a steady rate. In 1871, at the end of the Golden Age, the population in Ham had reached its peak of 255, an increase of 35 per cent since the beginning of the century. However, not every birth was a cause for celebration. Elizabeth Harding aged 22 and Emma Vivash aged 19 were both delivered of a boy in the Hungerford workhouse in 1869 and 1872 respectively.[113] Although neither child was specifically registered as illegitimate this would seem to have been the case. Fortunately the ending was not entirely unhappy. While both mothers disappeared from Ham, Elizabeth Harding's son Albert was looked after by his grandparents in the village, and Charles Vivash appears in the 1891 census as an agricultural labourer in Ham. The Vivashes, or Viveashes, became a well-known family in the area and one of Henry Deacon Woodman's daughters would marry a Viveash. A sadder story is that of Sarah Annett. In the 1891 census she is shown as the 28 year-old wife of Thomas Annett. Seven years later she gave birth to an illegitimate boy in the workhouse, but there is no record as to whom she went off the rails with or what happened to mother and son.[114]

Perhaps the harvest celebrations took place at either the Crown & Anchor or the Cross Keys Inn. It is not known exactly when either public house was built. Neither is clearly evident on the 1839 enclosure map but both are present on the 1877 Ordnance Survey map. However, the Crown & Anchor was certainly built by 1841, on the site of two cottages, as its innkeeper John Holdway is listed in the Ham census return that year as publican. The name of the inn derives from a gambling game with dice invented by sailors in the 18th century, in which four sides of the die were the four suits of playing cards – spades, hearts, etc – and the remaining two sides were a crown and an anchor. The Cross Keys Inn arrived later, possibly about 1850, and had a relatively short stay. It stood opposite the junction of Ham Road and Cutting Hill, but by the end of the 1880s it had gone, reputedly destroyed by fire, its inn sign – the symbol of St Peter's keys to the gates of Heaven – having failed to protect it. What happened to its innkeeper Henry Francis is not known, although a Thomas Francis, probably a son, was the publican of the Crown & Anchor at the end of the century. That Ham should have merited two public houses when it previously had none must have been partly due to the burgeoning population. It also seems to demonstrate happily that Ham was relatively prosperous in mid-century. However, in the 1870s fortunes in the farming world began to change once again and throughout the country the age-old Harvest Home would gradually die out as the purse strings of farmers tightened. By the end of the century it had become almost totally trans-formed into the religious celebration of Harvest Festival which is still part of the church calendar in Ham today.

Meanwhile the village had expanded. During the 1840s there was a surge in the number of adult agricultural labourers from 26 to 44. In 1861 this figure had settled back to 27, but in addition there was small army of ploughboys and stableboys – children under the age of 16 – as well as shepherds, foresters, carters and grooms, and taking these into account the two figures are not far apart. Away from the land a growing number of other trades had appeared and Ham had acquired a post office and shop to add to its school and public house. Kelly's Directory of 1848 included the following:

> John Holdway – publican, Crown & Anchor
> Reuben Hercomb – blacksmith
> Mrs Charlotte Blackmore – shopkeeper
> Enoch Fruen – post office receiver
> Mrs Sophie Whale – mistress of parochial school
> John Whale – boot and shoemaker
> James Knight – boot and shoemaker
> Thomas Habgood – carpenter and wheelwright

Twenty-five years later Reuben Hercomb would be succeeded as blacksmith by his widow Anne. It is doubtful whether she actually wielded a hammer, and it is more likely that she was in charge while her son and others did the hard work. The 1871 census shows Alice Hercomb aged 14, probably a granddaughter, as a nursemaid to the Woodman family at Ham Manor. By 1861 Prudence Pettit would be the shopkeeper. She later became the Sub-Postmistress and then the Post Mistress, but would die in the workhouse in 1911 at the age of 86.[115] Perhaps she suffered from dementia as workhouses also served as mental institutions. Another Ham resident to die in the workhouse was a tailor, Benjamin Brunsden. By the time he was 40 he had made his way to Ham, but he seems to have been unsuccessful in both trade and life dying unmarried and destitute at the age of 72.[116] Altogether six Ham residents died in the workhouse between 1866 and 1917 (the dates of extant workhouse records) – all of them women except for Brunsden. At first sight this appears to be a stain on Ham's record of looking after its own, especially as the

The Old Malthouse Cottages

workhouse with its deliberately harsh Dickensian regime was universally hated. But the reality was that after the 1834 Poor Law Amendment Act the practicalities of being 'on the parish' had changed, and the workhouse ironically represented the final welfare safety net for paupers, the mentally unstable and unmarried mothers.

Midway through the century Ham would also boast a village policeman and a maltster, George Hopkins. It seems likely that Hopkins was responsible for building what is now The Old Malthouse, but his trade there did not last long. By the time of the 1891 census the

Malthouse was occupied by John Bush, a carpenter, although another maltster would succeed him at the end of the century. In 1861 there were five carpenters and two basketmakers in the village, basketmaking being a popular trade in neighbouring Berkshire. Below stairs a sizeable troop of domestic servants – a butler and a total of 14 women – looked after the more prosperous householders in the village.

The 1840s had proved to be the ladder by which farming, both nationally and for Ham, had climbed to the broad sunny uplands of the 1850s and 1860s. In turn the 1870s would be the snake on which its fortunes slid down again. There were, however, two important events for the village before the recession struck deeply at the end of the century. The first of these was the building of the schoolhouse in 1874. It cost £400 and comprised a schoolroom of 29 feet 11 inches by 16 feet with separate outside lavatories for the boys and for the girls.[117] As time went by, a blanket strung across this large room was all that separated the infants from the older children. Annexed to the schoolroom was the master's house with a living room and kitchen downstairs and bedrooms upstairs. Like the children, the master had an outside lavatory. Henry Deacon Woodman provided the site which previously contained two cottages and also the money to build the school. Once it was built the school was placed in the care of the Church, although Woodman retained the title to the school and its grounds. The first master appointed on 31 May 1875 was William Alexander, 3rd Class Certificate. He continued in the post until May 1889 when the school was closed for one week, 'the master being ill'. Six weeks later he was replaced by Martha Brown, but she was evidently a stop-gap as J. Mahony took over in mid-September. Whether this succession of changes upset the children, or whether it was because William Alexander's teaching powers were in decline before his retirement through illness, the school received a scathing report from Woodman as the correspondent in 1890. By then Woodman was the squire at Ham Manor, and clearly a man of authority he pulled no punches in his report on the school he had built.[118]

> The present Master has been here about eight months, and keeps satisfactory order: but the Elementary subjects need much more attention. The Reading should be more fluent and more expressive, and the powers of the letters single and combined should be carefully taught, the writing is fairly uniform, spelling fair in the first standard, moderate in the second standard, very moderate in the fourth standard, and imperfect in the third, in which no child passed in spelling; while the Arithmetic is fair on the first, third and fifth standards, moderate in the second standard and imperfect in the fourth standard. Singing by year and needlework are fair, with no class subject brought forward the elementary standard should be better by next inspection. The supply of books should be more complete.

Whoever's fault it really was, the report effectively did for Mahony. By 1891 James Kavanagh had replaced him, and in November 1892 an Inspector of Schools paid a visit without notice and reported the 'School going on properly'. A religious report by the Reverend H. F. Gibson RDI the same month painted an even more glowing picture: 'The School continues to improve and passed a most satisfactory examination .... The children are bright, eager, in capital order'.[119]

The second event was the sale of the Ham Spray estate by public auction at the Three Swans Hotel, Hungerford on 27 May 1879. Charles Wright its owner had died, having left his mark on Ham with a white horse carved on the flank of Ham Hill beside Rivar Copse, now long since grown over as it was not infilled with chalk. The sale took place on the instructions of the High Court of Justice, Chancery Division, Charles Wright's Estate, Couling v. Goulter. That Charles Wright's estate should have been the subject of litigation in the High Court carries with it a faint whiff of Dickens's *Bleak House* and the saga of Jarndyce v. Jarndyce. However, neither this nor the rapidly worsening agricultural climate stopped the estate being described in the sale particulars as 'a most desirable agricultural & sporting property'.[120]

> The "Ham Spray Estate" lies within a ring fence. Situate in its centre, approached by a Lodge Entrance, through an Avenue of Elms is the Residence, which is charmingly placed in its own tastefully laid-out and well-planted grounds. Lawn and Shrubberies commanding views of the Picturesque Park and Park-like Grounds, and in a sheltered and warm position.
> The house comprises Entrance Hall; three Reception Rooms; nine Bed Rooms; Kitchen; Dairy; capital Underground Cellars; and all necessary and convenient Offices.
> Immediately adjacent are Carriage House and Stable accommodation, and Two productive Kitchen Gardens.
> The Farm Buildings include Barns; Stables; Cart House; Cow Shed; Piggeries; Granaries and Yard, and are necessary and suitable for the Estate.
> The Estate consists of wheat and bean arable, a good proportion of rich pasture, and some healthy Downland all being nicely intersected, and on some sides bounded by flourishing wood plantation and coppice.

This was Henry Deacon Woodman's opportunity to buy back Ham Spray. He had sold at the top of the market and now he would repurchase it 12 years later at the beginning of the next recession. It was largely due to chance but his timing was perfect.

In the 1880s and 1890s the agricultural recession was deep and bitter. In the aftermath of the American Civil War which had ended in 1865 the vast prairies of the Midwest came under increasing cultivation creating the so-called Corn Belt, and the railroads forged further

Painting of croquet being played on the lawn outside Ham Manor c.1880. In the foreground are three daughters of Henry Deacon Woodman from his first marriage

westwards enabling the grain to be transported to the coastal ports. As a result Britain was flooded with cheap American grain and the price of corn tumbled once again. The knock-on effect was that much of the land which had been arable during the boom years reverted to pasture or became what would now be termed set-aside. This in itself threw large numbers of agricultural labourers off the land; others became jobless as the farmers too were hit and bankruptcies became widespread. From August to October 1891 *The Daily News*, then the third most popular newspaper in the country, ran a series of articles by their special correspondent, George Mullin, about the plight of farming and especially the plight of the agricultural labourer.[121] Initially these were mainly concerned with the east of the country but then other counties including Berkshire and Wiltshire were also covered. This was an early example of investigative journalism and the articles provoked a voluminous and vigorous correspondence. The thrust of both articles and correspondence recited the low level of wages exacerbated by long periods of winter unemployment; inadequate and overcrowded accommodation, aggravated by lack of security of tenure; the dullness of rural life; and the tyranny of the squire compounded by the tyranny of the parson and even the parson's wife. All this caused a flight from the land by the young attracted by the excitement and better wages of the city, leaving the old to a living death 'for what has the poor man to look forward to but the hateful workhouse and a pauper's grave'. There were of course contrary views expressed. Writers of letters complained that these statements were exaggerated, work was available at reasonable wages, better wages would only be drunk in the tavern, no one was forced into the workhouse and the colonies were crying out for good active men.

The Daily News was not the only paper to recognise the problem. On 23 October 1891, in an article on the crop returns for that year, *The Times* commented in weightier tone:

> It cannot be said that this is a satisfactory picture of the year's progress, especially when we have the caution by Major Craigie that the increase in permanent pasture is due more to greater correctness in the returns than to fresh reclamation. It will be seen at a glance that, speaking in general terms, all crops which require the expenditure of much labour in their cultivation – even to the grass which requires curing into hay – show a great decrease, and this fact bears out the complaint which has become general in every part of the country that labour is now the great difficulty on the farm. The further reduction in corn crops has been brought about, no doubt, by the uncertainties of our climate and the low prices ruling as well, but even here the labour question must have been a further difficulty. At a time when fresh labourers' unions are being formed in various parts of the country it is well that the important bearing of these figures on the labour difficulty on the farm should be thoroughly realised.

So how did Ham fare in the face of these difficulties? According to *The Daily News* Wiltshire, together with Somerset and Dorset, was looked upon as one of the poorest and most poverty-stricken counties in England, and one of its letter-writers reported that 'in the Kennet Valley there are thousands of acres yielding annually the scantiest of pasture, with abundance of weeds and thistle seed'. When at the end of the century Henry Deacon Woodman purchased a parcel of land of 64 acres at Dove's Farm from the Reverend Coleman for £1,100 – he had previously purchased the bulk of the farm in 1880 for £5,000 – a third of its acreage was pasture or meadow, and half of that had recently reverted from arable.[122] Yet despite this ominous backdrop Ham seems to have ridden the storm remarkably well. From the census returns the number of adult agricultural labourers in the village remained almost unchanged: 34 in 1881, 32 in 1891 and 35 in 1901. The average age remained relatively constant too at around 37. In Ham it was common for agricultural labourers to go on working into their seventies – there was no such thing as a pension. This was balanced by a third of the workforce being aged between 16 and 25, which brought the overall average age down. Whilst each decade of census returns shows one or two retired agricultural workers as 'pauper' or 'on the parish', it is significant that no male agricultural labourer from Ham appears to have ended his existence in the workhouse. The constancy in numbers and ages also suggests that there was no flight of youth from the village to the towns or further afield through emigration.

There were both a Wiltshire Emigration Association and a Wiltshire Emigration Society operating during the 19th century, but while surviving records show many labourers from surrounding villages taking advantage of their assistance none appears to have come from Ham. Australia, America and Canada were the favourite destinations, and apart from the challenge of arriving in a new territory the voyage itself could be hazardous. In 1881 the *Marion* bound for Adelaide, South Australia with a full complement of emigrants – mostly agricultural labourers, including some from neighbouring Shalbourne – foundered on a reef before reaching port, but fortunately in this case without major loss of life. [123] However, although there were apparently no emigrants from Ham for forced economic reasons, the village does possess two intriguing emigration stories set nearly half a century apart.

Charles Hissey was the eldest son of Maurice Hissey, a yeoman farmer in Buttermere, and heir to his father's 550-acre Manor Farm (now Grange Farm) estate. In 1840, at the age of 35, he married 19 year-old Emily Mills, the daughter of a labourer in Ham. Weeks after their marriage at All Saints' Church the couple emigrated to South Australia, taking with them according to Hissey folklore Emily's parents and family. However, while Emily's siblings may well have accompanied her, the census returns make it clear that her parents, John and Elizabeth Mills, stayed firmly in Ham. Why Charles Hissey should have abandoned the prospect of his inheritance in Buttermere so abruptly is not known. Perhaps his family disapproved of him marrying a labourer's daughter, or perhaps he saw no future for farming in England. Photographs of the pair in middle age show Charles as a dour, craggy-faced and bearded man with a shaven upper lip, not unlike Abraham Lincoln, and Emily as a plain, stolid matron with a resigned expression on her face. They were nevertheless successful in at least one aspect of their marriage as a family gathering of their descendants in South Australia in 2007 numbered 254.[124]

Forty-six years later in 1886, William, known as Willie, Henry Deacon Woodman's only son by his first marriage, set sail for Chile at the age of 21 to set up a sheep farm in Patagonia with a business partner, the brother of a brother-in-law. On the voyage he met his future wife whom he married on arrival in Valparaiso. The sheep-farming venture flourished despite bitter Patagonian winters and unremitting wind for the rest of the year. Willie is reported to have taken several men from Ham with him, and also two maids. It seems likely that they came on a subsequent trip rather than the initial voyage. The men were said to have included a Bowley and a Levy. There were several adult male Bowleys by then in Ham but none of those in the census returns seems readily to fit the bill. The first appearance of the Levy family in the village from the census returns is in 1901, and the head of family is shown as Sarah Levy, a laundress aged 56. Ten years later she is shown as a widow, and it could be that her husband went to Patagonia but never returned. Willie Woodman himself did return to England because of his wife's ill health, but died not long afterwards at the early age of 43; he was survived by his wife and three children. Of the Ham men and women who had accompanied him, some apparently went to Australia but two men are said to have returned to Ham, where from their savings abroad they purchased a steam traction engine for hire which they named 'Patagonia'. In 1916 there is a reference in the village to Frank Levy, aged 37, as an engine driver, and perhaps he was the son of the Patagonian adventurer who failed to return and had then inherited his father's share of the traction engine. The maids are reported to have married shepherds in Patagonia. Why Willie Woodman like Charles Hissey should have chosen to emigrate when he was presumably heir to the lion's share of his father's estate remains unsolved. Possibly both father and son were gloomy about the prospects of farming in England, or perhaps Willie simply sought adventure abroad like many other young men of his generation. Willie predeceased his father and his widow and children do not feature in Henry Deacon Woodman's will – all the other surviving children of both marriages received legacies – so presumably Willie, or his widow, received his share earlier, and it may have been that which financed the Patagonian expedition.[125]

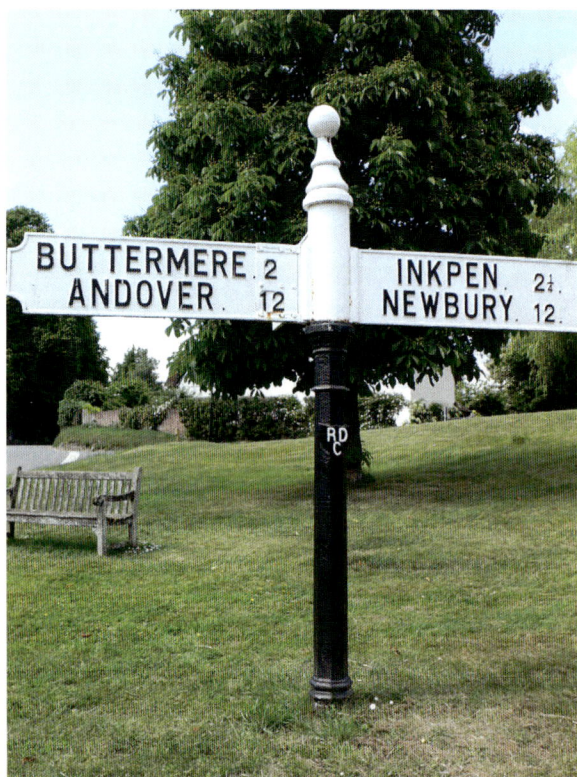

Signpost on the village green with the initials RDC for Rural District Council on the post

Henry Deacon Woodman was the key to what was happening in Ham in the 1880s and 1890s. The main target for attack in *The Daily News* articles and correspondence columns was the archetypal squire who was unconcerned by the miseries afflicting his workforce, but this was a label which could not be attached to Woodman. He was evidently a caring employer for his times, and he took his role as the *soi-disant* squire of Ham seriously. Not only was he the major landowner but he was also a long-serving churchwarden, correspondent for the village school and the first chairman of the Parish Meeting, the forerunner of the Parish Council, which was set up in 1894. Outside the village he was a Justice of the Peace, a member of the Board of Guardians of the Hungerford Workhouse and a District Councillor. Ham was part of Ramsbury Rural District Council which had been formed following the Local Government Act of 1894; the initials RDC can still be seen on the signpost on the village green. At home Woodman raised a large family in the Victorian tradition. He had six children, including the Patagonian adventurer, by his first wife Mary who died in 1886. Two years later he married Lilla, nearly 30 years his junior, by whom he had a further four children.

By all accounts he was a devoted father to his children and especially to his daughters, but despite this and his philanthropy in building the village school it would be unwise to cast him necessarily in the mould of an avuncular, benevolent patriarch of the village. He was arguably too much the astute businessman and instinctive autocrat for that. After all, he was a member of a high Victorian age in which status and outward appearances had become an obsession. No doubt deeply conscious of his origins as the illegitimate son of an ambitious local farmer, he would have been keen to maintain the standards expected of him both within and outside the village, and it is not surprising that he took particular pleasure in being transported about the countryside in his appropriately named Victoria – a light, four-wheeled two-seater – with his coachman perched up in front of him. But what he did for Ham was to steer it remarkably unscathed in comparison with the rest of southern England through a very difficult period for farming in the last two decades of the century. By the end of it he was exhausted and as the sale catalogue of his farming stock in 1901 put it, he was 'retiring from Agricultural Pursuits'. Canny as ever, he did not sell his estates at Ham Spray and Dove's Farm – and his other estates at Buttermere and Henley – until 1908 by which time the agricultural land market although far from rosy had considerably improved from the low point of the 1880s and 1890s.[126]

The second target in the *The Daily News* columns was the rector who was seen to be in the pocket of the squire and to bully his parishioners into attending church services they neither wanted nor understood. Again, for Ham, it would be wrong to attach that label to Charles Burder who was rector from 1864 to the end of the century. For a start, being a wealthy man he had no need to be in anyone's pocket. In 1839 the rector at Ham was allotted a rent charge of £435 to replace his tithes,[127] a not inconsiderable sum in those days, but Burder evidently had means of his own as in 1864, the year of his appointment, he replaced the west end of the

Rectory with 'a tall brick cross-wing built to designs by Waring & Blake of London'.[128] Despite this expense he and his wife would not live in the Rectory until some time in the 1880s. In the meantime the Rectory was occupied by a succession of curates who presumably carried out most of the pastoral work. These must have been busy times for the church: a decade earlier the census of 1851 showed 129 parishioners attending the morning service and 137 the after-noon service. Five years after Burder's appointment the patronage of All Saints' Church changed from the Bishop of Winchester to the Bishop of Salisbury.[129]

Rectors' wives also came under attack in the newspaper for being busybodies and interfer-ing dictatorially with the dispensing of charity in the village. Sarah, Charles Burder's wife, was a year older than her husband and would have been in her mid 50s by the time she came to live in Ham. Born and bred in London she would have been very much alive to her standing in soci-ety and the duties that emanated from her position as the rector's wife, but there is no reason to suggest that she was unreasonably officious in these. It is easy to forget that this was an era in which Cecil Frances Alexander, the wife of an Irish Anglican bishop, could write a hymn especially for the young which contained the verse:

> The rich man in his castle,
> The poor man at his gate,
> God made them, high or lowly,
> And order'd their estate.

This verse is now omitted from *All things bright and beautiful* in modern editions of hymnals, but in the late 19th century the hymn in its entirety was considered remarkable only for its charm; Mrs Alexander's *Hymns for Little Children* reached its 71st edition in 1900. What Sarah Burder set her mind to amongst other matters was training domestic staff. 'Parsonage trained' was a ready passport to domestic service elsewhere and the 1891 census shows Sarah Harris, aged 18, housemaid, and Edith Nash, aged 15, kitchenmaid, living in the Rectory.

Punch celebrated its Golden Jubilee in 1891. Fifty years on its satire directed at society's indif-ference to the plight of the poor was less frequent and less acid, and it did not comment on the issues raised by *The Daily News* and *The Times* directly. However, at the end of December that year it published verses referring to the establishment of county councils which picked up obliquely the points made in the newspaper articles. While once again the summary of tyran-nies outlined in the verses does not appear to have a strong echo in Ham, most of the village must have welcomed this move towards democracy which in 1894 resulted in the establish-ment of rural district councils and parish councils. However, even then these improvements did not in themselves produce the sudden transformation in rural life envisaged by *Punch's* tongue-in-cheek commentary.[130]

OUR VILLAGE

For centuries the Village was maintained, without cessation,
As 'a Squire and Parson's paddock,' just to keep poor yokels down,
But all that is to be altered, at the Radical's instigation,
We're settling on a village which shall have the charms of town.
It's shaped on Democratic lines, it is *in nubibus* [uncertain] yet,
But when Reform's set going, it's a horse that does not stop.
The House of Commons has pronounced, and old Tories fuss, yet
All understand the tyrant has the tip to shut up shop.

Chorus

In the Village, new Village, a healthy little spot,
The home of rural Hygiene, where nasty smells are not,
Where HODGE shan't be the thrall [slave]
Of the Vicarage and the Hall,
In the Village shaped on Democratic lines!

There bobbing to their 'betters' shall not be an institution
With the Jemmies and the Jessamies, as in the good old day;
There "Washhouses" shall civilise chawbacons – by ablution,
And Drink-shops shall not freely tithe the ploughman's paltry pay.
There shall be a Parish Council by the householders elected,
Who will snub "the Village tyrant" and will cut the Parson's comb;
And when once 'tis constituted such reform may be expected
That poor HODGE in all sincerity may sing his *"Home, Sweet Home!"*

Chorus

In the Village, new Village, the sanitary spot,
A small self-governed commune with full powers to 'allot',
A Free Library for all,
And a handsome Meeting Hall,
In the Village shaped on Democratic lines!

There the Labourer shall not half-starve on 'swankey' and thin pottage,
With a prospect of the Workhouse when no longer can he work;
And a voice in local business which the big-wigs cannot burke,
The rural working-man shall superintend his children's schooling,
And control long ill-used 'charities', and champion 'common rights,'
And, in fact, there'll be an end to Squire's sole sway and Parson's fooling,
And the rustics sole hope-beacon shall no more be 'London's Lights.'

Chorus: In the Village, new Village, etc

There the peasant politician with the Guardian shall grapple,
And keep up the rural standard, and keep down the local rates;
The haughty Church no longer shall lord it o'er the Chapel,
And the Voluntary School shall find the level it so hates.
In short, with Local Government invested, the whole Village
Shall grow vigorous, and virtuous, and prosperous, and proud,
And free from Landlord pressure, and the Parson's petty pillage,
The peasants shall no longer to the slums of London crowd.

Chorus
From the Village, new Village, a happy little spot,
A home of peace and plenty, where oppression may not plot;
Where there's room enough for all,
And the "hind" [skilled farmworker] is *not* a "thrall,"
In the Village shaped on Democratic lines!

In many other ways the 19th century was the coming of age for Ham. By the end of the century the village possessed a church, a school, a post office, a policeman and a police station – although the last seems to have been little more than the policeman's lodgings – as well as a shop, a public house, a blacksmith and a wheelwright. By the end of the next century only the church and the public house would remain. So not only was it a coming of age but the end of the century also marked the apogee of Ham as what many would regard as a quintessential rural village. In other facets of both village and national life the momentum of change would continue. In 1884 agricultural labourers were given the vote under the Reform Bill. At the beginning of that century few in the village would have been able to read or write, and their horizons would have been limited to daily tasks and the changing seasons. By its end an education was assured for their children. These advances would appear to have represented a victory for Hodge, and in one sense they were, but the reality was that Hodge who had borne the brunt of the agricultural vicissitudes of the 19th century was at the end of it a survivor rather than a victor, and even survival would prove tenuous as by the end of the following century the ranks of agricultural labourers would be depleted to an undreamt-of degree. In the meantime life in Ham was still firmly rooted in the land as the following list of 'object lessons' for the infants in the village school in 1897 clearly illustrates: [131]

1. A Plough	11. Butter
2. Wheat	12. The 4 Seasons
3. A Shop	13. Blacklead
4. Coal	14. Iron
5. Barley	15. A Carpenter
6. The Horse	16. The Potato
7. A Book	17. Leather
8. A Needle	18. Sugar
9. The Cow	19. The Butcher
10. A School	20. Money

Steam power was already present in farming but the great breakthrough of the internal combustion engine had still to come. On 17 September 1901 the agricultural stock of Ham Spray and Dove's Farms was sold by auction. Ten days later the stock of the Manor Farm went under the hammer. Both sales provide a valuable insight into farming practices at Ham at the end of the 19th century. The sale catalogue for Ham Spray and Dove's Farms lists 19 items of binders, corn drills, mowing machines, horse rakes, hay-making machines, chaff-cutters, root pulpers, cake crushers and seed barrows. There were also 36 lots of ploughs, drags, harrows and rollers. Ploughs and other such implements were now much more scientifically designed to cater for differing purposes and soils. However, to put this array of machinery into perspective, the combined sales of the farm stock also included 40 carts and wagons, numerous sets of harness and 40 horses The average sale price in the auctions for a horse was £39; the highest price achieved for an item of machinery was £19. There were no steam traction engines in either sale. The auctioneers offered luncheon at 2s a head refundable for purchases over £2. The lure evidently worked as including livestock the two sales made a total £5,145 18s.[132]

The sales reflected the sharp end of farming. In the background science was helping the farmer with the study of genetics to improve livestock strains, the cross-fertilisation of crop and pasture plants, and the identification of particular fertiliser requirements for different soils. It was also an age of agricultural associations and county shows where these new ideas and discoveries could be explored and exchanged. However, it is likely that reality fell well short of the ideal. In his book *Hodge and his Masters* published in 1880, Richard Jefferies, the Swindon nature writer, has one of his characters comment, 'I tell you that to introduce scientific farming in England, in the face of tradition, custom and prejudice, is a far harder task than overcoming the desert sand'. Even so, the compulsory collection of national statistics on farming had begun in 1866, and farming was no longer simply the province of individual landowners and farmers. By the end of the century it was a national enterprise, and Ham was part of it.

The final change for Ham in the 19th century probably took place largely unnoticed at the time by most of the village. In 1861 the estates belonging to the Dean and Chapter of Winchester became vested in the Ecclesiastical Commissioners.[133] Still less would anyone in Ham have realised at the close of the century that the Church's ownership of the manor of Ham, which had lasted for over 1,000 years, had only 14 more years to run.

HAM SPRAY,

4 Miles from Hungerford.

A CATALOGUE OF THE WHOLE OF THE HIGHLY VALUABLE

LIVE AND DEAD

Agricultural Stock,

INCLUDING THE HERD OF

134 Head of Superior SHORTHORN CATTLE,

VIZ.:—

63 In-calf HEIFERS (close to Calving),
42 Two and Three-years-old Fresh Barren HEIFERS,
24 Yearling HEIFERS and 1 STEER,
Yearling Shorthorn BULL,   3 In-calf Dairy COWS.

THE TEAMS OF

23 Powerful Cart GELDINGS & MARES,

AND CART COLTS,

TOGETHER WITH THE

Agricultural Implements, Machinery, Harness and Tools,

Which will be SOLD by AUCTION, by

MR. T. LAVINGTON

IN CONJUNCTION WITH

MR. A. HERBERT

On the Premises, as above, on

TUESDAY, SEPTEMBER 17th, 1901,

COMMENCING AT HALF-PAST 10 O'CLOCK PUNCTUALLY, by direction of Mr. H. D. WOODMAN, who is retiring from Agricultural Pursuits.

Luncheon will be provided at a charge of 2/- per head, to be refunded to Purchasers of £2 value and upwards.

Conveyances will leave the Three Swans Hotel, Hungerford, at half-past nine o'clock and half-past eleven o'clock on the morning of sale, and a conveyance will also meet the 9.47 down train and 9.59 up train at Grafton Station, to carry passengers to the Farm, at a moderate charge for the return journey.

Mr. WOODMAN'S SECOND SALE which will include the HAMPSHIRE DOWN BREEDING FLOCK, and 40 VALUABLE CART HORSES, will take place at "HAM MANOR FARM," on FRIDAY, SEPTEMBER 27th, 1901.

Catalogues may be obtained of Mr. T. Lavington, Auctioneer, Marlborough, or Mr. A. Herbert, Auctioneer, Andover.

Frontispiece of the auction catalogue of Ham Spray farm stock and equipment, 1901

14

TWO WORLD WARS

The beginning of the new century was marked by the death of Queen Victoria, ending a reign of nearly 64 years and one of the most remarkable periods of British history. The following year, 1902, saw the end of the Second Boer War which in its initial stages had been a humiliating chapter in Britain's military annals. To what extent these events impacted on Ham is not known. The only clue is the school log book which mentions 'The Rose, Shamrock and Thistle' and 'The Coronation' as being matters of common interest in 1902. The coronation of Edward VII would have been both a great national and international event. Victoria's children and grandchildren were sprinkled throughout the royal houses of Europe and included the Kaiser of Germany and the wife of the Tsar of All the Russias. However, the schoolmaster James Kavanagh might have had to tread a little more carefully in teaching the children about the national symbols, particularly in dodging round the vexed question of home rule for Ireland following the defeat of the two Home Rule Bills a few years earlier.

Of course what was of much more interest to Ham was Henry Deacon Woodman giving up farming in 1901. Thereafter, for Ham, the century splits naturally into two separate halves. The first half is dominated by the two world wars and their impact on the continuing fluctuating fortunes of farming. The second half reflects the divorce of the village from the land which had supported it for ten centuries.

Although he had given up farming Woodman did not put his Ham estates up for sale until 1908 and meanwhile continued to live in Ham Manor. He remained a churchwarden, an appointment he had held since 1862, and Chairman of the Parish Meeting. Under the Local Government Act of 1894 Ham had been given the option of having a Parish Meeting or a Parish Council; it chose by a majority of 15 to 2 to have a Parish Meeting, which would remain until 1976 when it became a Parish Council. Ham was now officially a parish and no longer a manor although its boundaries were unchanged. In the early years of the Parish Meeting its main task was to appoint two overseers of the poor of which Woodman was one. These were the successors to the overseers who had held considerable sway in the 18th century, but now their duties were circumscribed by government diktat – the workhouse system, although becoming much ameliorated, would continue in principle until its abolition in 1930. Parish Meetings were held in the school and on two occasions in 1899 and 1900 Woodman found himself the only attender.[134] This suggests that he was probably an autocratic chairman, and despite the debt owed to

Ham Manor c.1905

him for guiding the village through the dark times of the 1880s and 1890s, there is a hint of a sigh of relief when he stood down from his various appointments and left the village in 1909. Woodman then moved to Reading where he would later complain that the climate did not suit him or his wife. He died in 1915 at the age of 86 and is commemorated by a brass plaque on the north wall of All Saints' Church.

 Woodman's abandonment of farming created a vacuum at Ham and the man who would fill it was Samuel Farmer. Farmer was a partner of Stratton & Company and a major landowner. He owned the Henley Manor Estate and two other estates at Little Bedwyn and Froxfield, and either then or later he also owned land further west in Wiltshire.[135] Evidently a man of considerable energy, he is said to have been instrumental in persuading the Great Western Railway to continue its line beyond Hungerford, the original planned terminus, to Great Bedwyn. There is a lock on the Kennet & Avon Canal at Grafton named after him, and he is remembered in Little Bedwyn as a significant philanthropist. In 1901 Farmer took on the lease of the Woodman estates in Ham, some 1,135 acres, and over the next 25 years until his death in 1926 he would have a profound influence on affairs in Ham, although he himself would never live there – his home was Little Bedwyn Manor. One of his stipulations on entering the lease was for Woodman to spend a sum not exceeding £500 to provide cowsheds for not less than 50 cows, and because of that he is credited with introducing dairy farming to Ham.[136]

118

Henry Deacon Woodman with his second wife Lilla and their children c.1905, left to right: (standing) Ethel , Henry Deacon, Guy, (sitting) Freda, Hugh, Lilla

In 1908 Woodman finally sold his land at Ham. It was not all plain sailing. Farmer who purchased the Ham Manor estate and Dove's Farm haggled over what he felt was due to him under the Agricultural Land Holdings Act for improvements to the land during the period of the lease. A very small but evidently important side issue that occupied their respective solicitors was the knotty problem of the cesspit at Dove's House which was located on a different sale lot to the house. Terms however were agreed and completion took place at the end of September 1908; the price paid for Dove's Farm was £6,800. At Ham Spray the sale negotiations dragged on until April 1909, although a price of £7,000 plus an additional sum for the timber had been agreed much earlier.[137] Woodman reckoned that this delay was due to dilatoriness by the purchaser's solicitor, and that it was costing him 2–3 per cent in his potential investment return on cash due to fluctuations in the bond market since the previous autumn. The lawyer may well have been slow but the underlying reason appears to have been the ill-health of his client, Henry Wilson, and Woodman was shocked to learn that Wilson had died three days after the completion of the sale, remarking in a letter to his own solicitor on

24 April 'very glad to find Spray settled … such sad sad news of poor Mr Wilson's death'.[138] What happened next at Ham Spray is not clear. The estate was retained by Wilson's legatees and is shown as being owned by Messrs Wilson Brothers in Kelly's Directory of 1915, but by 1914 Samuel Farmer appears to have been overseeing it. Before his death Henry Wilson had promised to sell Ham Spray House and its garden to Stanley Pinniger, a solicitor from Newbury, and this was duly executed thus divorcing the house from the estate.[139] Pinniger would later serve as Chairman of the Parish Meeting for most of the war years. Ham Spray Cottage, described in the sale brochure as 'a modern cottage', was retained as a farm worker's cottage as part of the estate, and the farm manager, Fred Tucker, lived in the lodge.

Other changes in the major residences in Ham flowed from these sales. As Samuel Farmer did not live in Ham, the Manor House was rented to a Captain Frederick Brereton, late of the Royal Army Medical Corps.[140]

Brereton was a more remarkable man than this brief description might suggest. He had fought in the Boer War as a medical officer with the Second Battalion Scots Guards. Afterwards he became a prolific author of boys' adventure stories, largely related to Britain's colonial exploits, in the manner of the Victorian author G. A. Henty. His first book published in 1900 was *With Shield and Assegai: A Tale of the Zulu War*, and more than 50 other books would follow, many of them written at Ham Manor. A smaller claim to fame was his top of the range, 22 horsepower SCAT (Società Ceirano Automobili Torino) two-seater coupé in French grey with black coach lines, which was registered to him at Ham Manor in February 1914 with the Wiltshire number plate of AM3537. The first Wiltshire number plate AM1 had been issued in December 1903, and the rapid growth in the use of motor transport in the early part of the century can be partly gauged by the fact that in Wiltshire alone over 3,500 motor vehicles were licensed in the intervening 12 years. In 1914, like many of his contemporaries, Brereton enlisted in the army again at the age of 42 to fight in the First World War. He was promoted to lieutenant colonel and made a Commander of the Order of the British Empire (CBE) in 1919. It is not clear whether he returned to Ham Manor after the war, but it seems unlikely as Ralph Brown was living there by 1920. Brereton's first wife Ethel died in 1947 and he married again at the age of 81. He died in London in 1957.

Dove's House had been occupied by Annie and Mary (known as Polly) Woodman, the two unmarried daughters of Henry Deacon Woodman by his first marriage who were known locally as 'the Misses Woodman'. It now featured in the sale brochure as the 'Dove's Farm homestead'. Following the sale it became the residence of Farmer's estate manager Sidney Gauntlett, who was briefly elected Chairman of the Parish Meeting before relinquishing the appointment to Brereton a year later.[141] The displaced Misses Woodman then went live in Dove's Farm House, now Ham Cross, which their father had retained together with a meadow behind it. Determined not to be christened the 'Misses Doves' by the village, they changed the name of the house to Ivy Cottage.[142] Born and brought up in Victorian times and now in their late forties, the Misses Woodman were feisty chips off the old block and took a lively interest in the affairs of the village with Polly Woodman playing the organ in All Saints' Church amongst other things. Determined not to lose touch with the village, and to ensure that he would still enjoy some comfort on his visits to Ham after the Manor House had been sold, Henry Deacon Woodman raised the ceiling of his chosen bedroom in Ivy Cottage, in which he installed a very large half tester bed that required steps to climb into. He also retained the Old Malthouse Cottages, one of which would later become the village post office, shop and bakery.[143]

A missing link in these various transactions was East Court Farm, then known as Cannings. The *Victoria History* suggests that Henry Deacon Woodman acquired the farm prior to 1908 and that it formed part of his sales of land that year. However, the sales brochure for Ham Spray and Dove's Farm clearly shows the East Court land as belonging to 'Cannings Trustees', and in a note of August 1908 Woodman comments that a stream on the boundary between his and Mr Canning's (sic) properties belongs to him (Woodman).[144] What seems more likely is that both Woodman and Farmer in turn each rented East Court and also owned a small portion of it, before the greater portion was purchased subsequently by Samuel Farmer in 1918.

Ham Cross, the former Dove's farmhouse, known in the first half of the 20th century as Ivy Cottage. The dormer windows on the right were inserted when the roof was raised over the kitchen in 1908 to provide a bedroom for Henry Deacon Woodman

Once the dust had settled on the 1908 and 1909 sales, and on the death of the popular King Edward VII in 1910, there was a period of comparative calm. 1911 was marked by a blazing hot summer with the temperature in August reaching a record 100 degrees Fahrenheit, which resulted in a very early harvest. However, it was also marked by a series of strikes, and in Liverpool troops were called out and the Riot Act was read. The discontent was largely confined to urban labour which was well organised in trades unions. Agricultural labour lacked such unity and there is no evidence of unrest in Ham. In the following year, 1912, the only matter of note seems to have been a request to the Post Office to provide a Sunday delivery in Ham.[145] It was the lull before the storm, and Ham would have been oblivious of the manoeuvrings by the European states and Russia. Still less would it have appreciated the consequences of the assassination of an Austrian archduke it had never heard of by a Serbian teenager in an equally unknown Balkan city in June 1914.

Looking south from the green c. 1910. From left to right: Porch Cottages, Crown & Anchor, Rose Cottage (roof), Manor Cottages, Village School (roof), Reprieve Cottages (now Well Cottage)

After the storm had broken Ham found itself gripped by two parallel and competing vices: the war's increasingly insatiable appetite for men to serve in the armed forces and an increasing demand for domestic food. Farmer who already owned the leaseholds of the Ham Manor estate and Dove's Farm now purchased the freehold of the remaining part of the parish owned

The Ham Club parading past the Crown & Anchor on the occasion of a village fair c.1910

by the Church from the Ecclesiastical Commissioners in 1914[146] – the Ham Spray estate had already been disenfranchised in 1847. Wulfgar's near thousand year-old legacy of the manor of Ham to the Church was at an end. On a more immediate front, the exact relationship between Farmer and the owners of Ham Spray at that time is unclear, but he evidently exercised an over-all coordinating role in respect of the war effort. Farming was a reserved occupation, but as the need for military manpower grew, particularly after the slaughter on the Western Front in 1916, the screw tightened.

During the war a cynical ditty based on 'Sing a song of sixpence' was doing the rounds:

> Sing a song of Europe,
> Highly civilised.
> Four-and-twenty nations
> Thoroughly hypnotised.
> When the battles opened
> The bullets began to sing.
> Wasn't that a silly thing
> To do for any king?
> The kings were in the background
> Issuing commands;

> The queens were in the parlours
> By etiquette's demands;
> The bankers in the counting-house
> Busy multiplying;
> And all the rest were at the Front
> Doing all the dying.

It is doubtful whether the cynicism percolated to Ham. The village, as well as the wider county, was preoccupied with the tug-of-war between military conscription and the need to maintain the food supply. The Military Service Act had been passed in January 1916; it required unmarried men to enlist, ending the previous laissez-faire of voluntary enlistment. In December the same year, at a War Agriculture Committee meeting in Chippenham, the following guidelines for farm manpower levels in Wiltshire were drawn up:

> 1 carter for every 50 acres of arable land (vale)
> 1 carter for every 65 acres of arable land (hill)
> 1 milker for every 10 cows
> 1 man for every 50 head of cattle (fed)
> 1 shepherd for every 300 sheep (hurdled)
> 1 shepherd for every 500 sheep (grass)
> 1 extra day man for every 80–100 acres of arable land [147]

At that point ten farm workers from Ham had already volunteered or been called up and two of them had been killed in action. Joseph Hunt, a former milker at Ham, died in 1915 serving with 2nd Battalion The Royal Berkshire Regiment; he left a widow Alice in Hungerford. James Martin, a former carter, died in 1916 serving with the Royal Garrison Artillery. The other eight would survive the war; they included James Martin's brother and Wilfred Bowley, one of five Bowleys aged between 14 and 74 working on the various Ham farms in 1914, all of whom were descended from Charles Bowley.

At the end of 1916 there were 24 men, six boys and two women working on the farms.[148] The boys were aged 15–17, and one them who had been working on the farm for four years as a carter since the age of 13 was Sidney Waters. He would be killed in 1918 serving with 16th Battalion The Devonshire Regiment. Then there were 12 men in the critical 18–41 age group (the upper age limit for compulsory enlistment was not raised to 51 until April 1918) who were either exempt or temporarily exempt from military service because of their occupation or for medical reasons. Only two of them were medically graded 'A: fit for general service'. Of the others, one had been discharged from the army – possibly because of wounds, two had been rejected for service for medical reasons and the remainder were in one of the B or C medical categories and thus unfit for general service; it is not known whether any of them were eventually called up, but all survived the war.

Three other men from Ham who do not appear to have been employed in farming were also killed in the war. Fred Tucker, named after his father, the Ham Spray farm manager, and Herbert Pinn, the nephew of James Cripps, the head cowman living at East Court Farm House, then known as Cannings Farm House, were both killed in 1918 serving with The Royal Berkshire Regiment. The third, Thomas Chandler, serving in the same regiment, was killed earlier in 1915. The son of Sydney and Martha Chandler of Vernham Dean, he left a widow Elizabeth there and his connection with Ham is not clear.

William Barclay was born in Turriff, Aberdeenshire. At the age of 19 he enlisted in the Scots Guards and fought with them in the Boer War, where he would have been in the same battalion as its medical officer, Captain Frederick Brereton, later of Ham Manor. At the outbreak of the First World War he served in the Ypres Salient with the Second Battalion Scots Guards and was wounded in a failed night attack at Rouges Bancs on 18 December 1914, the week before the Christmas Truce that year. He was evacuated to Britain and returned to the front six months later. Promoted meanwhile to lance corporal, he was badly shellshocked at Ginchy in September 1916. Evacuated to Britain once again he was invalided out of the army being 'no longer physically fit for war service', and died in November 1917 in Aberdeen.[149] After his death his widow settled in Ham together with her four children, one of whom was born after her husband's death. She was coming home. Sarah Jane Barclay had been born and brought up in Ham and was the granddaughter of Charles Bowley, who had escaped the hangman's noose in the aftermath of the Captain Swing riots.

Little is known otherwise about Ham during the war, but it must have been a time of great stress. Farming as a reserved occupation would have been viewed by those who did not understand the true picture as a very cushy billet compared to the dangers and extreme discomforts of the trenches. At one level that implied gibe was justified, but the records show that very few of the able-bodied men in Ham, if any by the end of the war, escaped the war machine, and work on the farms was very largely carried out by a much reduced labour force of boys, the middle-aged and elderly and a few medically downgraded men, all of whom were ineligible for military service. Attendance at the village school dropped from the high 30s to the high 20s during the war, and there were a number of instances of boys missing school to work on the farms.[150] The School Attendance Officer was called to deal with the latter, but it was a two-edged sword. Nationally schoolchildren were encouraged to work on the farm out of school hours, and in February 1916 the War Agricultural Committee for Wiltshire appealed to the Education Committee to examine boys as early as possible so that they might be employed in agriculture.[151] There was absolutely no doubt that production of food was vital to the war effort. In the Spring of 1917 Britain was near starvation due to the success of German submarines, and a Food Control and Economy Sub-Committee for the parish was appointed at the request of Ramsbury Rural District Food Committee to cope with the food shortages; the sub-committee comprised Kate Poole (schoolmistress), Polly Woodman and Thomas Francis (publican at the Crown & Anchor), with the rector, the Reverend John Arkell, as correspondent.[152] There was already a national Food Controller, Lord Devonport, who asked the population to cut its consumption of bread by a quarter. In fact the village school did its bit. In July 1916 the school log recorded that the school had a 12-day holiday for haymaking, and in a later entry in September 1918 William Scammell, William Hutchins and James Levy were given a day off to help get in the harvest. In that same week, on three half-holidays, the children were taken to pick blackberries. They picked a staggering total of 196 ½ lbs and were paid 3d per lb – different times, different values. The person who wrote these delightful insights into school life was the headmistress Kate Agnes Poole who had taken over the school in 1904. Sadly 1918 would be her last year. On 13 January 1919 she was taken ill, and six days later she was dead from septic pneumonia.[153]

Eventually what became known as the Great War, 'the war to end all wars', ended in November 1918. The following year a special meeting of the Parish Meeting was convened to discuss the format of a Celebration of Peace. Thirty members of the village attended, a record for such parish meetings, and it was decided that the celebration should comprise tea, sports, entertainment and a bonfire. The school summer holidays were extended to include the King's Peace Week holiday, and with the rest of the nation the school observed the first two minutes silence on 11 November. Meanwhile a collection had taken place in the village to finance the War Memorial plaque now fixed to the north wall of All Saints' Church.

The war years left their mark in other ways. At the beginning of 1918 the Fourth Reform Bill had given the vote to single women over 30, largely as a result of the major contribution of women towards the war effort, although ironically many of the women who had taken part in the war were under that age. While full suffrage for women would not be enacted until 1928, this beginning became a catalyst for modest inroads into the hitherto entirely male administration of the parish. In 1919 Ham was startled to discover that Wiltshire County Council required one of the three candidates due to be submitted to it for the appointment of a new school manager, or correspondent, to be a woman. Also that year a Miss Fursby of Bedwyn was appointed Assistant Overseer in Ham at the princely sum of £5 per annum,[154] although her tenure would not be lengthy as Parliament ended the role of overseers in 1927. A few years later in 1925 the redoubtable Misses Woodman became active in the Parish Meeting.

Important though these initial assaults on Ham's male bastion were, they were overshadowed by yet another convulsion in the agricultural economy of the country. Despite the privations and food shortages the war had been a boom time for agriculture. In the later war years both prices and agricultural wages almost trebled from those in the immediate pre-war years.

Much of this was due to the Corn Production Act of 1917 which guaranteed minimum prices for wheat and oats and a minimum wage for farm workers of 25s a week. The euphoria of the peace kept prices high in 1919 and for the first half of 1920, but then prices tumbled by nearly 50 per cent. There were no longer armies to feed, food rationing had ended and large quantities of foodstuffs once again came from abroad. This precipitated an agricultural crisis compounded by the repeal of the Corn Production Act in 1921, a bill which was quickly labelled 'the great betrayal of agriculture'. Prices would not recover significantly until the next war 20 years later.

The records of the Parish Meeting make no reference to this crisis, which nevertheless would have had a severe impact on the economy of the village. Meetings were concerned with other more parochial matters. Ivy Dixon, now Ivy Hoare, was born in August 1916 at Moordown Farm. Most of the farm lay just outside the south-western parish boundary but at that time the farm was part of the Ham Manor estate. She went to school first in Ham and then with her sister in Buttermere, until she entered domestic service in Henley at the age of 14. Neither school had electric light and she walked to and from school, a distance of nearly two and a half miles each way, with in the case of Ham a steep climb up the hill on the return journey. The roads then were rough gravel and tarring the roads was one of the issues occupying the minds of the Parish Meeting. In 1922 the parish voted to tar the road through the village, but by 1927

A village outing c.1920

nothing had been achieved leading to a motion of censure against the parish's newly appointed councillor on the Ramsbury RDC, Mr Billington, for failing to take appropriate action. The tarring appears to have eventually taken place in 1929. The installation of a telephone in the village proceeded more swiftly. Having voted for one in 1923, a telephone had been installed by 1925 with the number Inkpen 7. However, it produced its own problems. The parish had given a guarantee that it would raise a specific minimum revenue from the telephone, and in both 1925 and 1926 there was a worrying deficit.

Other changes were afoot for Ham in the 1920s. In 1924 Lytton Strachey, Dora Carrington and Ralph Partridge came to live in Ham Spray House. Strachey was a leading member of a coterie of like-minded, avant–garde writers, intellectuals and artists which became known as the Bloomsbury Group. In part the group represented a reaction to its perception of the strait-jacket and humbug of Victorian values. Carrington was a promising young artist who had studied at the Slade; she would have been a pupil of the formidable Henry Tonks, whose descendant, James Eldridge now lives in Ham. She was not then a member of Bloomsbury as such but fell passionately in love with Strachey, which surprised their respective friends as Strachey was homosexual. They set up house together in 1917 at Tidmarsh near Pangbourne, and the following year Strachey's great work *Eminent Victorians* was published. After the war they were joined by Partridge, an ebullient heterosexual with a distinguished war record – he was promoted to major at the age of 23 and was awarded the Military Cross and Bar and the Croix de Guerre. Partridge and Carrington were married in 1921. In the autumn of 1923 the three of them were looking for a new home and led by Carrington they went to see Ham Spray House. It was evidently known territory to Carrington and Strachey as she remarks on Inkpen Beacon and Combe Gibbet in an earlier letter to him, and previously Carrington had come across Ham on a walking holiday. Her parents had moved to Ibthorpe House in 1914. Ibthorpe is some six miles as the crow flies over the hill from Ham and Carrington lived there until she moved to Tidmarsh with Strachey, so the downs would have been familiar to her. She described her excitement in a letter to her close friend and soulmate, Gerald Brenan:

> It is called Ham Spray House. That's a good title to begin with. It is within a mile of the village of Ham & the village of Inkpen and a stone's throw (if one threw well) from the most marvellous downs in the WHOLE WORLD – Tibet excluded – Inkpen Beacon. It is four miles from Hungerford, We saw a ram shackle Lodge, a long avenue of limes but all wuthering in appearance, bleak, & the road a grass track. Barns in decay, then the back of a rather forbidding farm house. We walked to the front of it & saw to our amazement in the blazing sun a perfect English country house. But with a view onto the downs before it that took our breaths away… The price I fear is prohibitive… [155]

Ham Spray House from the 1908 auction catalogue for the Ham Spray estate

The house was advertised in *Country Life* at the beginning of January the following year as a 'very charming country house' for £3,000. However, Strachey managed to negotiate the price down to £2,300, and by the end of the month he had bought it with help from Partridge – the house was registered in Partridge's name.[156] Carrington comments on the *Country Life* advertisement in her letters as a ploy by 'Mrs P' – presumably Stanley Pinniger's widow – to force up the price. Strachey, Carrington and Partridge would live together in Ham Spray House until Strachey's death in 1932. It was an unusual *ménage à trois* and complicated by both Partridge and Carrington being unfaithful to each other. By 1925 Partridge, an incorrigible philanderer, was firmly linked to Frances Marshall, a vivacious, dark-haired Cambridge bluestocking who was steeped in Bloomsbury from her childhood in Bedford Square and her association with its younger set at university. This development created a new tension in Ham Spray House. Although Carrington's marriage to Partridge was largely a sham, from then on the threesome became a markedly edgy foursome. Forming a backdrop to the various comings and goings during those eight years, Ham Spray House became a favourite haunt for Old Bloomsbury and the occupants' wider circle of friends. On the domestic side the household was looked after by Carrington assisted by Olive Martin, the daughter of the local carpenter, who came to Ham Spray House at the age of 15 in 1925 but left at the end of 1929 to join a family bakery. The two of them obviously got on well from the following description of tobogganing on Ham Hill, seen through Carrington's artist's eye:

> Yesterday afternoon I went tobogganing with Olive on the Downs. It was a most lovely afternoon. The sun was just setting, and the sky was a most delicate green tinged with pink and little clouds rose up from behind the crest of the downs, like balloons liberated by some hidden hand and floated up into the pale opal sky.
> . . . We had some lovely rushes down the hill. Olive had never been on a toboggan before.[157]

In various books about its occupants the house is described as modernised when they arrived in 1924, but there was no electricity and the 'modern drainage' described in the sales blurb turned out to be a misnomer. Carrington immediately set out to decorate what she described in one letter to Strachey as *la maison Jambon*, using paint and homemade hand-blocked wallpaper in bold colour tones. In 1928, flush with more funds from his publications, Strachey installed an electricity generator and central heating, and Carrington embarked on a new round of decoration. Other 'Bloomsberries' and their associates also left their mark on the house. Boris Anrep, the renowned Russian mosaicist, created a mosaic of a hermaphrodite on the fireplace in Strachey's bedroom. He later created another mosaic in the house to celebrate

Ham Spray House from the 2008 sale brochure

Ceramic panel of an owl and a fireplace tile depicting Carrington on her mare Belle, both painted by Carrington for Lytton Strachey's library in Ham Spray House

Ralph and Frances Partridge's marriage. Henry Lamb, a follower of Augustus John and a founder member of the Camden Town Group, left drawings in the house. Duncan Grant, a member of the Bloomsbury Group and one of Strachey's lovers, painted panels as did Vanessa Bell, another member of Bloomsbury who lived with Grant at Charleston Farmhouse. John Banting, the vorticist and later surrealist artist, also contributed a painting. All these contributions and most of Carrington's decorations have since vanished from the house; they were not to the taste of the new owners in the 1960s and they were first covered and then removed. Today, in what was Strachey's library, the survivors are a *trompe l'oeil* bookcase on a doorway, a painted ceramic panel of an owl standing on a book, and a fireplace with painted tiles, all done by Carrington. Although the losses are in many ways a sadness, Frances Partridge remarked at the end of the century to the then owners, Richard and Mary Gray, that she did not want the house to become a shrine to Bloomsbury.

What Ham made of it all is only patchily recorded, but the probable answer is not very much. For a start the house is the best part of a mile from the centre of the village, and then down a quarter of a mile of avenue which in those days was lined with wych elms (not limes as described by Carrington). Much later Frances Partridge would comment to her biographer, Anne Chisholm, that it was 'off the beaten track'. It is apparent that the Ham Spray House residents kept their bohemian lifestyle very much to themselves. They and their friends walked frequently on the downs and Carrington rode out on her mare Belle, a present from Strachey – 'It is exciting to see from the top of the Downs a little white horse walking across Huth's field and to know that it is Bellinda'.[158] Friends invited to Ham Spray House tended to be from their own intellectual circle, and this in turn reinforced the separation of the house and its goings-on from the rest of the village. Also, while Strachey had already become famous amongst the more literary public for his *Eminent Victorians*, the fame of the Bloomsbury Group as such and the almost prurient fascination in its louche sexual behaviour were much later phenomena.

However, not surprisingly the residents of Ham Spray House were regarded as strange neighbours by the rest of the village. In particular the tall, long-limbed and bearded Lytton Strachey was a scary figure to young children. Elsie Harding who lived with her parents at East Court Farm as a child recalled being 'frightened to death of the man, he was so odd. I used to go on the other side of the road when I saw him'. According to his biographer, Michael Holroyd, Strachey was christened 'God' by the village because of his beard and would sometimes sit on the green handing out 'forbidden cigarettes' to the local boys.[159] From today's perspective it is easy to imagine that there was an ulterior motive behind Strachey's largesse, but no lingering rumours exist to lend any substance to this suspicion. Shortly after their arrival in 1924 Partridge and Carrington had been invited to dine at Ham Manor as the married couple which outwardly they of course were – the Browns would have been their hosts – and discovered that the village viewed them as Bohemians and accordingly as foreigners. At that time Ham was still an insular village with a quiet, close-knit farming community. There were no buses and for most of the village a trip to Hungerford meant contacting Tom Bowley, at Littlefield Cottage on the Ham Road, who ran a horse and cart. He himself made a regular trip to Hungerford on a Wednesday, market day, and would run errands for other members of the village. The village was otherwise largely self-contained with a post office in one of the two cottages now forming the single Dove's House Cottage on the green, a grocery shop at the back of the Crown & Anchor run by the publican's wife Mrs Chandler, and another shop and bakery in the Old Malthouse run by Mr and Mrs Frederick Hatton.

It is quite possible that the news from the Ham Manor dinner reinforced the desire of the Ham Spray House residents to keep themselves to themselves. Nevertheless, it is apparent that Carrington did make an effort to meet the local inhabitants. In October 1924, some four months after her arrival at Ham Spray House, she writes amusingly about a visit to the Misses Woodman at Ivy Cottage.

> My call on the Miss Woodmans was fascinating. They are the most peculiar old ladies of about 63 and 66 years old. Do you know that they were born in *this* house, Ham Spray. Isn't that extraordinary. Their father built this house and made the garden, when he was a young man of 21. They had lived at Ham ever since they were born. They were full of information on every subject. They are so poor they have no servants, but do all their own work and the garden. They were very outspoken and natural because they had sunk below all pretensions.[160]

No doubt Annie and Polly Woodman were keen to impress their independence on Carrington, but perhaps they overdid it, or perhaps Carrington embroidered the story of her visit to spice up its telling in her letter. Either way her assumptions were wide of the mark. Henry Deacon

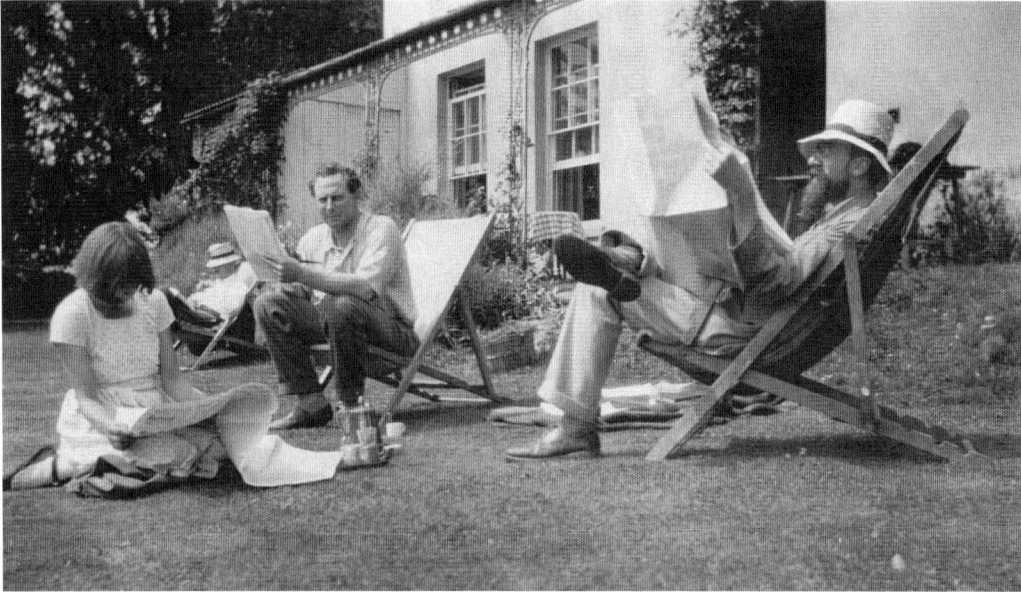

At Ham Spray House. Left to right: Dora Carrington, Saxon Sydney Turner, Ralph Partridge, Lytton Strachey

Woodman had taken pains to provide for his two unmarried daughters, and although they were not well off they were certainly not impoverished. They had domestic staff who lived in the Old Malthouse Cottages, including a gardener, William White. The sisters took great pride in their garden with its croquet lawn, heated greenhouse, fruit trees and vegetables. In their old age Annie and Polly Woodman would be looked after by Winnie and Jesse Bowley, and for their kindness to the two sisters they were given their part of the Old Malthouse Cottages on Polly's death in 1939; Norman Scutt, Winnie Bowley's brother, now lives there. Given the lifestyle of the inhabitants of Ham Spray House, Carrington's comments on the pretensions of the two sisters might appear surprising. In fact Strachey, Carrington and Partridge all came from comfortable homes where servants were the norm, and there was no question of not employing both indoor and outdoor staff at Ham Spray. Later, during the war, Frances Partridge would bemoan being bereft of domestic help. Back in 1924 Carrington was not alone in being impressed by her visit to Ivy Cottage; Polly Woodman confided afterwards to one of her half-sisters that 'the most peculiar people' were now living at Ham Spray.

There were very few people in the village for Carrington to call on other than the Browns at Ham Manor and the Misses Woodman. Dove's House was occupied by the Ham Manor estate manager who probably would not have been regarded as a social equal. This left the Reverend George Rodwell at the Rectory. Rodwell who had also arrived in the village in 1924 may well have made a welcoming pastoral visit to Ham Spray House, but if so it is likely to have fallen on

At Ham Spray House. Left to right: Dora Carrington, Marjorie Strachey, Frances Marshall (later Frances Partridge), Ralph Partridge

stony ground, as except for curiosity Strachey, Carrington and Partridge would have had no interest in All Saints' Church. In due course new neighbours would arrive, but initially the residents of Ham Spray House were probably more amused than troubled by being regarded as foreigners by the village.

Strachey died in January 1932 from stomach cancer. Prior to the previous Christmas it was clear that he was dying and various members of his family took up residence in the Bear Hotel in Hungerford. Initially Marshall joined them but then rented a room above what was then the post office in one of the Dove's House cottages on the green at Ham. Devastated by the loss of her one great love, Carrington shot herself at Ham Spray House two months later wrapped in Strachey's dressing gown. It was a particularly miserable end as she did not kill herself outright. She was a few days short of her thirty-ninth birthday. Despite her diaries and letters, a biography, and a recent film about her, Carrington as she was known – she deliberately dropped Dora – remains the most enigmatic of the Bloomsbury circle. She had been part of a golden generation of students at the Slade, and as well as the tragedy of her early death there is a regret that her talent as an artist never flowered in the same way that those of many of her contemporaries did. A year after Carrington's death Ralph Partridge married Frances Marshall and they continued to live in Ham Spray House until Ralph's death in 1960.

One of the casualties of the First World War was the merchant bank, or accepting house as it was known, Frederick Huth & Company. In danger of bankruptcy, the Bank of England rushed to shore it up in 1921, but although Huth's limped on until 1936 it was a broken reed. This impacted on the financial fortunes and future of Major Geoffrey Huth, Coldstream Guards, a scion of the Huth banking dynasty. Huth had fought both in the First World War and previously in the Boer War. Providing a bizarre footnote to life and times during the latter war, in one of his letters home to his mother Huth thanked her for the brace of grouse she had sent him which his batman had just cooked on a camp fire and which he pronounced delicious; the logistics of sending an edible brace of grouse from Britain to Cape Town and then into the field long before the days of air travel almost defies

Major Geoffrey Huth

belief. In 1907 he had married Gladys the daughter of another merchant banker, Sir Alexander Hargreaves Brown, and now, following the war and the collapse of the family bank, he turned his mind to farming. Having already purchased the 69-acre Lower Spray Farm in 1919 and 200 acres of the Inkpen Estate which included Church Farm a year later, he bought Ham Spray Farm in 1924. This consisted of land astride Bungum Lane on the eastern side of the parish boundary, and all three farms would in due course become known as Wansdyke Farms.

There was, however, a sad side to all this. Huth's brother had been killed at Ypres in the war, and seared by this, his own experiences in the war and the collapse of the family bank, Huth became a semi-recluse, a condition exacerbated by failing eyesight in his later years; he was virtually blind for the last ten years of his life. Allied to his depression Huth was a deeply religious man. Elsie Harding, whose father William Couling was employed by him, recalled him as a committed churchman who from time to time took services and preached as a lay reader. Largely self-taught, Harding had started to play the organ at All Saints at the age of 14, and on occasions Huth would take her up in his car to play the organ at Buttermere. On the return journey, if it were still light, he would always stop to admire the view, 'the best view in Wiltshire'. He would remain in her memory as a kind and modest man, and it is clear that despite his reclusive nature Huth took a keen interest in village affairs.

Another major event of the 1920s was the death in 1926 of Samuel Farmer. Although he was never a resident of Ham, he had nursed the village through the farming crisis of the First World War and its aftermath, in much the same way as Henry Deacon Woodman had nursed it through the last two decades of the previous century. Both now are largely forgotten heroes. By 1928 Farmer's estates at Ham had been acquired by (Samuel) Ralph Brown, and it is probable that he had purchased them several years before that. The records are incomplete but in any case on 28 June 1928 Brown then sold the estates by auction. Fortunately the sale brochure survives and it provides almost a Rosetta Stone in linking what was essentially a 19th century village with the modern village of today. With the exception of Huth's Ham Spray farms, Brown now owned the rest of the parish and most of the village except for a few scattered houses. The brochure listed 'six capital dairy and mixed farms' totalling some 1,350 acres. The core comprised Manor Farm of 324 acres, Dove's Farm of 267 acres, and East Court Farm – still known locally as Cannings – of 238 acres. The other three farms were New Buildings of 241 acres, situated mainly between Great Field and Ashley Drove and which for centuries had formed part of the Manor estate, and two small farms, Moordown Farm, 76 acres, and Bishop's Barn, 89 acres, both of which lay mostly outside the parish southern boundary.

The exact circumstances surrounding the sale are obscure, but for some reason – possibly because it did not reach its reserve at auction – Brown ended up retaining the Ham Manor estate. He and his wife were a popular couple in the village, taking part in the various village events which included dances in the village school. He himself was Chairman of the Parish Meeting for 45 years. During the First World War he had served in the Royal Navy and remained a keen sailor afterwards. A small man, he always managed to look as if he had slept in his suit, in strict contrast to his wife, Irene, a tall, slim woman with striking red curly hair who visited Paris regularly and liked to dress in the latest French fashions. They employed a housekeeper, chauffeur and gardener. Brown also retained Dove's Farm but sold it ten years later to Frederick Hill, who in turn sold it to Robin (later Viscount) Hudson in the 1940s. East Court Farm, now bolstered to 273 acres, was purchased for £3,350 by Huth who amalgamated it with Ham Spray, and although the farmhouse would retain the name this transaction ended East Court's long history as a separate farm which had begun with the entry in Domesday Book recording William Scudet's ownership. The remaining three farms became part of the Buttermere Manor Estate which itself would go under the hammer five years later in 1933.

The sale particulars included Ham Manor, described variously as 'a fine old Queen Anne Manor House' and an 'interesting old Manor House', and Dove's House, 'a fine old Queen Anne homestead'. The Manor House contained eight bedrooms, two them designated servants' bedrooms, but only one 'large bathroom'. There was no lavatory upstairs. Downstairs there was a WC in the Gentlemen's Cloakroom and another Servants' WC amongst the domestic offices. This general pattern was repeated at Dove's House where there were two richly

The drawing room at Ham Manor c.1920

panelled bedrooms, a 'bright and lofty Guest Chamber', two other family bedrooms and three secondary bedrooms. Again there was only one bathroom but this at least had a WC. However, downstairs it was necessary to cross a small flag-paved courtyard via the Back Lobby to find the only WC consorting with a large larder and the wood and coal store. Otherwise sanitation depended on chamber pots and commodes, and of course maids to empty them. Even a quarter way through the 20th century these scanty facilities were not unusual in old houses, and it would be another half century before the en suite bathroom would become a domestic priority for those who could afford it.

Not surprisingly the sale brochure concentrated on loftier themes: the splendid drawing rooms of both houses, and in the case of Ham Manor an oak-panelled library with 'rare old floor'. Outside, there were the manor house's 'charming pleasure grounds of 44 acres including a Park of about 23 acres and several useful paddocks', together with its dovecote, rose garden, orchard and heated greenhouse with 16 vines. Dove's House's 'pleasure grounds' included an excellent tennis lawn, a garage, harness room and stables. The 50 or so cottages being sold provide another barometer of the times. The figure of 50 is somewhat misleading from a 21st-century perspective as some of the cottages advertised no longer exist and others

Dove's House Cottages – then two semi-detached cottages – and Dove's House c.1910

were multiple occupancies of semi-detached buildings. Nevertheless, in total they represented 'the greater part of the Old-world Village of Ham' as the brochure succinctly put it.

An idea of the various changes that have taken place since can be gained from the following examples. Immediately north of Dove's House stood a block of three cottages and another pair of cottages. Only the latter has survived in the shape of Dove's Farm Cottage, which was created out of the two semi-derelict cottages in the 1970s by Nicholas Oppenheim. To the south, Dove's House Cottage, now within the curtilage of the main house, was formed in 1949 from two semi-detached cottages with separate gardens. Well Cottage was then three semi-detached cottages, as were Porch Cottages. Tudor Cottage was really two cottages although by then it was already occupied as a single dwelling. There were three condemned cottages where the Village Hall now stands, and Pond Cottage – two semi-detached cottages in the grounds of the Manor Farm buildings – was pulled down in the early 1940s as it was prone to flooding.

The descriptions of the various cottages in the brochure are often detailed. Little Field is listed as a 'picturesque thatched cottage: the cottage is detached, brick built and thatched and contains 4 good rooms, with a useful lean-to shed; E.C. (earth closet); it has a good supply of water from its own well and stands in a pretty old garden with an excellent paddock, in all about 1 acre 3 roods 18½ poles'. Forge Cottage was a 'charming old cottage and smithy: brick,

Reprieve Cottages – now Well Cottage – but then three cottages c.1910

timber and thatched cottage with 4 good rooms, timber and corrugated iron Shoeing Shed, Blacksmith's Shop and outhouse, having a good garden in the old-world style; N.B. a stone in the chimney states "I.C. 1689"; water from own well'. The cottage was let on a service tenancy to Mr Treasure but he himself may not have been the village blacksmith at that time. Nearly all the cottages were let on service tenancies, giving a glimpse of a vanishing semi-feudal village. The tenants held rights to an acre of allotment gardens abutting on to the north side of Pills Lane opposite the Poor Allotment on the other side of the lane. The sale also included a building plot of 37 acres, 'a most pleasant site for the erection of one or more residences', which was situated between Spray Road and Pills Lane at the north-east corner of the village, but in the event only Acorn Cottages were ever built on it sometime later. While the cottages in the village did not perhaps possess quite the chocolate-box appeal of Helen Allingham's 19th century paintings of idyllic cottages festooned with roses and hollyhocks, the sale descriptions and surviving photographs of the 1928 era nevertheless illustrate their undoubted rustic charm. It was only skin deep. The reality was that even in the early 20th century the cottages had no running water or electricity and sanitation depended on outside privies. Living at that level was still basic.

Electricity would come to the village in the next decade, but its introduction was spasmodic and initially there was a mixture of mains electricity, local generators and paraffin lamps. From 1931 until he was called up for war service in 1940 Norman Scutt lived in Forge

Pond Cottage (two semi-detached cottages) which stood in Manor Farm buildings and was demolished in the 1940s

Cottage together with his sister Winnie who would later marry Jesse Bowley. During that time the only lighting in the cottage was provided by Tilley lamps. There was still a working blacksmith's shop at Forge Cottage at that time, run by Dick Wiggin who was also the village blacksmith in Shalbourne. Before his call-up in the Royal Engineers where he served in bomb disposal, Scutt used to assist Wiggin at Forge Cottage, working the bellows and helping to shoe horses and mend cartwheels. Despite the increasing use of tractors, horses remained an integral part of the farming scene, and Forge Cottage would continue to be a working smithy until the 1950s when Ralph Brown sold Manor Farm.

In 1928 there was already a water pumping station for Manor Farm, which it is believed was originally put in by Henry Deacon Woodman at the end of the 19th century and driven then by a windmill. By 1928 it was also driven by a Hornsby oil engine and pumped water into an underground reservoir from where it reached its destinations by gravity feed. The pumping station can still be seen on the west side of the Fosbury road at the foot of Ham Hill. Later that same year an agreement was signed between Brown who owned the water and Huth and Annie Woodman to supply water for East Court Farm and Ivy Cottage respectively. This system continued to expand over the years to the rest of the village, except for Ham Spray which had its own supply and distribution system, until a catastrophe occurred in the hot summer of 1976. Somehow sewage leaked into the Manor Farm water system making half the

Forge Cottage, 1930s

village ill, and it had to be closed down, necessitating a bowser being stationed on the village green until mains water could be supplied to the village.

In the wake of the 1928 sale Ralph Brown made a gift to the village of a plot of land for a village hall. By 1930 a total of £118 had been collected towards its building. Fortuitously it was also discovered that the Rural District Council was holding £83 of Consols on behalf of the parish from the sale of the two parish cottages in 1882; the sale proceeds had originally been paid to the Guardians of the Poor of the Hungerford Union, and this may account for the fact the funds had become forgotten. As the net proceeds of the sale price of £90 had been invested in 3% Consols at the time, the investment seems to have been at best disappointing. The minutes of the Parish Meeting suggest that the £83 was added to the village hall fund, but seven years later the fund is shown as standing at only £165 8s 5d. Possibly this apparent discrepancy was due to architect's fees and other administrative expenses. In any case plans for building the hall at a cost of £150 were agreed the same year, 1937, and the hall was duly built by Ernest Gibbs who lived in The Beeches and Stanley Tucker.

The major outcome of the Ham Manor sale in 1928 was that once again there were only three farms: Manor Farm, Dove's Farm and now the largest of them, Ham Spray. Somehow they managed to survive the economic depression of the 1930s. The average price of an acre of

Well winding gear at Rose Cottage

agricultural land in England in the 1930s fell to £10–15, and there are local stories of land around Ham being sold for much less than that. After the war the average price had risen sharply to £88 by 1951, giving some idea of the difficulties facing farming in the 1930s. It was a gloomy time, and arguments have been advanced that nationally the inter-war years witnessed a general decline of the countryside and its traditional values and skills. Some of these arguments must have rung true in Ham. Like everywhere else machinery was overtaking man as well as horse. There was also a rash of building which reflected little of the surrounding countryside in the various designs of the houses.

Much of the building in Ham between the wars was due to Huth. As soon as he had purchased Ham Spray he set about finding himself a home. Since 1922 he had been living at Westcourt which was part of the Inkpen Estate – Westcourt was then a comparatively modest four-up, four-down village house – and he and his wife had provided Inkpen with its village hall, with the proviso that it was not to be used for anti-Christian or unconstitutional purposes. Ham Spray House, the traditional farmhouse for the Ham Spray estate, had been sold off in 1908 but now it was fortuitously on the market again following Stanley Pinniger's death and Huth was offered first refusal at a price of £2,000. Gladys Huth rejected it as being

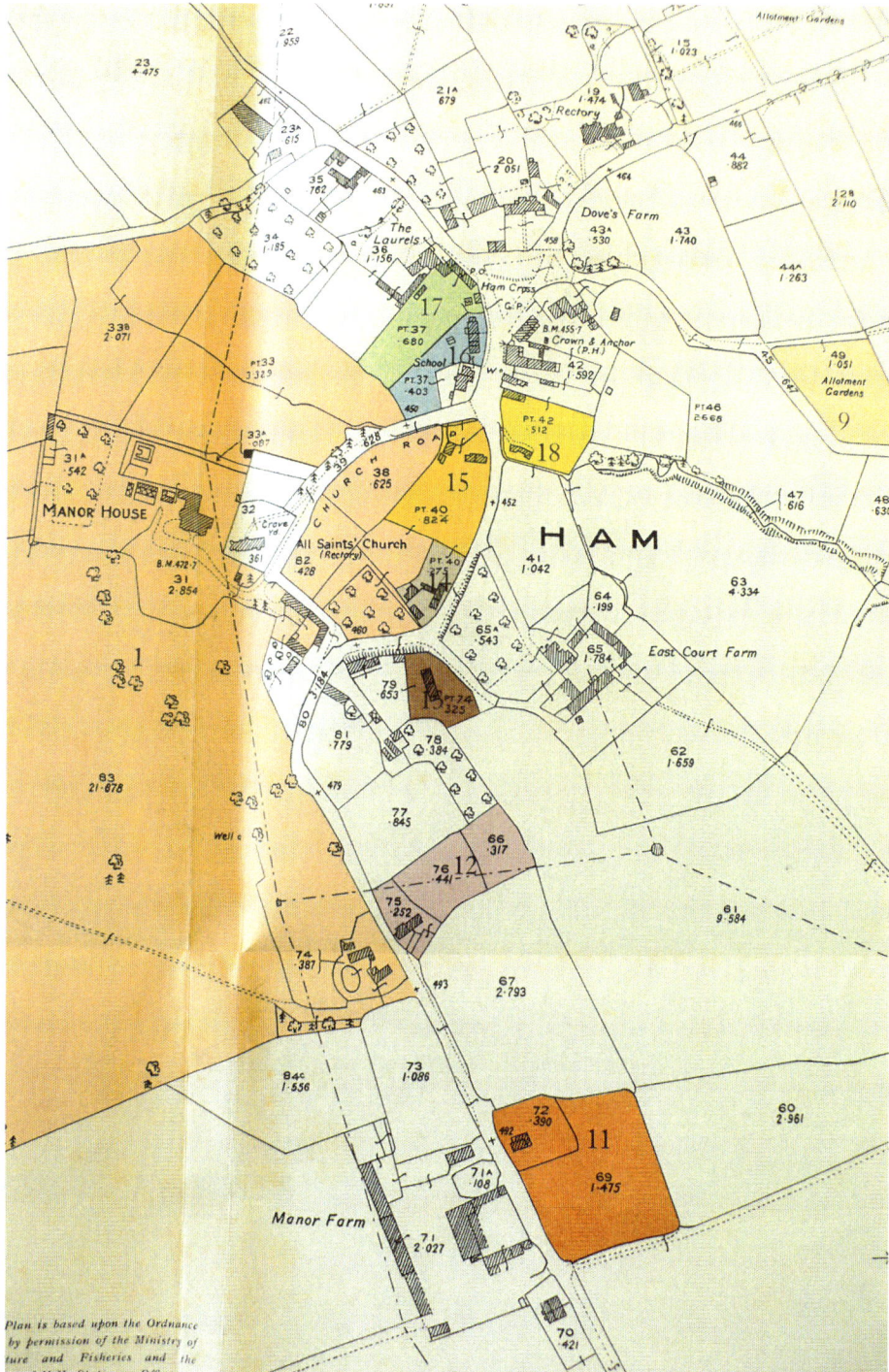

Plan of the village from the sale brochure of the Ham Manor estate, 1928

too near the farmyard, thereby in one of those twists of fortune leaving the door open for Lytton Strachey to purchase it. Gladys Huth's rejection of Ham Spray House led to the building of Wan's Dyke End, later renamed Wansdyke, at the eastern end of the village on the south side of Spray Road. Designed by Michael Waterhouse of London, the house was approved by Ramsbury RDC in 1924 and built in 1925. Despite its promising provenance the eventual result lacked architectural appeal, and although the house would stand for over 80 years it was pulled down in 2009 to make way for a new design.

Wan's Dyke End, later known as Wansdyke, built by Major Geoffrey Huth in 1924. It was demolished in 2009 and a new house – Coombe House – was built on the same site

Huth's next building project was to improve his stock of estate housing. In 1929 he converted a block of three run-down cottages on the village green known as Reprieve Cottages into a pair of labourers' cottages; 20 years later he would convert them again into the single property now called Well Cottage. In 1933 Garden Cottage and Greensand Cottage on Spray Road were approved, and these were followed by The Bothy, Wansdyke Cottages, Flax Lea Cottage and Drove Cottage – the last two being in Inkpen. Not everything went exactly to plan. In June 1938 he applied to Ramsbury RDC to build a pair of semi-detached cottages on Spray Road, the forerunners of Breach Cottages. At the hearing the designs were not approved, and Huth swept out in high dudgeon taking the plans with him, forcing the planning officer to place the following note on the file: *At the Council Meeting on the same date (1 June 1938) Major*

Huth collected all the plans submitted and took them away without my consent. Fortunately he missed one copy of the plan showing the plan of each floor with section and north elevation. A tart correspondence followed with the planning officer assuming that the removal of the plans meant that Huth had abandoned the application. He was wrong. Within the month Huth had returned to the attack with fresh designs, which were subsequently approved.[161] The building of these cottages was Huth's final round before the war. After it he would build Acorn Cottages in 1945.

By then Ramsbury RDC had already built the two westerly pairs of council houses at the Severalls. The case for more houses in Ham had first been raised at a Parish Meeting in 1925, when it was feared that Ham's dwindling population might lead to the closure of the school. At that time it was proposed that 12 houses should be applied for, but the application was subsequently reduced to four. These events sparked an even wider building spree in Ham. In 1933 the Rectory was sold and a new rectory, now Vale House, was later built on the site of allotment gardens. Although not nearly as large or distinguished as its predecessor the new rectory was still spacious by modern clerical standards, comprising five bedrooms, a drawing room, dining room and study. However, there were metal Crittall windows instead of sash windows, there was no central heating, only open fires, and a pump in a special room next door to the pantry drew up water from the rectory's own borehole. The back door was labelled 'Trades' on the architect's plans, suggesting the perceived lifestyle of a rector in the 1930s, and while it could not compete with the gardens and glebe land of the old rectory, there was a large garden, again evidence that the rector was expected to employ a gardener in addition to indoor domestic help. The former rectory was purchased by Mrs Whatton, the widow of Hugh Whatton of Rockley Manor, near Marlborough. She renamed it The Lodge and immediately built a pair of semi-detached cottages on its eastern side where she installed Polden her gardener and Dawes her chauffeur who drove her about in a shiny black limousine. Remembered as a bad-tempered woman always dressed in black who disliked children, Mrs Whatton quarrelled with her neighbours in Ivy Cottage over the line of the boundary between the two properties; eventually the dispute was settled in favour of Ivy Cottage. She kept a noisy peacock and a poorly controlled Dalmation dog called Wongo, both of which managed to irritate the village. Poor Mrs Whatton, it seems that she had an unfortunate knack of rubbing up the village the wrong way, but in 1939 she redeemed herself by offering the grounds of her house for a fête to raise funds for the village hall, an offer that was quickly accepted.

To the north of the village a bungalow, Happy Valley, was built by Robert Mander on the Hungerford Road in 1936. He would establish a large nursery garden on the land behind it. Two years later another bungalow, Elston Lodge, was built for Jim Spowage, a local policeman, on the east side of the Fosbury road. Then in 1939 Manor Farm Cottages were built for Dove's Farm by Frederick Hill on the opposite side of the Fosbury road. Today it is tempting to wonder how all these houses were built so easily. The Town and Country Planning Act would

Aerial view of the green and Spray Road, May 1934. Ham Rectory can be identified by its semi-circular drive above the green; it had just been sold but the new rectory (Vale House) and the Old Rectory Cottages had yet to be built. 1–4 The Severalls can be seen on the extreme right

not be passed until 1947; the act required planning permission to develop land and amongst other aspects was designed to protect agricultural land and the countryside. Before the war owners of land or building plots had it much their own way, provided in the case of Ramsbury RDC that houses had a supply of potable water and conformed to its design criteria. No formal opinion was sought from the parish. The bar for acceptable design was set at a low level and the results were unfortunately often numbingly banal. Gone were the intricately patterned brickwork, alternating panels of flint and brick, and high gables or thatch of the previous century, and in their place came mostly drab houses of plain red brick lacking any echo of the vernacular architecture of the village. The inter-war years produced few buildings of architectural merit and Ramsbury RDC was not alone in approving such depressing designs. The 1930s were both a decade of economic recession and the birth of an era of functional utilitarianism in architecture, and in many cases the applicant could only afford to build a simple, inexpensive dwelling. In 1934 an application was made to build a bungalow on the site of what would become known as Hayfield at the junction of Ham Road and Cutting Hill, but it was refused on the grounds that the building material was not brick. The plot-holder appealed that he could not afford to build in brick, and he was subsequently allowed to build what was then called The Bungalow in timber and asbestos as set out in his original application.

There was, however, the Restriction of Ribbon Development Act of 1935. The 1930s were also the new age of the motorcar and by mid-decade the Government was alarmed that the annual tally of road deaths was now being measured in thousands. Part of this was put down to houses being built on the edge of roads which created congestion and accidents, and so although there was an aesthetic purpose recognised in the Bill, it was also designed to ensure that in future houses would be set back from roads to ease the flow of traffic. After the enactment of the Bill planning applications required the completion of two extra forms, but so far as Ham was concerned this added hoop appeared to do little to stop development creeping out along its approach roads.

When it came the impact of the Second World War on farming was gentler than its predecessor. For a start planning had begun as early as 1936 when the first small storm clouds had appeared on the horizon. A Food (Defence Plans) Department was created in the Board of Trade and the Beveridge Report which set out the parameters for feeding the country in war was commissioned. In the event the first phase of food rationing was not introduced until January 1940. Farming was again a reserved occupation: men over 21 and fully employed in farming were reserved, as were those aged between 18 and 21 if they held key jobs. This did not of course prevent agricultural labourers from volunteering for the armed forces, but nationally the farm labour force did not begin to feel the pinch until Spring 1941. One man who was not called up was Tom Walter who had been Huth's gamekeeper since 1936. When Huth learnt that his age group was due to be called up and that Walter's six brothers were already serving, he told Walter that he would ask for him to be excused, and true to his word 'being an Army man himself, he did', as Walter would later relate. As well as being a gamekeeper Walter became an expert mole catcher. Challenged by Huth to do something about the moles, ten dozen mole traps were purchased for him and in five years he calculated that he had caught 4,000 moles;

his record was 92 in four days in a 15-acre field. Walter left Wansdyke in 1946 when Huth gave up shooting.

By 1941 the Women's Land Army (WLA) had begun to pick up some of the strain. The WLA had featured in the First World War but only towards the end when its limited numbers made little impact, except to provide delightful material for cartoons in *Punch*. Land Girls would continue to provide a rich vein for cartoon material in the Second World War, and an even richer vein of quite unprintable jokes based largely on the real or imagined innocence of young women brought up in an urban environment when faced with the trickier aspects of bovine anatomy. In the Second World War the WLA was up and running before the war had started. By the end of December 1941 there were 412 Land Girls registered in Wiltshire, and two years later this number had risen to 1,762, boosted significantly by the requirement in 1941 for women aged 20–21 to register for war work.[162] Vita Sackville-West, the writer who was involved with the Bloomsbury Group through her passionate love affair with Virginia Woolf, was engaged to write a booklet about the WLA in 1943, in which she extolled the accomplishments of the Land-girls (her spelling) in carrying out their various farming tasks, including forestry in the Timber Corps and thatching. No county records have survived of where the Land Girls in Wiltshire were sent, but Ham had its share. Frances Partridge who had herself been briefly a Land Girl at Castle Howard in the summer of 1918 mentions in her diaries Land Girls helping to put out a fire in the dairy at Upper Spray. The girls were billeted with William Couling, the foreman of Wansdyke Farms, who lived at East Court farmhouse which was still called Cannings at that time. Other Land Girls worked at Manor Farm and one of them stayed with Winnie and Jesse Bowley at the Malthouse Cottage.

Another source of help on farms was Italian prisoners of war following Italy's co-belligerent status in 1943, and Frances Partridge's diaries mention Hudson's Italian prisoner of war helping with school sports on VE Day. (Although Robin Hudson did not purchase Dove's House until 1946, he appears to have purchased Dove's Farm from Frederick Hill at some time before that.) Wiltshire records show that those Italian prisoners of war who were designated 'co-operators' were given considerable freedom. Although not allowed access to pubs, they could visit shops and cinemas and were allowed to drive farm tractors on public roads. At the end of the war some 60,000 German prisoners of war were also employed in agriculture and forestry, but while a number were billeted on farms in Buttermere, Inkpen and Shalbourne, none appears to have worked in Ham.

A more fundamental aid to farming during the war was the exponential increase in the use of the tractor, which in itself amounted to a mini-agricultural revolution. Tractors were not new and they too had been introduced in increasing numbers towards the end of the First World War, but the numbers then were still too small and the cost too high – £4–500 for most marques whether of British or United States manufacture – to have any real impact on farming. Numbers increased further between the wars but the jury was still out on the feasibility of them taking over entirely from horses. A book entitled *Agriculture in the Twentieth Century* by Sir Daniel Hall, published in 1939, contained an essay which compared the costs of running six horses – three teams of two horses – and the costs of running a tractor for one year. The question posed at the end of the essay was whether a tractor could do more than four times as much work as six horses to make the running costs of the tractor an economically viable proposition. Today the answer would seem obvious, but then with the effectiveness and versatility of tractors still not fully proven no answer was even attempted. At the outbreak of the Second World War the number of tractors in England and Wales was estimated at about 50,000; the number of farm horses was about 700,000. By 1942 the number of tractors had doubled and by the end of the war it had nearly doubled again. On the heels of tractors came the combine harvester, but this was still a rare beast before the war. In 1929/30 the first two combine harvesters arrived in Britain from the United States, and one of them went to Linkenholt, some five miles over the hill. It was towed by a crawler tractor with caterpillar tracks driven by Alfred Stockley – whose son John lives in Inkpen – on the strength of his expertise as a tank driver in the First World War.

One source of what actually happened in Ham during the war is Frances Partridge's diaries. However, these are coloured by the stance of both Ralph and Frances Partridge as pacifists, leading to her diaries of the war years being titled *A Pacifist's War*. In late 1942 Ralph was called up for military service, and despite his enviable service record in the First World War – he was known locally as Major Partridge, and christened 'the major' or 'the Major Bird' by the inner Bloomsbury circle – he asked to be registered as a conscientious objector. He argued that war was irrational, that he had resigned from the army immediately the First World War had ended, and that he had become a pacifist at that point. At first his request was refused but later it was granted on appeal. It is difficult to reconcile Ralph Partridge's apparent Damascene conversion to pacifism at the end of the First World War with reports of him as a happy warrior during the war itself and his continued use of his wartime military rank. Most of the Bloomsbury Group were, however, instinctively pacifist, as indeed was Frances Partridge, so whatever his own initial feelings might have been Ralph would have become immersed in their beliefs and arguments. Overall it smacked of the self-indulgence which was one of the less attractive traits of the Bloomsbury set. Once their views became known both Ralph and Frances discovered a distinct coolness from the grandes dames of Ham and Inkpen, amongst whom Mrs Hill who lived in Dove's House was prominent, as was 'Mrs G., the Queen of Inkpen'.[163] The latter was Honor Goodhart who lived at New Mill, and as both her sons were serving in the Royal Navy and her daughter in the Women's Timber Corps, her antipathy was hardly surprising. Their next door neighbour Huth was also incensed and at one point cut off the water supply to Ham Spray House to register his displeasure. Strangely Frances Partridge does not mention this event, and as she relates a perfectly amicable discussion about water shortages in the Ham Spray supply with Colonel Boord, Huth's son-in-law, a couple of years later, it may need to be taken with a pinch of salt. The general hostility towards them at that time is, however, undisputed, and it caused the Partridges to withdraw further into their own circle of friends outside Ham. As a result, life in the village itself receives few mentions in the diaries. Despite all this, the Partridges took in refugees from London both at the outset of the war and a year later during the blitz. The subject of taking in refugees had first been broached with Frances by one of Huth's daughters early in 1939, but ironically when it happened the organiser for the distribution of refugees in Ham was the disapproving Mrs Hill. Later, Ham Spray House also became a temporary billet for troops exercising in the area.

Ham was not a target for air attack but Newbury was, and Frances Partridge recalled searchlights in the sky above the downs – there was a searchlight sited at Buttermere – and on one occasion four German bombers flying straight over the house en route for Newbury. On that occasion there were no casualties but Newbury was later bombed again with 18 people being killed. On 4 November 1940 a stray stick of bombs fell on Ham from an aircraft which had evidently become lost, and one of the bombs made a crater beside Spray Road near the end of the avenue leading to Ham Spray House. Another of the bombs fell in fields near the Poultry Farm bungalow on the Ham Road – the fields were then part of the parish of Shalbourne. Fortunately there were no casualties although apparently a small boy was found asleep under debris from the blast. Otherwise the diaries record more prosaic events. There was an ice storm in January 1940 which destroyed many trees; in April 1942 a fire in the dairy in the farm buildings behind Ham Spray House was successfully put out by the fire brigade using water from the farm pond; and later the same year there was the rare treat of a circus in Hungerford.

Perhaps because they were too mundane, there are only the briefest of glimpses in the diaries of the ordinary, everyday wartime privations and restrictions which would have affected life in Ham. Frances Partridge mentions making a blackout curtain while listening to Beethoven, there are problems with her son Burgo practising putting on his gas mask, and there is a brief reference to food, clothing and petrol rationing. Possibly another reason why the diaries deal so lightly with this aspect of the war is that she shunned discussing such matters as part of her pacifist stance; she could be vituperative in her diaries about people who cheerfully accepted these privations and the myriad of regulations that accompanied them, as their contribution to supporting the war effort. There was a regulation for almost every facet of life. Frances records Ralph slaughtering a pig on two occasions, and these would have been subject to a controversial slaughtering policy for livestock.

To be fair to Frances Partridge, if her diaries deal sparsely with the village, the minutes of the Parish Meeting scarcely reflect that there was a war at all. In May 1939 several Air Raid Precautions notices were read out and it was decided to ask Mrs Whatton to advise on casualty service training, evidence that the country at village level was gearing itself for the likelihood of war. In 1940 £5 was given to the Spitfire Fund from the £18 raised by the Ham and Buttermere Flower Show, and in 1941 and 1942 there are mentions of scrap iron collections for the war effort. There are no minutes at all for 1943 and 1944. Unfortunately the school log book covering the war years is recorded as missing from its shelf in the school at the end of the war. As a farming community living partly off the land and removed from the fear of nightly bombing raids and from V1 flying bombs ('doodle-bugs') and V2 rockets later in the war – although Frances Partridge records a stray doodle-bug exploding on Inkpen Beacon in July 1944 – Ham probably fared better than many other villages in southern England. Much of life continued as normal. Valerie Barker, a granddaughter of Henry Deacon Woodman, lived at Ivy Cottage for the first year of the war, and for her it was a matter of cycling each day to Hungerford to catch the train to Newbury where she went to school. Back at Ivy Cottage her principal fear was to avoid being sucked down into the well inside the kitchen from which water was still being drawn. This apparent normality was not unusual at that stage of the war. Writing in August 1940, Vita Sackville-West commented, 'A new phrase creeps into letters of friends and acquaintances living in some parts of England, Scotland and Wales. It varies little in the wording, and is apologetic rather than boastful. It runs, "You would scarcely believe here, that a war is going on."'[164] Later, as most people in the village grew vegetables and many kept chickens, Ham was shielded from some of the worst aspects of food rationing. Rabbits also added to the meagre meat ration, and at harvest time the various farms were allowed to distribute extra rations to those bringing in the harvest. Beyond the issue of food supply there was a spirit of 'make do and mend' in the village in tune with the national slogan.

Nevertheless, there was still the anxiety for those in the village who had husbands, sons, daughters or sweethearts serving in the armed forces. Four men from Ham would become casualties of the war. Two of them, great friends, had joined the Volunteer Reserve of the Royal Air Force. Sergeant John Chandler served with 214 Squadron which operated various types of medium bombers. He was killed aged 20 in July 1943; his body was recovered from the sea off the Frisian Islands and later buried in the military cemetery at Oldenburg, Lower Saxony. His father was Joseph Chandler then the publican at the Crown & Anchor. In January 1945 Sergeant William Bartholomew, a wireless operator and rear gunner with 619 Squadron which flew heavy Lancaster bombers, was killed over France aged 19. He is buried at Soulac-sur-Mer, some 80 kilometres north-west of Bordeaux, one of four British servicemen to be buried there. He was the son of Billy Bartholomew who was the gardener at Wansdyke Farms.

Men of Ham served in the Royal Artillery in the Napoleonic Wars and in the First World War, and they did so again in this war. Gunner Reginald Taylor was serving with the regiment when he died in May 1941 at the age of 20. He was the son of John and Martha Taylor in the village and is buried in All Saints' churchyard. Lance Bombardier Walter Couling served with

112 The West Somerset Yeomanry Field Regiment, one of many Royal Artillery territorial regiments to be mobilised in the war. He was 29 when he died in October 1943 from tuberculosis, leaving a widow Lydia. She was initially refused a war widow's pension as the War Office ruled that his death was not due to war service, but following a campaign by *The Daily Mirror* this decision was reversed. His father was William Couling, the foreman at Wansdyke Farms. All four are remembered on the war memorial on the south wall of All Saints' Church. A separate memorial in the church records the death of Cyril Wheeler, an officer in the Royal Navy who was killed in action at sea in 1940. He was the son of the rector, the Reverend Charles Wheeler.

On the home front a platoon of the Home Guard was based on Ham. It was part of D Company, 6th Wiltshire Battalion Home Guard, which initially had its headquarters in Shalbourne but later moved to Wilton. Battalion Headquarters was in Marlborough and the battalion's mission was to hold Marlborough and a number of villages as centres of resistance to delay the expected enemy advance. It is doubtful whether Ham was one of the designated villages, particularly as D Company had a specific task to guard a sector of the 'Blue Line', the line of the Kennet and Avon Canal, which was an important secondary line of defence in the event of invasion. D Company's sector lay between Burbage and Froxfield. [165] Following the successful exploitation of the D-Day landings and the removal of the threat of invasion, the Home Guard was stood down in December 1944. The Ham platoon included most of the able-bodied men left in the village. Ralph Brown of Ham Manor was the platoon commander and Jesse Bowley was the corporal. Other Bowleys also served in the platoon, as did Reg Haines, Jim Turner and Leonard Cummins. The platoon met in the large barn now belonging to South House at Weldermill, and practised rifle firing at a range at the foot of Ham Hill in the far south-east field of Wansdyke Farms which lies across the parish and county boundary; the field is still known as Field Firing Range. It has become fashionable to deride the contribution made by the Home Guard to the defence of Britain, on the grounds that it was ill-equipped and under-trained and, therefore, ineffective. Of course, embedded in the national consciousness is the television comedy series *Dad's Army*, recounting the hilariously bumbling antics of Captain Mainwaring and his Home Guard platoon in the fictitious Walmington-on-Sea, and there are real-life tales of exercises between the Ham platoon and the Inkpen platoon when both sides came to blows. Some of the current criticisms of the shortcomings of the Home Guard are certainly justified, but that should not detract from the role it played as a citizen army throughout most of the war. The Ham platoon amongst others would have taken its training very seriously, and its mission as part of the defence of the Blue Line in the event of invasion was certainly not window-dressing. Now, nearly 70 years after the Home Guard was disbanded, the ghostly outlines of the wartime field firing range can still be made out on aerial photographs.

15

SEA CHANGE

Full fathom five thy father lies;
　　Of his bones are coral made;
Those are pearls that were his eyes:
　　Nothing of him that doth fade
But doth suffer a sea-change
Into something rich and strange.

The Tempest, William Shakespeare

A soldier who did return to Ham from the war was Cecil Hoare. Born in 1914, he came as a child to live in Fosbury where his grandfather was the postmaster. He went to school in Oxenwood, and on leaving school at the age of 14 his first job was to cart flints to the road menders, which had been collected in the fields by the women and children. In 1935 he joined the Royal Artillery and was stationed initially in India. When war broke out he served in Iraq, Syria and the Western Desert, taking part in the battle of El Alamein. All Saints' Church probably joined with the rest of the country's churches in ringing its bells on Sunday, 15 November 1942 to celebrate El Alamein, Britain's first land victory of the war, although there is some doubt as to whether the delicate state of the bell cradle in the tower would have allowed it. It was the first time since war had been declared that church bells had been rung, as they had previously been reserved as a national signal to warn of invasion. Home on leave in 1944 Hoare married Ivy Dixon, but he was unable to set up married life with her until after the war and his demobilisation in December 1945.[166]

Soldiers returning from the war were to have a marked effect on the future politics of Britain. Despite the carnage of the First World War which swept away much of a whole generation of young men, one of the war's few saving graces had been to ease the pressure created by the simmering social discontent throughout the country. The Second World War would continue the cathartic dismantling of the previously rigid class structure in Britain. In 1945 a Labour administration was catapulted into power with the help of the Services' vote, confounding pre-election predictions. Armed with a significant majority in parliament – the first overall majority for the Labour Party – Clement Atlee and his cabinet set about creating a new socialist Britain based on state ownership and state provision of welfare. They would, however, become frustrated by the lack of money to do so, and although the National Health Service was introduced and the foundations of the modern welfare state were laid, these significant achievements were carried out at the expense of reviving the post-war economy. The middle classes felt victimised and following what was termed the 'revolt of the suburbs' Labour was able to cling to power only by its fingernails in the General Election of 1950. It was not enough and by the end of 1951 a Conservative government was back in office with a slim majority of 17.

Ham was the antithesis of the suburbs, but cracks of a different kind had already started to appear in its own social structure. The sale prospectus of the Ham Manor estate in 1928 had revealed a village where apart from a handful of houses every building was owned by one or other of the two major landowners. Half a dozen years later there were once again three landowners but otherwise little had changed, and the council rates list for 1934 shows 25 houses registered as agricultural cottages. Eleven years after that, with the war in between, the 1945 rates list showed that the number of agricultural cottages had reduced to 18. Amongst the cottages then registered as dwelling houses was Bridge Cottage (now Candlemas Cottage) which was owned by Squadron Leader Abercromby. His wife was co-opted to serve as one of the managers of the village school, and faced with an alien name the schoolchildren were swift to christen her Mrs Apple Crumble – or at least that was the polite version! Forge Cottage was also privately owned but would continue to house a working blacksmith's shop for a few more years. Both Bridge Cottage and Forge Cottage, and also Yew Tree Cottage, had in fact been sold before the war in 1938 as part of a larger sale of property, with an average sale price was £260. After the war this move towards privately owned residential property in the village was reinforced when in 1947 Huth wrote to Ramsbury RDC to inform them that he intended to convert the two Reprieve Cottages into a single three-bedroom dwelling, having moved the two families there into new cottages; he had built Acorn Cottages in 1945 as additional housing for his estate workers. This provoked a sharp response from Wiltshire County Council:

> I have to draw your attention to the additional condition contained in Section 5 (1) of the Housing (Rural Workers) Amendment Act, 1938, which provides that all reasonable steps shall be taken to secure the maintenance of dwellings so as to be in all respects fit for habitation as dwellings by persons of the working classes for the period of twenty years from the date on which they first became fit for occupation, and I shall be glad, therefore, if you will kindly let me know when the cottages have been reoccupied.

Huth retaliated with a letter occupying a complete page of foolscap starting with the sentence, 'I have been interested in the building of cottages for the working classes for some years now, and since 1920 have built over 30 cottages, both at Inkpen and Ham and also in the town of

Hungerford'. He was granted his licence and duly sold the cottage to Mrs Ivy Tarratt for £3,625 in 1949. His victory was complete when he received £100 from Wiltshire County Council towards the renovation of each of the two previous cottages. It is interesting to compare the post-war sale price of the renovated cottage with the average sale price of £260 achieved for each of Bridge, Forge and Yew Tree Cottages 11 years earlier. At the time Reprieve Cottages were being converted Huth ran a competition in the village for a new name for the completed cottage. It was won by George Mills, the baker in the Old Malthouse, who came up with the name of Well Cottage by which it is still known.

There were also housing problems of a different kind. In 1946 Ivy Hoare became house-keeper to the Partridges. This later entailed her moving into the nursery wing of Ham Spray House in 1950 together with her husband Cecil who by then had a job with a firm in Hunger-ford making aircraft components and also her mother. This was not satisfactory from either side, and to give them independence Ralph Partridge, almost certainly with Huth's support, agitated for more council houses. The result was the building of the third semi-detached coun-cil house in the Severalls, which the Hoares occupied in 1954 and where Ivy Hoare still lives. The Partridges continued to live in Ham Spray House until Ralph's death in 1960. Stricken by his death and the thought of living alone in a large house with its attendant financial pressures, Frances Partridge sold Ham Spray in 1961 to Major and Mrs Guy Elwes, apparently for the asking price of £9,500. Ivy Hoare who had got on well with the Partridges would continue as housekeeper for the Elwes. With Frances Partridge's departure Ham lost the last of its most famous residents. However, the measure of vicarious fame which the Bloomsbury residents brought to Ham did not emerge until the publication from the late Sixties onwards of a stream of books about them. Frances Partridge would herself become a grande dame – in her case a grande dame of the literary world as one of the century's distinguished diarists – whilst still retaining her captivating charm. The first of her diaries, *A Pacifist's War,* was published in 1978. This brought her critical acclaim and the wartime unpopularity of her pacifist views caused few ripples. The latter was not surprising as the Second World War was becoming a distant memory, the highly unpopular Vietnam War had ended three years earlier, and the Cold War still posed the threat of nuclear annihilation. As a result the national mood was unambigu-ously anti-war. She would go on to write a dozen books altogether, as well as writing literary reviews for *The Spectator*. But, as much as anything else, she was a tireless keeper of the flame for Old Bloomsbury. At the age of 99 she was awarded a CBE for her services to literature, and she would die just short of her 104th birthday.

Looking back, if there were any regrets for Ham in all this, it is that the Bloomsbury resi-dents of Ham Spray House lived in Ham but were never part of the village, unlike their prede-cessors and successors at Ham Spray. It may not have been all one-sided, but fundamentally village life did not feature in the Bloomsbury ethos; the interests of the group lay elsewhere. As her biographer, Anne Chisholm, would later comment, Frances Partridge was not a joiner. Even so, a common thread running through both Frances Partridge's and Carrington's diaries and letters is their love of Ham Spray House as a refuge from the rest of the world, and equally their love of the achingly beautiful countryside that surrounds it.

The war would touch Ham in other ways. Magda Slazenger was born in a village near Budapest in Hungary. Her parents were goldsmiths and they were also Jews. In the late 1930s Hungary passed a series of draconian anti-Jewish acts and in 1940 joined the Axis powers, but it proved to be an awkward member of the alliance and this provoked an invasion by Germany in 1944. After the invasion nearly half a million Hungarian Jews were transported to the extermination camps at Auschwitz in Poland. Whether then or earlier, the exact sequence of events is hazy, Magda together with her parents and her sister and three brothers were sent to Auschwitz. Her parents were gassed straight away but Magda survived despite being subjected to horrific medical experiments. She would bear those scars and the concentration camp identification number tattooed on her arm for the rest of her life. The Soviet forces over-ran Auschwitz in January 1945. Before then in the face of the Soviet advance, the Nazis began dismantling the camps and the majority of the inmates were forced on a death march to the west, the survivors being sent by train to the concentration camp at Belsen. The British forces liberated Belsen in April 1945, and British Red Cross medical teams were soon involved with giving aid to the 60,000 surviving inmates. The survivors were in the jargon of the day DPs, displaced persons, and throughout the following year British Red Cross relief teams struggled frantically with this problem and the thousands of German refugees who had flooded into the British zone to escape the Soviet forces.

At some point in this chaos of war-torn Germany Magda was discovered and befriended by Lady Dunlop, one of the British Red Cross workers, who brought her to England where she initially became the housekeeper for the Dunlop family at their home in Speen near Newbury. Lady Dunlop also happened to be a great friend of Huth and in due course Magda became the cook at Wan's Dyke End. While there Magda met and married Norman Bird from Shalbourne where she would spend the rest of her life. Magda and Norman had two sons, Micky and Bill, who both built up successful construction businesses. Bill who was at one time Chairman of Shalbourne Parish Council now lives in Ham at Happy Valley, from where he runs his agricultural construction company, BK Grain Handling Engineers, which is the holder of a Royal Warrant. By one of those grim coincidences Magda fell and broke her hip on the 45th anniversary of the liberation of Auschwitz. She did not recover and died soon afterwards. A remarkably kind and generous woman, she would never talk about her terrible wartime experiences. Perhaps for the same reason she suppressed her Jewish faith for the rest of her life, and it was the Reverend Derek Ryder, the Shalbourne and Ham rector, who said Kaddish for her at her end.

William Chant was another soldier from Ham to return from the war, although he was invalided out of the army immediately afterwards suffering from tuberculosis. He would later become a Special Constable. Before the war he had married Lilian, the youngest child of Sarah Barclay, the widow of Scots Guardsman William Barclay. By then Granny Barclay, as she was known to the Chant family, was living in the Severalls and was one of the Ham residents who took in evacuees from the Blitz. In February 1944 Lilian had become cook and household help to the Partridges, breaking the wartime drought of no indoor staff at Ham Spray House. The following year, with the Soviet Army encircling Berlin, and a photograph in a newspaper of a German mother and the two children she had killed before committing suicide herself, Frances Partridge records an impassioned comment by Lilian on the war, 'How terrible it's been! How glad we shall be when it is all over!'[167] The two got on well together, and on another occasion Frances Partridge remarks in her diaries on Lilian's naughty pussycat smile while relating a story about her brother-in-law returning from Germany with some very minor loot. With a husband back from the war with TB and a young family to bring up, Lilian stopped working at Ham Spray House at the end of 1945. In later years she would remember the Partridges affectionately as generous employers.

The Chants had three children, Doreen who as a small child would sometimes accompany her mother when she worked at Ham Spray House, and John and Anne. They went to school in Ham under the eagle eye of Miss Kemp, who was quick to administer corporal punishment to any child unwary enough to cross her. Discipline was strict at home too, and in that the children's home life probably mirrored the experiences of many other families of that era. They lived in one half of Manor Cottages, and until the cottages were refurbished by Ralph Brown in 1956 bath time was a tin tub in front of the Rayburn in the kitchen, and the lavatory was a shed at the bottom of the garden, next door to a similar shed belonging to their neighbours Rupert and Kate Rolfe. Privacy was at a premium. Rupert Rolfe with his shock of white hair and string tied round his trousers below the knee worked at Dove's Farm, where he drove a green Field-Marshall tractor which had to be started with a cartridge owing to its heavy flywheel – the bang of the cartridge being fired was one of the familiar sounds in Ham in those days.

In the immediate post-war years there was little for young children to do in Ham by today's standards. There was no television in the Chant home, and like many other households their father rented a set for the Coronation in 1953. Nevertheless, the village green and the fields and lanes around Ham were a wonderful playground, and the children had their private haunts and secret rat-runs to get about the village. As they grew up their horizons broadened. A weekly youth club for teenagers was run in the Village Hall; the leading light in organising this was Brigadier Edward Stileman. In Hungerford there was the Regent cinema plus excellent dances on a Saturday night in the Town Hall. Getting to Hungerford, however, was a problem as there were still no buses and it was largely a matter of walking or cycling. The only regular bus

John Haines at the door of Rose Cottage c.1900

service from the village was to Newbury. It ran on Thursdays and Saturdays along the back road via Inkpen. This was operated by Mr Stout of Shalbourne, and his series of Bedford Duple buses, initially with wooden seats and then shiny brown leather ones, began their journey in Shalbourne at the King's Arms, the former pub that later became Valentine House.

Robin Tubb, now the Hungerford Bellman and Town Crier, was born in Inkpen and was taught by Elsie Harding who by then was the primary school teacher at Inkpen School. After the war he was a frequent visitor to Ham as his great-aunt Jean (Tucker) lived at Rose Cottage. Her husband who Tubb remembers as a true rustic character worked at Shalbourne Manor. Next door at Tudor Cottage lived his great-uncle Reg (Haines), the gardener at Ham Manor. Reg Haines was also an expert fiddle player, holding the fiddle in the old country way with the butt against his chest and not tucked under the chin. Both he and his father John before him were much involved with All Saints' Church, and in 1914 John acquired the church's set of hand bells which still remains in the family. Rickyard Meadow behind Tudor Cottage and the other fields and woods around Ham provided the same fascination for Tubb as they did for the Chant children. Pills Lane offered a tempting short cut between Inkpen and Ham, and Tubb recalls being chased off it by Huth's men. His route would take him past Ham Spray House, as it had done before the war for boys from Ham who used to sneak down Pills Lane to spy on the occupants of Ham Spray House and their friends bathing nude in the swimming pool. Tubb's memories of the Partridges are more innocent. He was entranced by the cut of Ralph Partridge's tweed jacket and Ralph would remain for him a lasting icon of sartorial elegance.

A decade later in the 1960s, as a young girl Charlotte Wood was a frequent visitor to Ham, staying at weekends with her grandparents, the Jamesons, at Ham Cross. For Charlotte and other children in the village of her age the green was a particular Eden. Photographs of the green at the beginning of the century show it looking much as it does today except for a couple of large trees, and in 1939 Arthur Mee, writing in his book on Wiltshire in *The King's England* series, remarked on children on the 'tiny green'. Before the Second World War the green was also the setting for Louis Black's Fair. This travelling fair was a great annual event for the village, with a coconut shy, a palm reader and other stalls on the green, and swing-boats erected in front of the school. By the 1960s the green had become overgrown. Elm trees had begun to grow at the eastern end, and these together with bushes and brambles made it an exciting jungle to play in. The verges around the green were unkempt and Dove's farmyard next door to Ham Cross spilled out onto the road, so that the small wilderness on the green enhanced the distinctively agricultural atmosphere at the heart of the village. Later her grandfather would clear the jungle from the green and start to make it once again a smooth sward.

Charlotte's grandfather was Rear Admiral Sir William Jameson, and he and his wife Elizabeth had come to live at Ham Cross in 1959. The cottage had been retained by the Woodman family after Polly Woodman died in 1939. For much of the 1940s it was let to a Captain Biggs and his two unmarried sisters who were Woodman relatives. It was then lived in briefly by Hugh Woodman, one of Henry Deacon's sons by his second marriage, before being sold to a Mr and Mrs Murray who changed its name from Ivy Cottage to Ham Cross. During his distinguished naval career Jameson had been the Assistant Naval Attaché in Washington in the early part of the Second World War, and there he would have had a ringside seat as the United States entered the war following the Japanese pre-emptive attack on the US Pacific Fleet at Pearl Harbor in 1941. Following his retirement from the Royal Navy he had stood unsuccessfully as the National Liberal and Conservative candidate for North Norfolk before coming to Ham. He then wrote a series of books about the navy including *The Fleet that Jack Built*, a history of the making of the modern navy by Admiral of the Fleet Lord 'Jackie' Fisher and his fellow admirals. Jameson had joined the Grand Fleet as a young midshipman in 1915, the same year that Fisher resigned as First Sea Lord over Gallipoli, and the following year he took part in the Battle of Jutland on HMS Canada.

The Jamesons' only child Felicity married Humphrey Wood, a partner in the London-based architectural practice Renton Howard Wood Levin. Amongst Wood's *chefs-d'oeuvres* was

The village green with Dove's Yard and Ivy Cottage (now Ham Cross) in the background, c.1910

the Crucible Theatre in Sheffield, now popularly known for hosting televised snooker champi-
onships. In the 1970s the Woods purchased Well Cottage from a Miss Sweet and moved to Ham
with their three children, Susanna, Charlotte and Flora. Humphrey Wood would later become
Chairman of the Parish Council and a formidable protector of the architecture and ambience
of the village. After Elizabeth Jameson died in 1995 having outlived her husband by nearly 30
years, Ham Cross was initially let for a short period before it became the home of Charlotte
and her husband Ben Lowsley-Williams. The house was later sold in 2009 and the Lowsley-
Williams moved to Lynch Farm in Shalbourne, the former smithy which a century and a half
earlier had been the home of blacksmith James Aldridge whose forebears had also come from
Ham. Another wheel in Ham's story had turned a half circle.

Next door, Ernest Opperman and his wife Josephine had purchased The Lodge in 1954
from Mrs Whatton and renamed it The Old Rectory. They had been forced to leave their previous house at Greenham Common near Newbury, when it was compulsorily purchased to
provide the Commandant's residence for the new United States Air Force base that had been
established at the wartime air station there. Much later, in the closing years of the Cold War, the
base, still operated by the USAF, would acquire a degree of notoriety when it housed nuclear
cruise missiles and became a focus of protest for the Peace Women encamped outside its main
gate. Opperman had trained as an engineer and served in the war as a major in the Royal Elec-
trical and Mechanical Engineers. After the war he took over the family business of Opperman

The village green, 2010. Dove's Yard has been replaced by Ham Green Cottage

Gears Limited in Newbury from his father. The firm had been started in 1860 by his grandfather who had come to London from Hanover, and after a bumpy ride during the recession in the 1920s it became heavily involved in defence work in the war. This included making undercarriages for Wellington bombers, and the firm is also credited with coming up with the original concept for the DUKW, the amphibious military vehicle developed during the war by the United States.

With The Old Rectory Opperman inherited Mrs Whatton's gardener Polden, a delightful man and an excellent gardener of the old school. Unfortunately he led a sad and unhappy home life, and one Saturday he hanged himself in the potting shed at The Old Rectory, leaving a note that he regretted being a bitter disappointment to his wife. He was discovered by the chauffeur Hillebrand who summoned Opperman for assistance, but they were too late to save him. Opperman owned variously a Rolls Royce or a Bentley, and Hillebrand's main duty, in theory, was to drive his employer to and from the firm in Newbury, but such was Opperman's fanatical enthusiasm when it came to motorcars that it was he who drove the car with Hillebrand sitting beside him in the passenger seat dressed in his chauffeur's cap and uniform.

Opperman's elder son Michael would later take over the family business. At the time of the family's arrival in Ham Michael had been to university and had completed his National Service. A keen amateur steeplechase jockey and the holder of a recently acquired pilot's licence, he

161

was evidently a young man of dash and spirit. One summer with his parents away on a business trip to the United States, and having persuaded the maid Betsy Anne Bowley to hand over the key to his father's wine cellar, he decided to have a party at The Old Rectory for a few friends from London. The pièce de résistance was to be a brief flying display, and having hired an Auster from Thruxton his plan was to swoop down over The Old Rectory, touch his wheels on the lawn behind it, avoiding the beech trees and a large oak on either side, and then climb swiftly again to miss the trees at the far end of the garden. Although the trees are now much higher than they were then, it would still have been no mean feat given the height of the house and the length of the lawn. The manoeuvre was, however, safely accomplished bar some foliage becoming entangled in the landing gear, and Michael flew triumphantly back to Thruxton. Returning to The Old Rectory and expecting a hero's welcome, he was greeted by a scene that today might have been a stage set from a period drama of that era. In the study he found his parents who had returned unexpectedly early from their American trip, his group of friends now sheepishly shuffling from one foot to the other, and an embarrassed elderly police constable. Robin Hudson who lived at Dove's House was also present. One of Michael Opperman's guests, his girlfriend of the moment, managed to break the ice by asking the police constable whether there had been any interesting cases locally. 'Oh yes', replied the constable, delighted to be temporarily let off the hook from the duty ahead of him, 'We've had a most interesting case of bestiality …,' which he proceeded to describe in all its lurid detail.

Hudson's role in this drama added to its almost Wodehousian surrealism. Earlier that summer he had been driving his combine harvester on Dove's Farm, when Monty Hine who lived in Buttermere had sneaked up behind him at low level in his Auster. Turning round, Hudson had suddenly seen the aircraft approaching him at what seemed head height. Unnerved he had leapt off the combine harvester, breaking an ankle in the process. The combine harvester had meanwhile careered onwards, ending up in a ditch with a broken axle. Having witnessed Michael Opperman buzzing The Old Rectory, Hudson was convinced that it was Monty Hine, and scenting revenge had contacted the police, only to be mortified to discover that he had shopped the wrong man. The upshot of the whole affair, which was reported in the press, was that Michael Opperman had his pilot's licence suspended for three years and never flew an aircraft again.

In 1964 Ernest Opperman sold The Old Rectory to the Darwins for £27,000. He had originally purchased it for £6,000, the fourfold increase in the sale price reflecting the rapid general increase in house prices over the intervening ten years. He then moved to Alton where he had bought a farm and would eventually die at the age of 102. Robert Darwin, always known as Robin, was a great-grandson of the famous naturalist Charles Darwin. His father had donated the Darwin archive to Cambridge University, and later in life Robin Darwin would become embroiled in a dispute over the future disposition of a so-called missing box of papers from

Ham Rectory (now The Old Rectory), 1905

the archive. Trained at the Slade he was a painter of landscapes and portraits and before the war had taught at Eton where he had been at school. After the war in 1948 he became at the comparatively early age of 38 the Principal (later Rector) of the Royal College of Art (RCA), where he placed a greater emphasis on product and specialist design, including graphics and fashion. Under his direction the college gained full university status, and he was awarded the CBE in 1954 and knighted ten years later. His portrait by Ruskin Spear hangs in the RCA, and he himself continued to paint in retirement at The Old Rectory, building a studio attached to the garage when he could no longer manage the climb to his previous studio at the top of the house. He is remembered in the village driving around in his Bentley and peering through its narrow windscreen in his glasses, looking not unlike the illustration of Mr Toad in *The Wind in the Willows*. After his death in 1974 his widow Ginette, a gifted and imaginative hostess, went on living in The Old Rectory for some years before moving to Pewsey. The house was then owned for a short time by the Harrisons before being purchased by Nicholas Baring, banker and philanthropist, and his wife Diana, literary agent and fellow philanthropist, who had come from Shalbourne.

That Ham should have become home for not one but two Rectors of the prestigious Royal College of Art may seem a surprising coincidence, but like many other coincidences at that time it had its origin in the war years. During the Second World War the Ministry of Home Security established the Camouflage Directorate, to which was recruited a small but distinguished coterie of artists and designers. It was said, perhaps apocryphally, that amongst the cognoscenti it was possible to tell who had been responsible for the camouflaging of a particular ship or aircraft hangar from the distinctively idiosyncratic design of its disruptive camouflage pattern. Darwin had served in the Camouflage Directorate and one of his colleagues there was Richard (Dick) Guyatt, who before the war had been a successful freelance designer – at the age of 19 he had created posters for Shell-Mex and BP. In 1940 Guyatt was made the Camouflage Officer for Region 11 in the United Kingdom with Darwin designated as his assistant. Darwin did not relish the prospect of being number two to Guyatt and engineered his appointment as secretary to the Camouflage Committee, for whom he would later write an influential paper, 'notes on the role of Artists in Camouflage'.

After the war Darwin appointed Guyatt as Professor of Graphic Art at the RCA. Guyatt was then 34 years old: this was a young, reforming team at the college. At the time of his appointment the department was known as the School of Design for Publicity, but stung by criticism of the title in an article in *The Times* Guyatt coined the term 'graphic design' which has now become universal currency. In 1951 he was the co-designer of the Lion and Unicorn Pavilion for the Festival of Britain. The festival which opened on 3 May and was held on the 100th anniversary of the Great Exhibition caught the public imagination. There were over eight million visitors to the South Bank exhibition, and on 24 May the children at Ham School listened to a BBC broadcast of an Empire Day Service at the Festival of Britain Church. Not surprisingly Guyatt's commissions in 1953 for a suite of table china for the Goldsmiths' Company and a Coronation mug for Wedgwood both vividly echo the iconic Festival of Britain design style for which he was largely responsible. He continued as a design consultant for Wedgwood and won a large number of other commissions, many of them celebrating royal anniversaries. He was made CBE in 1969 and following in Darwin's footsteps later became the Rector of the RCA. In retirement he came to live at Forge Cottage. He was married to Elizabeth (Lizzie) Corsellis, an illustrator in her own right who predeceased him. In 2000 at the age of 86 Guyatt was awarded the Misha Black Memorial Medal for his services to design education. In his address at the presentation ceremony the then Rector of the RCA, Sir Christopher Frayling, quoted Ruskin's famous dictum, 'Fine Art is that in which the hand, the head, and the heart of man go together'. It had been the title of Guyatt's inaugural lecture at the RCA, and serves as an excellent memorial to both him and Darwin. Guyatt died at Forge Cottage in 2007.

Alongside these changes in the village, the husbandry and ownership of the land around it was changing too although at a different pace. Both before and after the war drillings were carried out in Ham to look for oil, but nothing of consequence was discovered. Instead the two dominating influences were, first, the continuing mechanisation of farming and, secondly, the advent of the Common Agricultural Policy which replaced the previous system in Britain of guaranteed prices for cattle and grain. The CAP had been instituted in the 1960s but did not affect the United Kingdom until the latter joined the Common Market in 1973, and even then its measures did not really start to bite in Ham until the 1980s.

Well before then Ralph Brown had sold Manor Farm in the late 1950s. The sale of the farm machinery, which included the blacksmith's tools and equipment from Forge Cottage, took place in the field next to Orchard House. A parcel of the land was bought by Huth, but most of it was sold to the Miller brothers. At the end of the century this larger element was purchased by John Lee, so that what was once Manor Farm eventually became wholly absorbed into Wansdyke Farms. Brown continued to live in Ham Manor until the mid 1960s when his wife died, and he himself died eight years later in 1973. They are buried side by side in Ham church-yard. Ralph Brown is remembered with affection both for his energy in the village's affairs and for his generosity. His 45 years as chairman of the Parish Meeting spanned the Second World War, and while he may not have had to deal with the same degree of difficulties faced by Samuel Farmer in the previous war, he undoubtedly saw the village through another period of national upheaval and adversity. The schoolchildren in the village also had particular reason to mourn his departure. Each Christmas he had given them a party in the school and in the summer he funded an outing to the seaside by bus.

When Brown left Ham Manor it was purchased by Dudley and the Hon Angela Delev-ingne,[168] who stayed for only three years. It is rumoured that they left because they felt the house was haunted. During their stay they altered the windows at the front of the house, removing the ground floor oriel windows, and they also removed the balustrade below the clock tower. They were followed by Sir William and Lady Beale; Sir William had earlier been engaged in building the present South House on the site of its original 16th century cottage, but when Ham Manor became available they sold South House to Janie Hague whose daughter, Melanie Melsom, still lives there. Sir William was a director of Maples, the former furniture retailer, and the manor benefited from a blitz of Maples carpets. The Beales, however, like their predecessors would stay for a brief three years, and in 1971 the manor was bought by Jeremy and Susan (Susie) Philipps who lived there for the next 20 years. Susie who now lives at Manor Farm House is a painter of jewel-like oils of fruit and flowers, and both her daughters, Clare and Nicola (Nicky), are also well known artists, Nicky achieving national acclaim in 2010 for her double portrait of the two royal princes, William and Harry, for the National Portrait Gallery. In 1993 the Philipps sold Ham Manor to Hans and Anna de Gier, and Anna, now Anna Wintermans, still lives there.

Meanwhile, in 1967 Major Geoffrey Huth died. As the major landowner he had dominated

Acorn Cottages, built in 1945, the last of Major Geoffrey Huth's building projects

life in the village for over 40 years, and his death marked the end of another chapter in Ham's story. There is no memorial to him in All Saints' Church – his ashes were scattered on Ham Hill – but during his lifetime he erected the plain stone cross that stands beside the church porch with its simple inscription, 'In remembrance that Christ died for thee'. It is clear that he was capable of great acts of kindness and generosity in which his humanity shone through. He also had the foresight and courage of his convictions to invest in farming during the agricultural depression of the 1930s, particularly in building modern cottages for his estate workers outside the traditional centre of the village. At the same time there was a darker side to his nature driven by his depression and his subsequent reclusiveness, and despite his many other attributes it is this aspect for which, however unfairly, he is now chiefly remembered. He was instinctively authoritarian and combative – within his family circle he was christened 'The Emperor' – and he managed to pick quarrels with most of his neighbours and the village at large, many of which developed into feuds. Some of these have become legendary as the following two stories illustrate.

In 1963, in what were still the early years of silage production, Huth decided he needed a silage clamp, and without any consultation he gouged out a large area on the south side of Spray Road which is still visible today. This caused an uproar in the village, and his retrospective planning application to the Marlborough and Ramsbury Rural District Council was refused following a public meeting in the Village Hall. Local tradition has it that the meeting adjourned for lunch to the Crown & Anchor, where the publican convinced the chairman of the meeting that effluent from the silage clamp would ruin the best ale in his cellar. Whether the entire story is true or not, a formal complaint about possible contamination to the Crown & Anchor is on record in the Council's files. Huth appealed against the decision but to his fury that was turned down too.[169]

Pills Lane is an ancient cart track which runs roughly parallel to and south of Spray Road, starting beside where Brook House now stands. Shortly before reaching Ham Spray House, the lane turns due south to end in the fields on the edge of the downs. The lane is marked on the early 19th century enclosure maps and later Ordnance Survey maps of the village, and whatever the exact legal status of the lane might once have been, the village had long regarded it as a right of way. So when Huth effectively closed the lane by chasing off it what he considered to be trespassers, his actions caused great resentment in the village. After the Second World War when its usefulness as a cart track had declined the lane was allowed to decay, and by the end of the century most of it had become unusable. Huth came from an age long before rambling and the right to roam had become a public issue, and initially he would have had public sentiment on his side, as around and after the turn of the previous century there were plenty of commentators willing to take the side of farmers against what were viewed as the inconsiderate actions of trespassers in the countryside, and particularly the depredations of their dogs. What Huth failed to appreciate, however, was that villages have traditions and long memories. The whole issue of rights of way was a topic of considerable interest for the village throughout the century. In 1934 the Parish Meeting formed a committee to trace footpaths and bridleways and to forward the results to the 'proper quarter'. The starting point was the 1828 Enclosure Award, which listed a footpath running from Manor Farm House to the Lynch, and a bridleway running from a 'private road' east of Manor Farm diagonally across the face of Ham Hill to the ridgeway. By 1950 a total of four footpaths and two bridleways had been successfully recorded and blessed by officialdom, and by 1993 the total had risen to eight – but Pills Lane was not amongst them. Spurred on by expert advice, at the end of the century the Parish Council under the leadership of its chairman Humphrey Wood then decided to enter a claim that Pills Lane was an ancient right of way.

This later proved to be fraught with difficulties. The 19th century maps were not sufficient evidence on their own, and it was impossible to find anyone who could recall using the whole length of the lane in the previous 20 years; by then, apart from the initial 300 metres, the lane had become choked by vegetation and barbed wire. Another difficulty was that the new owners of Brook House, who had acquired the property in 1996, were alarmed at the prospect of a right of way being established a few feet away from the front of their house and objected. Both sides took legal advice, respective counsels were briefed and the matter went to adjudication. The subsequent inquiry did not support the village's claim, and although the Parish Council appealed the judgement stood. It had been a costly exercise and it was left to a few stalwart individuals to settle the legal fees. It was not, however, a complete rout, as alongside the claim to reopen Pills Lane the Parish Council had argued that there should also be a right of way along the farm track – the private road in the 1828 Enclosure Award – to link up with the bridleway running diagonally up the face of Ham Hill, and this was upheld.

On the lighter side there is an amusing tailpiece to Huth's later years at Wansdyke. In 1956 Ham became a combined benefice with Shalbourne and in the wake of this event the second

Vale House, the former rectory, in its earlier form, 1980

rectory was sold. Its new owner was Geoffrey Webb who renamed it Vale House. Webb together with Edward Mason had been the script-writer for the popular BBC radio series *Dick Barton*, the dramatic adventures of Dick Barton, Special Agent, and his assistants Jock and Snowy, with each instalment leaving its eponymous hero stranded in some new, perilous and seemingly irretrievable situation. At the time Webb purchased Vale House he was again teamed up with Mason as a script-writer for what has become one of the longest and most popular of BBC radio soap operas, *The Archers*, 'an everyday story of country folk', that had begun in 1951. Webb was a regular at the Crown & Anchor, and while the fictional Ambridge is set in the West Midlands much of the farming lore in the programme at that time is believed to be based on Ham and surrounding farms in the area. Certainly Huth thought so. He was an avid listener to the programme every evening and demanded silence in the house when the programme was being broadcast.

Webb's son Quentin has confirmed Ham's role in providing a large part of the farming background for *The Archers*, but poured cold water on another Ham tradition that Ted Whitlock from Buttermere, a fellow regular of Webb in the Crown & Anchor, was the model for Walter Gabriel in the series. In fact the character of Walter Gabriel had been created prior to Webb's arrival in Ham. Nevertheless, Whitlock undoubtedly added colour to the local scene. Most evenings he careered down the steep hill from Buttermere on his bicycle using his hobnailed boots to brake his progress, and once inside the Crown & Anchor he would sometimes reveal a ferret curled up in the capacious pocket of his raincoat, enhancing his reputation as a local poacher. The publican at the time was Ginger (Harold) Wheedon who was convinced that he had seen a pair of red shoes without a body walking down the stairs of the pub and that the pub was haunted. Some of this colour may have filtered down into *The Archers*. Webb and Mason took it in turns to write a month's worth of scripts for the series under the umbrella of a jointly agreed framework overseen by the editor, Godfrey Baseley. When it was his turn Webb would rush down to Hungerford on an almost daily basis to post off his scripts. On one of these journeys Webb's car suffered a tyre blow-out and in the traffic accident that followed he was tragically killed.

Earlier, in 1958, Huth had made over Wansdyke Farms to his elder daughter Julia Boord. He then continued to farm the estate in partnership with her, although so far as the actual business of farming was concerned Julia was a sleeping partner. Following Huth's death a number of events occurred in rapid succession. In the autumn of 1967 Julia Boord's husband died, and in the following spring Huth's widow Gladys also died. As a result, Julia's son Gerald, then aged 25 and working in Johannesburg as an accountant, was summoned home to take charge of Wansdyke Farms. Huth's other grandson, the son of his daughter Lydia, is the well-known local naturalist Charles Flower who grows wildflower seeds at Flower Farms in Shalbourne.

When Gerald Boord took it over in 1968 the estate was mainly arable with two dairies at Ham Spray and Lower Spray. The team which he inherited was headed by the foreman John Couling, whose wife Margaret had been Huth's secretary and would now become the estate secretary. Two cowmen plus a relief, assisted by two former Barnado's boys, operated the dairies – there had originally been three Barnado's boys whom Huth had installed in The Lodge with a lady to look after them. On the arable side there were three tractor drivers and a mechanic, Alan Jackson. A gamekeeper and a gardener completed the workforce of 12. Forty years later the workforce had shrunk to a farm manager, three full-time farm workers, and the seasonal summer addition of four more workers; between them this team was also responsible for farming an estate of similar size at Chieveley. This significant reduction mirrored what was happening elsewhere in the country. Between 1960 and the end of the century the number of men and women in the United Kingdom working in agriculture halved. Amongst other factors, new farming technology and increasingly sophisticated and powerful agricultural machinery had made the previous manpower levels redundant. This evolution is vividly illustrated by a recent local statistic. In the summer of 2010 a total of 154 acres of wheat at Wansdyke Farms was harvested in one 25-hour stretch.

Long before that, in the 1970s, Boord had purchased Town Farm at Buttermere, adding a further 132 acres to Wansdyke Farms; the house and four acres at Town Farm were sold on at the time. Later, in 1986, he sold Wansdyke Farms to John and Sandra Lee who in due course bought Manor Farm from the Miller brothers, bringing the estate up to its current total holding of 1,786 acres.

When Boord arrived at Wansdyke Farms in 1968, his mother Julia initially came to live with him at Wan's Dyke End which he subsequently renamed Wansdyke. In 1974 Julia moved to East Court farmhouse which had been renovated. She died in 1990 and East Court was then sold on the open market. It would be the last of the original farmhouses of the three historic farms in Ham – Ham Manor, Dove's Farm and now East Court – to be detached from its land. Prior to 1974 the farmhouse had been rented by Bernard Venables. His obituary described him as fisherman, artist, writer and environmentalist. Trained at the Croydon School of Art and afterwards employed in a commercial art studio, Venables was successful enough as a painter in his own right to exhibit at the Royal Academy. However, it was as a professional fisherman and writer on angling that he achieved national fame. In 1946 he joined *The Daily Mirror* and his daily cartoon strip *Mr Crabtree Goes Fishing* quickly caught the public imagination. It was published in book form in 1948 and became the best selling angling book after Isaak Walton's *The Compleat Angler*, selling over two million copies. Unfortunately for Venables the royalties of the book went to *The Daily Mirror* and not to him, and in 1953 he left the newspaper to be the co-founder of the highly successful *Angling Times*. He died in Salisbury in 2001 at the age of 91.

The pattern was different at Dove's Farm. In 1958 Paul Marriage, a grain dealer who lived in Newbury, purchased the farm together with Dove's House, which had been known as The Laurels, from Viscount Hudson. Marriage then sold Dove's House back to the Hudsons. Robin Hudson's father had been the Minister of Agriculture during the war and was created Viscount Hudson of Pewsey afterwards. Robin (properly Robert like his father) who inherited the title in 1957 had earlier married a very pretty French woman, Marie-Claire Schmitt, but she left him to become Duncan Sandys' second wife. Sandys was Secretary of State for Commonwealth Relations at the time and a year after their marriage became embroiled in the notorious divorce of the Duke and Duchess of Argyll, as he was rumoured to be the 'headless man' in an explicitly compromising photograph of the Duchess. That same year, 1963, Hudson died at the early age of 41. Throughout the rest of the century Dove's House would be owned in turn by the Honourable Jacob and Serena (now Lord and Lady) Rothschild, Mrs Phillips who was one of the Guinness family and added the orangery to the house, Julian and Emma Sainty who did much to renovate and redecorate the house,[170] and finally Simon and Helen Green. As a result, while the farmyard continued to operate on the north-west corner of the green, what had been called the Dove's Farm homestead was now separate from its estate. The farm manager in 1958 was Monty Hansford who lived in The Beeches. He was assisted by Rupert Rolfe, by now living in Dove's Farm Cottage, and Jim Turner who was born in 1900 and worked on the farm until the age of 84. The farm possessed three tractors and a combine harvester. There were no horses, and by then nationally in the wake of the tractor revolution of the war years tractors outnumbered horses on farms by two to one. Fifty years later, such were the technological advances in farm machinery that Dove's Farm required only one tractor and a share in a combine harvester.

In 1974 Andrew Blake took over as farm manager, living at Orchard House which was built at that time at a cost of £25,000. Three years afterwards Michael Marriage succeeded his father and on Blake's retirement he and his wife Clare took up residence in Orchard House. Inspired by a talk he immediately converted Dove's Farm into an organic farm, becoming one of the pioneers in Britain of this school of farming. Finding, however, that no one was interested in his first organic crop, he started milling on his own account as Doves Farm Foods, initially in the farmyard on the village green and later in a new mill on the Salisbury Road. Like Wansdyke Farms, Dove's Farm was largely arable with some cattle, although the cattle were later replaced by sheep, returning the land to its earlier rhythm of sheep-corn husbandry. For much of the post-war years barley was the predominant cereal crop on the Berkshire Downs, but in the 1980s this changed to wheat. By now the Common Agricultural Policy was starting to have a major influence on farming, and by the end of the century from Marriage's perspective many farmers had become reliant on CAP payments for up to half their income. The net result was that the smaller farmer, farming some 300 acres such as Dove's Farm, found himself financially squeezed with his comparative earnings in the marketplace dropping well below what he had enjoyed in the 1960s.

When the Tories came back into power in 1951, they strove to fulfil their election pledge of building 300,000 new houses a year despite the scarcity of resources. Most of the eventual recipients were content with their new homes, but for many other people there were downsides to this strategy. In particular, commentators in the press railed at the steady erosion of the countryside, caused by the proliferation of new housing estates and the building of new towns. Although the North Wessex Downs would not be designated as an Area of Outstanding Natural Beauty until 1972, Ham was in any case fortunately well removed from any significant centre of population or industry and as a result escaped unscathed from this 1950s race to build new houses. Nevertheless, there was a flurry of building activity in the next decade. Three bungalows were built along the north side of Spray Road – Field House, Pettits and Fernedown, and beyond Happy Valley a series of bungalows was built along Cutting Hill, although the latter would not belong to the parish of Ham until the boundary change in 1980. Two of them, Windy Ridge and Lilac Bank, were built on sites previously occupied by two eccentric sisters, the Misses Forbes. One of them lived in a tent and the other in a derelict single-deck bus. They had been rescued by ambulance in the ferocious winter of 1962/3 and never returned. Beyond the Misses Forbes three small wooden bungalows had already been built before the war.

At the end of the 1980s there was a further building flurry, but this time it was in the centre of the village. An application was made for three detached houses and two semi-detached houses to be built on the site of Dove's farmyard on the north side of the green. In the end this was reduced to three detached houses, and Sunningdale, Staddlestones and Ham Green Cottage were duly built. The centre of the village had been designated a conservation area in 1973, and because of its location directly overlooking the green Ham Green Cottage was required to echo the vernacular architecture of other houses on the green. Dove's farmyard had meanwhile been moved to its current location beyond Dove's Farm Cottage in time for the new barns to be battered by the storm of 1987, and in 1990 planning consent was granted for a farmhouse on the new farmyard site. Although the farmyard had moved only a few hundred yards, the move had much deeper repercussions. There was no longer a farmyard at the heart of the village, and with that the last intimate bond between the village and the farming world around it had been broken.

While the number of houses in Ham had been increasing by modest degrees in the second half of the 20th century, parts of the village's established infrastructure were vanishing at the same time. Before the war Ham could boast what might almost be termed a miniature shopping precinct around the green. There was the post office in one of the Dove's House Cottages. Next door was a butcher's shop in the Reprieve Cottage nearest the Crown & Anchor. Then across the road there was a shop at the back of the pub, which sold sweets, tinned items and knick-knacks. A more general store and bakery operated in The Old Malthouse. At the end of the war the butcher's shop disappeared, and when Hudson converted the two Dove's House Cottages into one cottage in 1947, the post office was combined with the general store and bakery in The Old Malthouse, with the manual switchboard for the local telephone exchange on one side of it. The shop at the rear of the Crown & Anchor would continue until the early 1960s leaving the shop-cum-bakery and post office in the Malthouse Cottages as the grand survivor. This shop was run by the Hattons for many years, and Frederick Hatton had been the baker since the beginning of the century. In 1947 Frederick Hatton bought the freehold of The Old Malthouse from the Woodman family, and a decade later Norman and Rose Lansley took

Presentation of the Best Kept Village Award 1963. Left to right: Daisy Aldred, her granddaughter Carol Hanks, and The Hon Mrs Anthony Methuen, President Elect of the Wiltshire WI

it over. Sundays were kept free, partly so that Norman could play the organ in All Saints' Church with Rose working the bellows, helped from time to time by teenager Quentin Webb.

The bakery was at the heart of the shop. Baking the bread started at five in the morning, the dough having been made the night before, and by half-past ten the two vans were on the road to the surrounding villages operating on two circuits on alternate days, Mondays to Saturdays. It was a fiercely competitive business, with Spackman's of Hungerford and Oxenwood Stores, amongst others, snapping at the Ham bakery's heels. Any newcomer to one of the villages could expect a swift call from the Ham bakery anxious to claim them as a customer. Among those who worked in the shop were Reg Stevens who arrived in the village in the late 1950s, his wife Brenda after their marriage, and also the three Chant children. The post office element of the shop was another cherished lifeline for the village, and it acquired a brief blaze of local fame following an attempted robbery which was foiled by Rose Lansley. Her bravery in forcing the intruder to flee was recognised by the Post Office who awarded her a medal. In 1970 the Lansleys sold the shop to Colin and Lilian Cripps, and it was not long before the Cripps discovered that they had acquired a much more demanding taskmaster than they had bargained for.

173

Ham School group shortly before the school closed. Back row: Miss Millicent Strange, Paul Langton, Zarack Mussel, Alison Wright, Clive Tooth, Colin Mouland, Miss Dorothy Wescott. Middle row: Matthew Stockley, Tracey, Alexander Blake, Sarah Wright, Alison Stevens, Nicola Snell, Justin Hale, Rebecca Lambourn. Front row: Justin Bagma, Paul Stevens, Tina Smith, Roland Blandthorn, Sarah Stockley, Duncan Blandthorn

In addition to the long hours the shop had become run down and needed major refurbishment. Items from the 1930s and 1940s were still lurking in the shop, and upstairs there was even stuff from the previous century. On top of that there was a small crisis when Ham was hit by severe flooding in 1971. By then the baker came on a daily basis from Newbury, and while the flood lasted he was only able to reach the village with great difficulty and many of the deliveries had to be curtailed. Exhausted by all this the Cripps sold the shop to the Baileys the following year. Shortly afterwards the shop closed and Ham was without a village store, bakery or post office – and without its famous lardy cake.

In 1980 the village school closed. Concerns about this possibility had been voiced as long ago as 1925, when the topic of the village's shrinking population was raised at a Parish Meeting. It was agreed then to apply for 12 houses to be built to remedy the situation, but this recommendation never got off the ground. In 1932 the school roll was sufficiently buoyant for discussions to take place on enlarging the School House, but it was decided to build a hut on the land adjacent to the school instead. Five years later soundings suggested that the possibility of closure was 'unlikely for some years'. The school weathered the war years and in 1944 received a small boost when Buttermere school closed and the Buttermere children came to Ham. In company with most other schools the school closed in May 1945 for two days for the VE Day celebrations. The early years after the war were a boom time with the infants overflowing into the Village Hall, and on 2 June 1953 the children danced and sang to celebrate Coronation Day. The later 1950s, however, proved to be a low point for numbers, the school roll sinking to the 20s, largely due to children aged over 11 being transferred to Hungerford from 1953. By the beginning of the 1970s the school roll had risen again to the low 40s, but it was a false dawn and by the end of the decade with Dorothy Wescott as headmistress numbers were once more down to the low 20s. Closure could no longer be averted and on 11 July 1980 the final school assembly took place, followed by a service attended by Lady Jameson, Chairman of the Governors. Four of the remaining children went to Marlborough Comprehensive and 13 went to Shalbourne Primary School. In the wake of the school closure it was thought unlikely that the Woodman family could still prove title to the School House, and plans were made to move the Village Hall into the school. However, this proposal had to be aborted when the Woodman family did indeed prove title, and the school subsequently became two semi-detached houses.

For some of the older residents in the village the closure of the school represented the final nail in the coffin of Ham as a close-knit, working class community. It had taken 50 years from the time of Ralph Brown's sale for Ham to be transformed from a semi-feudal, agricultural village into what might be crudely described as one of the numerous smaller satellites of London on the outer edge of the metropolis's rapidly expanding commuter belt. This transformation had accelerated in the aftermath of the war, as agricultural employment shrank and farming was no longer the *raison d'être* of the village. Mobility, too, had reached a different level.

Owning a private car had ceased to be accessible only by a privileged minority, and a regular bus service now ran to and from the village. As a result shops, and later supermarkets, were only a few minutes away. The building of the M4 motorway in the late 1960s meant that there was a high-speed road link to London in addition to the railway, and this increased the desirability of Ham both as a commutable home and as an easily accessible weekend retreat. The trend for home ownership had meanwhile gathered pace, creating a shortage of property and fuelling an escalating increase in house prices. In Ham cottages which had once been agricultural tenancies were being modernised and changing hands for what before the war would have seemed untold riches. In 1928 Ham was described as being 'in the much sought and well favoured residential area of Hungerford – one of the few remaining districts within the 60–70 mile radius of London left unspoiled in all its old-world charm, wherein all the traditional pursuits of the countryside may be followed'. By the end of the century estate agents were saying much the same thing but to a more varied audience, and never ones to miss a trick were talking of the village as being in the centre of a 'Golden Triangle'. However, their sales brochures no longer boasted that hunting was available three days a week with the Craven Fox Hounds and the Tedworth Hounds, as they had done before the war. In all this Ham was simply mirroring what was happening to hundreds of other rural villages in the south of England.

One bulwark of the village which did not crumble was All Saints' Church, but for a time it was badly shaken. Immediately after the war Ham still had its own rector and rectory, which helped to make the church a centre of village life. One of the rectors was a particularly charismatic man who attracted large congregations on Sundays with his powerful hellfire sermons. Unfortunately his charisma proved to be his undoing, as one evening when the owner of The Old Rectory was walking his dogs in the paddock on the other side of Spray Road, he came across the rector beneath a hedge in the arms of a woman who was decidedly not his wife. The woman in question was the headmistress of the village school who was required to relinquish her appointment when the affair was discovered. The scandal must have blazed brightly at the time, but it was shortlived and few can now even recall it. What really shook the village was not the scandal but the loss of its own rector and its rectory in the mid 1950s, when the parish became part of a combined benefice with Shalbourne. Whether it was due to this drop in status, or whether it was a symptom of other changes in the underlying pattern of village life, or both, church and churchyard drifted into neglect and decay over the next two decades.

In the early 1980s came two sharp jolts to rattle the parish out of this lethargy. The first was a threat that the church might face closure by the Salisbury diocese if it were unable to prove it was playing an active role in the community. At the time only a third of the adult population was on the church electoral roll and the church funds were in deficit. Alarmed at this prospect the Parochial Church Council wrote to every householder urging better support. Hard on the heels of this threat it was learnt that the church fabric needed repairing. At first this was a minor jolt only, as the cost appeared to be of the order of £12,000, but five years later this had risen inexorably to nearly £60,000 and a major fundraising operation was underway master-minded by the PCC treasurer, Ronnie Watson. The high point was a highly successful dance on a rock'n' roll theme, the Ham Hop, organised by Richard Gray, Michael Marriage and Andrew Melsom and held in the Dove's Farm mill on the Salisbury Road. Eventually the fundraising target was met with the help of a substantial grant from English Heritage. The work which mainly consisted of renewing the roof, the electric wiring and the lighting, and repainting the interior, was completed in 1990, and a special service was held in the church to celebrate the restoration.

The celebration, however, proved to be premature. A crisis emerged, and no ordinary crisis for a small village as almost inevitably Murphy's Law became rampant too. English Heritage discovered that the interior of the church had been painted with white emulsion rather than limewash and withheld the final tranche of its grant until this had been put right. The cost of correcting this mistake was estimated to be significant, and while the PCC blamed the architects, the architects blamed English Heritage for failing to make their instructions clear, and everyone stood their ground. Meanwhile the builders issued a writ for their overdue final payment. Fortunately this last problem was temporarily solved with a loan from the diocese. Legal advice was then taken, and letters were written to the Chief Executive of English Heritage and to the local Member of Parliament, but it would take nearly another five years before the crisis was finally resolved and the emulsion had been replaced by limewash. Once the furore had died down, another part of the church in need of restoration was tackled. The bell cradle in the tower had been unserviceable since the war, and perhaps even before then. The cradle was successfully repaired and a service of rededication was held in December 2000. Now, at long last, the bells could once again ring out in renewed celebration, as they had first done three centuries ago to celebrate the restoration of the monarchy and the return of the Anglican form of worship to All Saints' Church.

16

CODA

History is relentless, riding roughshod over the ends of centuries and never pausing to draw breath. Like fine wine, it tastes best when allowed a decade or two of bottle age before being set down in cold print, and so even though the first decade of the new century is already over, this part of Ham's story ends in the closing years of the 20th century. As it happens, the end of that century marks the culmination of the sea change in Ham's society, a sea change where – as Shakespeare put it – beneath the changes on the surface the past remains but in different forms. There are those still living in the village who mourn the passing of earlier times when for them the village was a simpler, more closely knit and less material society. A wistfulness for the past is nothing new. In 1877 Richard Jefferies, a passionate chronicler of the north Wiltshire countryside in the late 19th century, wrote this description of a model parish.

> A rural parish, if a well-selected specimen, forms of itself a miniature state, and contains representatives of the chief varieties of human life. It has its political boundaries, within which it enjoys considerable self-government. These have been carefully surveyed and mapped, and the map is preserved in the local archives. It has its constitution, and its geography – brooks in the place of rivers, coppices for forests – and one or more special products for export. The vestry forms an independent local council. Not many years since the resemblance was still more complete, when unpaid labour was expended upon the internal roads; each farmer taking his turn with waggons, horses, and men, to repair them. The poor of the place were relieved upon the spot, and the administration of that relief gave to the overseers an indirect power. At the same time there existed a local *esprit de corps*. [171]

In 1877 the internal combustion engine had only just become a commercially viable proposition, and it would be several decades before it made its critical impact on the farming world. This passage was also written before the introduction of parish councils under the Local Government Act of 1894. Yet it is still tinged with nostalgia for a former way of life. What is more remarkable is how much of the framework of Jefferies' miniature state can still be recognised in the Ham of today, although unlike his model parish Ham's *esprit de corps* has survived. Ninety years ago the talk in Ham was of tarring roads and the need for a village telephone;

today it is about traffic calming and the need for faster broadband. As for the land around the village, while farming is no longer central to the life of the village it is still the dominating influence in the wider parish, and as always, despite the advances of science, nature remains the great leveller.

It is easy to dwell on the 19th and 20th centuries, especially the latter, and they occupy half of Ham's story when set down on the printed page. This simply reflects the increasing availability of records and in more recent times the vibrancy of living memory. The earlier centuries which chart the genesis of the village and its frequent struggles for survival are inevitably more distant drums. Fortunately in Ham it is still possible with a little imagination to reach out and touch those earlier centuries.

One winter's evening go and sit in All Saints' Church in the dark. Let the darkness and the cold seep into you. Then imagine the altar a blaze of candlelight at the far end. Candles also illuminate a statue of the Virgin Mary, the soft light burnishing the gilding on her halo. Other candles dimly light the nave. Before the altar stands the tonsured priest urging, pleading with the congregation to repent of their sins. Long ago he became accustomed to the stink rising from their unwashed bodies and clothing. But they are restless. It is cold, numbingly cold, and the adults are frightened, none of them wanting to believe that two of the Four Horsemen of the Apocalypse in the shape of the Black Death are galloping towards them at relentless speed. The male youths of the village, the fuzz of their nascent beards hardly darkening their cheeks, are only present under threat of dire punishment from their fathers. They too are frightened, but in a show of bravado they are openly ogling the older girls. In turn the girls, standing loosely with their parents, are trying to hide their giggles behind the palms of their hands while exchanging glances of sly complicity with their fellows, each one wondering which of the callow, pimply youths will one day be the first to tumble them in the hay.

Then choose a sunny day with large clouds racing across the sky to walk up Ham Hill. Take the footpath which veers off the Fosbury road before the nature reserve, and which centuries ago was possibly Burghard's *anstig* or steep hill path. Pause at the bottom and wonder how many feet trod that path in ancient times, and how many men, women and children cursed at the thought of that steep climb yet again in the course of their daily toil, whether in the heat of summer, in the wind and rain, or in the frost and snow of winter. The path is little more than a sheep track and then higher up a gentle indentation on the flank of the hill, reflecting how few feet tread it now. At the top you are on the ridgeway, the *herepath*, which must have been trodden by yet thousands more feet back to the very beginning of man's existence in that countryside. It would have been deeply rutted in past centuries as wagons were laboriously drawn along it in all weathers. It is still rutted today, but that it is largely due to a band of four-by-four enthusiasts intent on exercising their right to drive their vehicles along a byway without concern for the damage they do. Walk eastwards along it until you are abreast of Ham Spray

House. The track dips slightly at this point and swings to the right. Ahead of you is Rivar Copse, the Bull's Tail. Directly to your left you will see the pale green-washed south front of the house built by Henry Deacon Woodman in about 1850. A century later Frances Partridge wrote about 'its charming pink-washed Jane Austen front', but few people can now remember the house that colour as for most of the second half of the 20th century it was painted white. In the 1920s Dora Carrington would have ridden out from the house on her little white mare Belle to where you stand. Down below are the slopes where she once tobogganed with the laughing teenaged Olive Martin.

Now look half left (north-east) and in the middle distance you will see the tower of Inkpen church. Come forward of that and two fields away in the valley below you will see the line of a stream heading straight towards you. The stream disappears behind a line of woodland which is Inwood Copse. Two knuckles to the right of Inwood Copse, in the same field as the stream, is the site of the Roman villa. Wait until a shaft of sunlight washes over the field, and then imagine the walls and colonnades of the villa gleaming in its brightness.

Continue along the ridgeway until you reach the summit of Oswald's Hill. There is a byway marker post at this point. Turn sharp left off the ridgeway and walk 50 paces between the two lines of fences. Twenty paces directly in front of you, just inside the edge of Rivar Copse, is the bowl-barrow. It has been there for two and a half thousand years and is now half submerged in the tangle of scrub. Even so, it is still possible to visualise it as the last resting place of two Celtic warriors, who in their prime hunted in the forest below.

The ancient forest is long gone, but look westwards: the village of today is masked by trees and other woodlands still stud the landscape of the manor of Ham, which the first King of England gave to his loyal thane Wulfgar.

ILLUSTRATION CREDITS

Map of Parish of Ham with Saxon boundary markers (*Susie Eldridge*)

Aerial photograph of Ham Hill, June 1967 (*UK MOD Crown Copy Copyright 2011*)

Saxon boundary charter of 931 (*The British Library Board*)

Ham Manor mowing account for 1733 (*Berkshire Record Office*)

Drawing of memorial to John and Christian Hunt in All Saints' Church (*English Heritage*)

Rent roll for Ham, 1644 (*Berkshire Record Office*)

Petition opposing the opening of an alehouse in Ham, 1720 (*Wiltshire and Swindon Archives*)

Ham Manor farm accounts January–March 1754 (*Berkshire Record Office*)

Land tax list for Ham and Henley, 1780 (*Wiltshire and Swindon Archives*)

Drawing of Ham Manor, 1787 (*Susan Philipps*)

All Saints' Church from a watercolour by John Buckler, 1806 (*English Heritage*)

John Haines at the door of Rose Cottage (*Robin Tubb*)

Painting of Ham Manor by J.Adam, c.1880 (*Polly Woodman*)

Ham Manor c.1905 (*Valerie Barker*)

Henry Deacon Woodman with his second wife Lilla and family (*Valerie Barker*)

Ham Spray House, 2008 (*Richard Greenly*)

Dora Carrington, Saxon Sydney Turner, Ralph Partridge, Lytton Strachey (*National Portrait Gallery, London*)

Ceramic owl panel and fireplace tile, Ham Spray House (*Richard Greenly*)

Wansdyke (Wan's Dyke End) (*Richard Greenly*)

Major Geoffrey Huth (*Gerald Boord*)

NOTES

Abbreviations Used

BRO: Berkshire Record Office

HRO: Hampshire Record Office

VHCE-W: Victoria History of the Counties of England – A History of Wiltshire: unless otherwise stated this reference is to the history of Ham in Volume 11.

WSHC: Wiltshire and Swindon History Centre

1. In the early stages of the Second World War it was forbidden to ring church bells, as the ringing of church bells was a national signal that the invasion of Britain by Germany had begun. Church bells were, however, rung in 1942 as a national celebration of the victory at the battle of El Alamein. The state of the church bells cradle in the tower of All Saints' Church was already giving cause for concern during the war and would be repaired at the end of the century.

2. Details of Royal Observer Corps bunkers can be found on the internet.

3. VHCE-W Volume 1; map reference 34856202.

4. VHCE-W Volume 1.

5. VHCE-W Volume 1; map reference 349626.

6 Article on The Saxon Land Charters of Wiltshire by G. B. Grundy in The Archaeological Journal, Volume LXXVI, Second Series XXVI, 1919.

7. Map reference 34986250.

8. The original charter is held in the British Library: Cotton Charter VIII. 16. Dr Scot McKendrick, Head of Western Manuscripts, comments: 'According to the experts, this is an authentic contemporary charter. Some Anglo-Saxon charters survive only in later copies, and are occasionally medieval forgeries.' The British Library also holds a 12th century copy, entered in the cartulary of the Old Minster, Winchester: Additional MS. 1350, ff. 81v–83r.

9. Dorothy Whitelock (Ed), The Anglo-Saxon Chronicle.

10. From the translation by Kevin Crossley-Holland, The Anglo-Saxon World.

11. A modern text of the medieval Latin and Old English is recorded in W.de G. Birch's Cartularium Saxonicum, Volume 2, 1887. Another version can be found on the internet: Anglo-Saxons.net.S416.

12. This boundary marker is referred to in G.B. Grundy's The Saxon Land Charters of Wiltshire, published in The Archaeological Journal, Volume LXXVI, Second Series XXVI, 1919.

13. Another source gives this as the 'Pond of the Green Quarry': A.F. Major quoting G.B. Grundy in The Wiltshire Archaeological & Natural History Magazine, Volume XLII, December 1924.

14. F.W. Maitland, Domesday Book and Beyond.

15. VHCE-W.

16. As above.

17. Marriage settlement dated 30 November 1676 set out as a Trust Deed from the Dean and Chapter of Winton. Ham Parish church records.

18. Will of John Hunt proved at Marlborough, 27 June 1750. WSHC.

19. Counterpart lease between The Dean of Winchester Cathedral and John Hunt Watts, dated 25 November 1779. HRO.

20. Wiltshire Feet of Fines, 1249 and 1250. WSHC.

21. VHCE-W.

22. Inquisitions Post Mortem Temp. Henry III to Edward II. WSHC.

23. Victoria History of Berkshire, Volume 4.

24. VHCE-W.

25. Indenture dated 1666, part of a bundle of papers headed 'In the Manor of Ham at the Court of the Manor there holden'. WSHC.

26. VHCE-W.

27. As above.

28. Plan of the Manor of Ham in the County of Wilts, the property of the Dean and Chapter of Winchester, 1810. HRO.

29. Enclosure Maps of Ham, 1828 and 1839. WSHC.

30. VHCE-W.

31. Original accounts of 1732 and 1733 held at BRO.

32. Richard Jefferies, *The Contents of Ten Acres – May 1883* from John Pearson (Ed), *Landscape and Labour*.
33. Will of John Aldridge of Ham in the County of Wilts Yeoman, dated 24 May 1753 and proved on 15 December 1753. WSHC.
34. Assignment dated 12 May 1762. WSHC.
35. Shalbourne tithe roll of 1845.
36. *English Episcopal Acta Vol VIII, Winchester 1070–1204*; Acta of Henry of Blois; 6 January 1171: final disposition to his monks, Winchester, cathedral priory of St Swithun.
37. J.R.H. Moorman, *Church Life in the Thirteenth Century*.
38. *VHCE-W*.
39. Wiltshire Feet of Fines, Edward I and II; 1362. WSHC.
40. Register of Wykeham. HRO.
41. Register of William Edington, Bishop of Winchester 1346–1366.
42. Geoffrey Chaucer, *The Canterbury Tales: The Prologue*.
43. Wiltshire Tax List of 1332. WSHC.
44. *VHCE-W*, Volume 4.
45. List of Rectors in All Saints' Church.
46. Reproduced from *A History of Wiltshire, Vol. 11*, (Oxford University Press, 1980) p.155, by permission of the Executive Editor.
47. Custumal of St Swithun's Priory, collated and translated by J.S. Drew. HRO.
48. As above.
49. B. Gummer, *The Scourging Angel – The Black Death in the British Isles*, page 153.
50. J.R. Lumby (Ed), *Chronicon Henrici Knighton vel Cnitthon monachi Leycestrensis*, 2 Vols, Rolls Series, 1889–95, II, pages 57–8.
51. J. Tait (Ed), *Chronica Johannis de Reading et Anonymi Cantuariensis 1346–67*, 1914, pages 88–9.
52. Register of William Edington, Bishop of Winchester, 1346–1366.
53. P.Vinogradoff, *Oxford Studies in Social and Legal History*, Volume V.
54. Mark Page (Ed), *The Pipe Roll of the Bishopric of Winchester 1301–2 and 1409–10*, Hampshire County Council, 1999.
55. *VHCE-W*, Volume 4.
56. A. Luders et al (Ed), *Statutes of the Realm 1101–1713*, 11Vols, 1810–28, Volume1 pages 307–8.
57. Joan Greatrex (Ed), *The Register of the Common Seal of the Priory of St Swithun*, 1978.
58. Taxation List of 1545. WSHC.
59. Taxation List of 1576. WSHC.
60. Facsimile (dated 1855) of a 17th century list of fines levied on Wiltshire gentlemen for not taking a knighthood at the coronation of Charles 1. WSHC.
61. Subsidy List Wiltshire, James 1, 23 Mar 8 (1608). WSHC.
62. Injunction 28 of 1547.
63. *VHCE-W*.
64. Salisbury Diocese R.O., Detecta Bk. 1550–3, f.141. (*VHCE-W*)
65. Ham Parish Meeting minutes of 6 April 1911. The cottages had been sold by permission of the Board of Guardians (Hungerford and Ramsbury Union) and the Local Government Board to a Mr W J Pocock for the sum of £90; the net proceeds of the sale were invested in 3% Consols.
66. *A Rent-roll (Ham) for ye Dean & Chapt. Wint. 1644*. BRO.
67. Additional manuscripts 22084 and 22085, from the books of the Wiltshire County Committee giving charges against the clergy 1645–6.
68. A.G. Matthews, *Walker Revised*.
69. As above.
70. *Parliamentary Church Survey in Wilts 1649–50*. WSHC.
71. A.G. Matthews, *Walker Revised*.
72. As above
73. Wiltshire Record Society, *Wiltshire Glebe Terrier 1588–1827*, December 1677.
74. Part of a letter (undated) to the President of (?)Trinity College from the Bishop of Winchester. HRO.
75. A.G. Matthews, *Walker Revised*.
76. Indenture, catalogue no 334/4. WSHC.
77. A.G. Matthews, *Walker Revised*.
78. H.G. Rawlinson, *Three Letters of Dr. Richard Traffles*.
79. Document A1/190/1 dated 1720 in a later hand. WSHC.
80. Research paper on licensing of innkeepers in the 18th century. WSHC.
81. N. Rees, *Epitaphs*. In the 19th century the following couplet was added, but it detracts from the charm of the original verse:
My Fire-dried corpse lies here at rest,
And, Smoke-like, soars up to be bless'd.
82. Will of Matthew Hunt. WSHC.
83. Ham Poor Fund accounts 1683–1797. WSHC.
84. Ham Estate Accounts Book 1749–1759. BRO.
85. Land Tax Assessment 1780. WSHC.

86. Ham Enclosure Act of 1827. WSHC.

87. *VHCE-W*, Volume 4.

88. Extract from Ham parish minutes.

89. *VHCE-W*.

90. The communion cup and cover and paten are recorded in J.E. Nightingale, *Church Plate of County of Wilts*, 1891. The maker's mark on the cup and cover of a sun in full splendour is recorded in I. Pickford (Ed), *Jackson's Silver and Gold Marks of England, Scotland and Ireland*; the entry refers to a communion cup which presumably is the Ham cup. The dates of both items are given as spanning two years, as the hallmark date letter formerly changed on St Dunstan's Day, 19 May, and not 1 January as it does now.

91. All three men would later become in-pensioners of the Royal Hospital Chelsea.

92. Captain Swing was the *nom de plume* of the leader of the rioters, but whether he was an actual person or whether it was a generic name for the leadership is not known. The name appeared as a signature on various handbills setting out the rioters' grievances.

93. National Archives.

94. *The Times*, 10 January 1831.

95. As above.

96. *The Times*, 2 November 1830.

97. *The Times*, 19 January 1830.

98. Act of 21 March 1827. WSHC.

99. Land Tax Assessment for Ham, 1800.

100. A Terrier of Ham, 1810. HRO.

101. Farm accounts for Ham Spray. Woodman family papers.

102. Land Tax Assessment for Ham, 1839.

103. *VHCE-W*.

104. Woodman family papers.

105. As above.

106. *VHCE-W*.

107. Mortgage dated 29 August 1857; reconveyance dated 29 August 1868. Woodman family papers.

108. Ham Spray farm accounts (Woodman family papers) and table of national wages, Lord Ernle, *English Farming Past and Present*.

109. Lord Ernle, *English Farming Past and Present*.

110. *VHCE-W*.

111. Ham School log book. WSHC.

112. Quoted in David Hoseason Morgan, *Harvesters and Harvesting 1840–1900. A study of the Rural Proletariat*.

113. *Hungerford Union: Workhouse Births and Deaths 1866–1914*, published in 2005 by The Eureka Partnership based on information held by the BRO.

114. As above.

115. As above.

116. As above.

117. Plans of school. WSHC.

118. Ham School log book. WSHC.

119. As above.

120. Ham Spray estate sale brochure of 1879. WSHC.

121. *Life In The Victorian Village: "The Daily News" Survey of 1891. Vols 1 and 2*, published by Caliban Books.

122. Sale particulars of Dove's Farm, 1900. WSHC.

123. Wiltshire Emigration Society records held by WSHC.

124. Hissey family records based on a family publication *A Shepherd Came From Buttermere – The Family Tree of Charles Hissey*.

125. Woodman family papers.

126. Sale brochures, Woodman family papers.

127. *VHCE-W*.

128. As above.

129. As above.

130. *Punch*, 19 December 1891.

131. Ham School log book. WSHC.

132. Woodman family papers.

133. *VHCE-W*.

134. Ham Parish Meeting minutes.

135. Agricultural returns. WSHC.

136. *VHCE-W* and Ham estate papers, WSHC.

137. Ham estate papers. WSHC.

138. As above.

139. As above.

140. Kelly's Directory and 1911 census return for Ham.

141. Ham Parish Meeting minutes.

142. Woodman family papers.

143. Woodman papers. WSHC.

144. As above.

145. Ham Parish Meeting minutes.

146. *VHCE-W*.

147. Loose leaf minute of Wiltshire War Agriculture Committee; agricultural census 11 December 1916 – with Ham agricultural returns. WSHC.

148. Manuscript return of Samuel Farmer, December 1916 – with Ham agricultural returns. WSHC.

149. Scots Guards records.

150. Ham School log book. WSHC.

151. P.E. Dewey, *British Agriculture in the First World War*.

152. Ham Parish Meeting minutes.

153. Ham School log book. WSHC.

154. Ham Parish Meeting minutes.

155. D de H Carrington, *Carrington: Letters and Extracts from her Diaries*, letter from Carrington to Gerald Brenan, 23 October 1923. Reproduced by permission of A P Wyatt on behalf of The Executors of the Estate of David Garnett and Sophie Partridge.

156. M. Holroyd, *Lytton Strachey: A Critical Biography, Volume 2*. Other sources give the purchase price as £2,100 and £2,000. The only precise factor is the asking price of £3,000 advertised by Harrods Estate Office in *Country Life*, and it seems unlikely that Strachey would have been able to beat the price down below £2,300.

157. D de H Carrington, *Carrington: Letters and Extracts from her Diaries*, letter from Carrington to Gerald Brenan, 22 January 1927. Reproduced by permission of A P Wyatt on behalf of The Executors of the Estate of David Garnett and Sophie Partridge.

158. As above, page 341. Reproduced by permission of A P Wyatt on behalf The Executors of the Estate of David Garnett and Sophie Partridge.

159. M. Holroyd, *Lytton Strachey: A Critical Biography, Volume 2*, page 480

160. D de H Carrington, *Carrington: Letters and Extracts from her Diaries*, letter from Carrington to Gerald Brenan, 19 October 1924. Reproduced by permission of A P Wyatt on behalf of The Executors of the Estate of David Garnett and Sophie Partridge.

161. Marlborough and Ramsbury Rural District Council planning records. WSHC.

162. V. Sackville-West, *The Women's Land Army*.

163. F. Partridge, *A Pacifist's War*, page 48.

164. V. Sackville-West, *Country Notes in Wartime*.

165. Major E.A. Mackay (Ed), *The History of the Wiltshire Home Guard* (1946).

166. Cecil Hoare died in 2011.

167. F. Partridge, *A Pacifist's War*, entry for 30 April 1945.

168. There are two portraits of the Hon. Angela Delevingne (née Greenwood) in the National Portrait Gallery.

169. Ramsbury Rural District Council planning records. WSHC.

170. Dove's House was profiled in *House and Garden*, March 2007.

171. R. Jefferies, *Landscape and Labour*, essay: *The Future of Country Society*, 1877.

BIBLIOGRAPHY

Adamson, J, *The Noble Revolt – The Overthrow of Charles I*, Phoenix, 2007

Birch, W. de G, *Cartulorium Saxonicum: a collection of charters relating to Anglo-Saxon History. Volume 2*, Whiting, 1885–93

Brigden, R, *Victorian Farms*, Ramsbury – Crowood Press, 1986

Caliban Books, *Life in the Victorian Village: The Daily News Survey of 1891 –Volumes 1 and 2*, Caliban, 1999

Campbell, J, *The Anglo-Saxon State*, Hambledon and London, 2000

Carrington, D de H,*Carrington: letters and extracts from her diaries/ chosen and with an introduction by David Garnett, with a biographical note by Noel Carrington*, Jonathan Cape, 1970

Chisholm, A, *Frances Partridge, The Biography*, Weidenfeld & Nicholson, 2009

Crittal, E. (Ed), *Victoria History of the Counties of England – A History of Wiltshire*, Volume 4, Oxford: for the Institute of Historical Research by Boydell & Brewer, 1959

Crossley-Holland, K, *The Anglo-Saxon World*, The Boydell Press, 1982

Crowley, D. A. (Ed), *Victoria History of the Counties of England – A History of Wiltshire*, Volume X1, Oxford University Press, 1980

Cutler, C. (Ed), *Kintbury Through The Ages*, Kintbury Volunteer Group, 2004

Day, J, *Gloucester & Newbury 1643, The Turning Point of the Civil War*, Pen and Sword, 2007

Dewey, P. E, *British Agriculture In The First World War*, Routledge, 1989

Domesday Book, The Folio Society, 2003

Dove, P.E, *Domesday Studies*, Longmans, Green & Co, 1886

Duffy, E, *The Stripping of the Altars: Traditional Religion in England c1400–c1580*, Yale University Press, 1992

Enfield, R. R, *Agricultural Crisis 1920–23*, Longmans, Green & Co, 1924

Ernle, Lord, *English Farming Past and Present*, Longmans, Green & Co, 1919 (2nd Edition)

Fennel, R, *The Common Agricultural Policy*, Clarendon Press, Oxford, 1997

Fleming, A. and Hingley, R, (Ed), *Prehistoric and Roman Landscapes*, Windgather Press, 2007

Gaunt, W, *English Rural Life in the 18th Century*, The Connoisseur, 1925

Gentles, I, *The English Revolution & The Wars in the Three Kingdoms 1638–1652*, Pearson Longman, 2007

Gerzina, G, *Carrington, A Life of Dora Carrington 1893–1932*, John Murray, 1989

Goodden, H, *Camouflage and Art – Design for Deception in World War 2*, Unicorn Press, 2007

Gummer, B, *The Scourging Angel – The Black Death in the British Isles*, Bodley Head, 2009

Hammond, R. J, *Food and Agriculture in Britain 1939–45: Aspects of Wartime Control*, Stanford University Press, 1954

Holroyd, M, *Lytton Strachey, A Critical Biography*, Volume 2, Heinemann, 1968

Hooke, D. (Ed), *Anglo-Saxon Settlements*, Blackwell, 1988

Hooke, D, *The Landscape of Anglo-Saxon England*, Leicester University Press, 1998

Horrox, R, (Translated and Ed), *The Black Death*, Manchester University Press, 1994

Jefferies, R, *Hodge And His Masters*, Smith, Elder & Co, 1880

Jefferies, R, *Landscape and Labour*, essays and letters collected by John Pearson, Moonraker Press, 1979

Keats-Rohan, K. S. B, *Domesday People*, The Boysdell Press, 1999

Kumin, B, *The Shaping of a Community: the Rise & Reformation of the English Parish c.1400–1560*, Scolar Press, 1996

Kynaston, D, *Austerity Britain 1945–51*, Bloomsbury, 2007

Kynaston, D, *Family Britain 1951–57*, Bloomsbury, 2009

Laing, L, *Celtic Britain*, Routledge & Kegan Paul, 1979

Maitland, F. W, *Domesday Book and Beyond*, University Press, 1897

Margary, I. D, *Roads in Roman Britain*, Dial House, 1967

Morgan, D. H, *Harvesters and Harvesting 1840–1900, A Study in the Rural Proletariat*, Croom Helm, 1982

Moorman, J.R.H, *Church Life in England in the Thirteenth Century*, Cambridge University Press, 1945

Morrill, J. (Ed), *Reactions to the English Civil War 1642–1649*, Macmillan, 1982

Partridge, F, *A Pacifist's War*, The Hogarth Press, 1978

Partridge, F, *Everything To Lose, Diaries 1945–1960*, Victor Gollanz Ltd, 1985

Partridge, F, (Edited by Rebecca Wilson), *Diaries 1939–1972*, Weidenfeld & Nicholson, 2000

Pugh, R.B. and Crittal,E. (Ed), *Victoria History of the Counties of England – A History of Wiltshire*, Volume 1, 1957, and Volume 2, 1955, Oxford: for the Institute of Historical Research by Boydell & Brewer

Purkiss, D, *The English Civil War: A People's History*, Harper Press, 2006

Rees, N, *Epitaphs: a dictionary of grave epigrams and memorial eloquence*, Bloomsbury, 1993

Rogers, J. E. T, *History of Agriculture & Prices in England, Volume VII 1703–93. Part II*, 1902

Sackville-West,V, *Country Notes in Wartime*, The Hogarth Press, 1940

Sackville-West,V, *The Women's Land Army*, Michael Joseph, 1944

Shalbourne to the Millennium, Antony Rowe Ltd, 1999

Snyder, C. A, *The Britons*, Blackwell, 2003

Stenton, F. M, *The Oxford History of England: Anglo-Saxon England*, Oxford University Press, 1947

Stratton, J. M, *Agricultural Records 220–1968*, J.Baker, 1969

Surman, C.E, *A.G. Matthews' Walker Revised (being a revision of John Walker's Sufferings of the Clergy during the Grand Rebellion 1642–60)*, Dr Williams's Trust, 1956

Thorn, C and F (Ed), *Domesday Book, Wiltshire*, Phillimore, 1979

Trevelyan, G. M, *British History in the 19th Century and After (1782–1919)*, Longmans Green& Co Ltd, 1937

Vinogradoff, P, *Oxford Studies in Social and Legal History*, Volume V, Clarendon Press, 1916

Wade Martins, S, *Farmers, Landlords and Landscapes (Rural Britain 1720 to 1870)*, Windgather Press, 2004

Warner, G. T. and Marten, C.H.K, *The Groundwork of British History*, Blackie, 1923

White, R. H, *Britannia Prima*, Tempus, 2007

Whitelock, D (Ed), *The Anglo-Saxon Chronicle*, Eyre and Spottiswoode, 1965

Williamson, T, *The Transformation of Rural England – Farming and the Landscape 1700–1870*, University of Exeter Press, 2002

Wilt, A.F, *Food For War – Agriculture and Rearmament in Britain before the Second World War*, Oxford University Press, 2001

Woolrych, A, *Battles of the English Civil War*, Batsford, 1961

Wroughton, J, *An Unhappy Civil War: The Experiences of Ordinary People in Gloucestershire, Somerset and Wiltshire 1642–46*, Lansdown Press, 1999

Ziegler, P, *The Black Death*, Readers Union, 1969

INDEX

Figures in bold denote illustrations

Abercromby, Squadron Leader and Mrs
  154
Acorn Cottages 24, 139, 145, 154, **166**
Acre 28
Æffe 25
Æthelstan 9, 20–1
Agricultural Revolution 81–3, 90
Albert, Prince 87
Aldridge, James 43, 160
Aldridge, John 43
Alexander, William 105
Alfred the Great 10, 19–20
All Saints' Church 10, 33, 44–7, **45**, 49, 53,
  55, 60–1, 65, 86–9, 93, 118, 126, 134,
  152–3, 158, 166, 176–7, 179
American Civil War 106
Andrews and Dury map 39
Annett, Sarah 102
Annett, Thomas 102
Anrep, Boris 130
Archers, The 168–9
Arkell, Rev John 126
Ashley Coppice 24
Ashley Drove 24, 29, 41, 50, 86, 136
Atrebates 13

Baer 22–3
Baileys 175
Baker, William 97
Bakewell, Robert 90
Banting, John 131
Barclay, Sarah Jane 125, 157
Barclay, William 125, 157
Baring, Diana 163
Baring, Nicholas 163
Barker, Valerie 151
Barnes, George 94
Barnes, William 92
Bartholomew, Billy 151
Bartholomew, Sergeant William 151
Batt (widow) 66
Beale, Sir William and Lady 165
Bear Hotel (Inn), Hungerford 94, 134
Bedewynd, Williamus de 45
Bedwyn, Little 118
Bedwyn, Great 10, 14, 63, 118
Beeches, The 141, 171
Bell, Vanessa 131
Bennet 84
Bennet (Benet), Michael 65, 87
Bennet, Ann 65
Bennet, Grace 66
Bennet, Robert 77
Beowulf 20, 24–5
Beveridge Report 147

Biggs, Captain 159
Billington 128
Bird, Bill 156
Bird, Micky 156
Bishop's Barn 50, 136
Black Death 31, 45, 47–8, 52–7, 84
Blackbirds 88
Blackmore, Charlotte 103
Blake, Andrew 171
Blake, John 58
Blois, Henry of 44
Bloody Assizes 69
Bloomsbury Group 9, 128–134, 148, 155–6
Blundy 84
Blundy, Robert 90
Boord, Colonel 150
Boord, Gerald 169–70
Boord, Julia 169–70
Bothy, The 144
Bowl-barrow 12, **15**, 23, 180
Bowley 109
Bowley, Betsy Anne 162
Bowley, Charles 92–3, 124–5
Bowley, George 93
Bowley, Henry 97
Bowley, Hester 93
Bowley, Jesse 133, 140, 148, 152
Bowley, Tom 132
Bowley, Wilfred 124
Bowley, Winnie 133, 140, 148
Bowling Drove 42
Boyler, Thomas 57–8
Breach Cottages 144
Brereton, Captain Frederick 120, 125
Bridge Cottage – see Candlemas Cottage
Bright, Robert 41, 65, 76, 82, 84
Britannia Prima 16
Bronze Age 12, 13
Brook House 88, 167
Brookes, John 43
Brotherton family 43
Brotherton, Thomas William 39
Brotherton, William Browne 38–9, 82
Brown, Arthur 88
Brown, Marion 88
Brown, Martha 105
Brown, Ralph 132–3, 136, 140–1, 152, 165,
  175
Brownjohn, Katherine 68
Brunsden, Benjamin 104
Bull's Tail 22, 180
Bungalow, The 147
Bunggy de Buttermere, William 33, 49
Bungum Lane 14, **18**
Burder, Rev Charles 111–2

Burder, Sarah 112
Burghard 22–3, 29, 179
Bush, John 105
Bushel's copyhold 94
Bushell, John 39, 82
Bushnell, Rev John 39, 82
Buttermere 13, 21, 23, 33, 36, 80, 109, 127,
  151, 162, 169–70, 175

Caesar, Julius 12, 13
Can(n)on, Thomas 57–8
Candlemas Cottage 85, 154
Canning, John 39
Cannings 38, 121
Canterbury, Archbishop of 55
Canute 19
Captain Swing Riots 80, 92–3, 125
Carrington, Dora 128–34, **133**, **134**, 156,
  180
Celts 10, 12, 13, 16, 23, 30
Chalff, John 48
Chandler, Joseph 151
Chandler, Mrs 132
Chandler, Sergeant John 151
Chandler, Thomas 125
Chant, Anne 157, 173
Chant, Doreen 157, 173
Chant, John 157, 173
Chant, Lilian 157
Chant, William 157
Chaplin, Edith 58
Charles I 58, 62–3, 66, 68
Charles II 69, 87
Chaucer, William 47
Chilbolton 50
Chisholm, Anne 131, 156
Church Road 42
Churchscot 50
Civil War 31, 37, 62–71, 87
Clarke, John 39
Clarke, Richard 39, 57–8
Claudius, Emperor 13
Clayton, George 97
Clerke, John le 38, 48–9
Clubmen 64
Cobbet, William 91, 93, 96
Cobbett's Rural Rides 96
Coke, Thomas 90
Coleman, Rev 108
Collingbourne 21
Combe Gibbet 128
Common Agricultural Policy 165, 171
Commonwealth 31, 67–71
Communion cup 89, **89**, note 90
Cooper, Francis 82

Cooper, John 65
Cooper, William 67
Cooper's copyhold 94
Corn Law(s) 92, 99
Corn Production Act 1917 127
Corporation of Sons of the Clergy 89
Corpus Christi College, Oxford 67–8
Cottager 29, 51
Couling, John 169
Couling, Margaret 169
Couling, Walter 151–2
Couling, William 135, 148, 152
Court of the Manor of Ham 94
Covenant, Thomas 48
Cowderoy, Thomas 35, 39, 94
Cowley, James 94
Cowley's Copse 41
Cripps, Colin and Lilian 173–4
Cripps, James 125
Cripps, Jane (aka Watts) 99
Crofton 36–7
Cross Keys Inn 72, 102–3
Crown & Anchor 41, 72, 85, 88, 102–3,
    122, 123, 132, 167, 168, 172
Cuckoo's Nest 102
Cummins 84
Cummins, Leonard 152
Cummins, Samuel 96
Curle 65
Cutting Hill 22, 73, 103, 147, 172
Cynegilis 17

D'Avenant, Rev Thomas 94
Daily News, The 107–8, 111–2
Danes 10, 17, 19
Daniel's Lane 17
Darwin, Ginette 163
Darwin, Sir Robin 162–4
Dasevyle, John 48
Deacon, Martha 97
Delevingne, Dudley and the Hon Angela
    69, 165
Denford 21
Digweed, George 97
Digweed, John 97
Diocletian, Emperor 16
Directory of Worship 67
Dixon (Hoare), Ivy 127, 153
Domesday Book 20, 25–30, 36, 52, 136
Dove, Daniel 39
Dove's Farm 32, 35, 39, 49, 58, 85, 108, 115,
    119, 136, 141, 145, 162, 170–1, 177
Dove's Farm Cottage 85, 138, 171–2
Doves Farm Foods 171
Dove's Farmhouse 85
Dove's House 35, 85, **85**, 97–8, 119–20,
    133–4, 148–9, 171
Dove's House Cottages 132, 134, 138, **138**,
    172
Dove's Yard 39, 159, **160**, 172

Drove Cottage 144
Dyer, Richard 65, 77

East Court Farm 27, 32, 35–9, **38**, 43, 49,
    58, 86, 94, 121, 125, 132, 136, 140, 148, 170
Edington, William of 47, 53
Education Act 1870 100
Edward the Confessor 26
Edward the Elder 20
Edward VI 60
Edward VII 117, 122
Elizabeth I 60
Elizabethan Poor Law 1601 76, 92
Elson, Thomas 82
Elstob and Everleigh Hundred 27
Elston Lodge 145
Elton, William 65, 77, 88
Elwes, Major and Mrs Guy 155
Enclosure Act 1827 82–3
Enclosure Act Award 1828 94, **95**, 167–8

Faccombe 68–9
Faller, Thomas 33, 57
Farmer, Samuel 118–9, 121–3, 136
Fawler (see Faller)
Fernedown 172
Festival of Britain 164
Field Firing Range 152
Field House 41, 172
Field Lane 24, 42–3
Field Names:
    Aldridge's Ground 43
    Beow's Meadow 22, 24–5
    Breach Meadow 41
    Brights Meadow 41
    Cocks Balls 41
    Cow Leaze 41
    Cowleaze Severalls 41
    Culvers Meadow 41, 88
    Flaxlea 22, 25
    Further Down 13, 23
    Further Severalls 41
    Great Field 24, 41 83, 136
    Grubbed Mead 41
    Haying Field 41
    Hoglands 41
    Home Meadow 83
    How Mead 43
    Lashmoor 24, 41
    Little Field 83
    Lower Ashley Field 24
    Middles Severalls 41
    Milking Ground 41
    Pidget Corner 23
    Pidget's Field 23, 41, 43, 83
    Pool Meadow 24
    Rickyard Field 41, 158
    Several Mead 83
    Severalls 41

Square Mead 43
    The Down 41
    The Old Meadow 42
    Upper Blacklands 15
Flaxlea Cottage 144
Flewell, Harriet 96
Flewell, John 96
Flewell, Richard 94, 96
Flower, Charles 169
Foghel, Henry 48
Forbes, Misses 172
Forde, Henricus de 46–7
Foreman, Geoffrey 48
Forge Cottage 74, 86, 138–9, 141, 154–5,
    164
Fosbury (Road) 13, 24, 86, 145, 179
Fowlmere 22, 24
Francis, Henry 103
Francis, Thomas 103, 126
Fruen, Enoch 103
Furlong 26, 28
Fursby, Miss 126

Garden Cottage 144
Gauntlett, Sidney 120
Gibbs, Ernest 141
Gillingham, Mary 88
Gillingham, Rev Richard 74, 77, 88–9
Goddard 84
Godden, Professor Malcolm 21, 25
Godnynge, Adam 48
Godwin 19
Goldsmiths' Company 164
Gomm, Rev William 94
Goodhart, Honor 149
Grant, Duncan 131
Gray, Mary 131
Gray, Richard 131, 177
Green, Simon and Helen 171
Greensand Cottage 144
Grendel 24
Grendel's Mere 22, 24–5
Grey, Lord 93
Grym, John 48
Gunter, Ferdinand 38
Gunter, Margaret 38
Gunter, Thomas 37–8
Guyatt, Richard 164

Habgood 84
Habgood, John 82
Habgood, Richard 82
Habgood, Thomas 103
Hadham, Nicholas 46–7
Hague, Janie 165
Haines, John 158, **158**
Haines, Reg 70, 152, 158
Haines, Richard 96
Halydaye, Ricardus 60
Ham Cross 39, 121, 159–60, **160**, 161

Ham Green Cottage **161**, 172
Ham Hill 10, 13, 17, 23–4, 50, 81, 100, 106 (white horse), 130, 140, 166–8, 179
Ham Hill Nature Reserve 13, 16
Ham Manor (manor house) 29, 32, 39, 69, 75, 85, **86**, **107**, 117, **118**, 120, 132–3, 136–7, **137**, 165
Ham Manor estate 9, 33–5, 42, **42**, 49, 58, 78, **79**, 81, 94, 99–100, 119, 122, 127, 136, 141, 154, 170
Ham Road 22, 24, 29, 73, 103, 132, 147
Ham Spray (estate) 32, 39, 94, 96, **97**, 99–100, 106, 115, **116**, 119, 121, 123, 136, 140–2, 154, 169
Ham Spray Cottage 120
Ham Spray House 86, 98, 120, 128–9, **129**, **130**, 131, **131**–4, 142, 144, 149–50, 155–7, 167, 179
Ham Spray Lodge 120
Ham, Isabel of 36
Ham, John of 36
Ham, Walter of 36–7, 49
Ham, William of 36
Hamm 29
Hamme, Ralph of 47, 53, 55
Hansford, Monty 171
Happy Valley 145, 156, 172
Harald, John 56
Harding, Elizabeth 102
Harding, Elsie 132, 135, 158
Harding, John 82
Harris, Sarah 112
Harvest 101–2
Harvest Festival 103
Harvest Home 103
Hatton, Frederick 132, 172
Haxton 57
Hayfield 147
Hayward 50–1
Hayward, Philip 77
Henley 23, 57
Henry III 36, 60
Henry VIII 60
Herbagium 51
Hercomb 84
Hercomb, Alice 103
Hercomb, Anne 103
Hercomb, Joseph 72, 77
Hercomb, Mary 72, 77
Hercomb, Reuben 103
Hide 26–7
Hill House 86
Hill, Frederick 136, 145, 148
Hill, Mrs 149–50
Hillebrand 161
Hissey, Charles 109–10
Hissey, Maurice 109
Hitchman 84
Hitchman, William 77
Hoare, Cecil 153

Hoare, George 97
Hoare, Ivy 127, 155
Hobbs, Richard 77
Hodge 90–1, 113–4
Hodges, Michael 65
Holdway, John 103
Home Guard 152
Hopkins 77
Hopkins, George 104
Hore, Elizabeth 87
Hore, William 58, 87
Hudson, Viscount (Robin) 136, 148, 162, 170
Humphris, William 96
Hungerford 29, 50, 63–4, 80, 118, 132, 150, 155, 157–8, 169, 173, 176
Hungerford Poor Law Union 99, 141
Hungerford Workhouse 99, 104, 111
Hunt 33, 84
Hunt, Christian 33, 61, **61**
Hunt, Edward 34, 82
Hunt, Henry 34, 68
Hunt, John 33–4, 57–8, **59**, 60–1, **61**, 63, 65, 68, 75, 77–8, 87–9
Hunt, Joseph 124
Hunt, Laurence 65
Hunt, Matthew 65–6, 74–6
Hunt, Thomas 68
Hunt, William 87
Hutchins, William 126
Huth, Gladys 135, 142, 144, 169
Huth, Major Geoffrey 131, 135–6, **135**, 142, 144–5, 147, 149–50, 154–6, 165–7, 169

Ibthorpe House 128
Industrial Revolution 91
Inkpen 14, 21–2, 29, 35, 52, 142, 144, 148–9, 154, 158
Inkpen Beacon 10, 128
Inkpen Ridgeway 50, 179
Inwood Copse 14, **18**, 23, 180
Isabel, Lady – daughter of Edward III 36, 46
Ivy Cottage 121, **121**, 132–3, 140, 145, 151, 160, **161**

Jackass (severall) 94
Jackson, Alan 169
James I 58
Jameson, Lady (Elizabeth) 159–60, 175
Jameson, Rear Admiral Sir William 159
Jefferies, Richard 115, 178, note 32

Kavanagh, James 106
Kemp, Miss 157
Kennet and Avon Canal 10, 118, 152
King 84
Kintbury 144, 80, 92
Kinwardstone Hundred 27
Knight 77

Knight, James 103
Knights Templar 15, 49

Lamb, Henry 131
Lansley, Norman and Rose 172–3
Laud, Archbishop 66
Laurels, The (see Dove's House)
Lee, John 165, 170
Lee, Sandra 170
Levett, Professor Elizabeth 54–5
Levick, Henry 98
Levy 109
Levy, Frank 110
Levy, James 126
Levy, Sarah 109
Lewdon, Katherine 57
Lewenden, John 58
Lilac Bank 172
Linkenholt 149
Little Field 86, 138
Littlefield Cottage 24
Locrix, Matilda 51
Lodge, The 145
Long 84
Lower Spray 24, 41, 169
Lowsley-Williams, Ben and Charlotte 160
Luton 20
Lynch Farm (Shalbourne) 43, 160
Lynch, The 24, 29, 167

Mackrell, James 77, 80, 82
Mahony, J 105–6
Malthouse Cottage 148
Mander, Robert 145
Manor Cottages 85, **122**, 157
Manor Farm 32, 115, 136, 138, 141, 148, 165, 167, 170
Manor Farm Cottages 61, 86, 145
Manor Farm House 34, 39, 86, 140, 165, 167
Marchman, Samuel 43
Marlborough 63, 80, 166
Marriage, Clare 171
Marriage, Michael 171, 177
Marriage, Paul 170
Marshall, Frances (see also Frances Partridge) 129, 134, **134**
Martin, James 124
Martin, Olive 129–30, 180
Martyn, Thomas 57
Martyn, William 57
Mary, Queen 60
Melsom, Andrew 177
Melsom, Melanie 165
Mercia 19, 20
Merriot, Robert 65
Miller (brothers) 165, 170
Mills, Elizabeth 109
Mills, Emily 109
Mills, George 155

Mills, John 109
Mills, William 82
Moordown Farm 36, 127, 136
Mortymer, John 48
Mortymer, Roger 48
Mount Prosperous 17
Mr Crabtree Goes Fishing 170
Mulle, Walter atte 36, 48–9
Mulleward, Thomas de Shereborne 46
Mullin, George 107

Nash, Edith 112
Netherfield 72
New Buildings 86, 136
New Minster, Winchester 27
Newbury 63, 150, 158
Newbury, battles of 62, 64–5
Newlin, Rev Henry 67, 87
Newlin, Nicholas 67
Newlin, Rev Robert 67–8, 74
Norman Conquest 10, 26, 44, 48
Norman, William 48
Northumbria 20, 23

Old Dyke Lane 17, **18**, 22, 24
Old English 29
Old Malthouse, The (Old Malthouse
    Cottages) 84, 104, **104**, 121, 132–3, 155,
    172
Old Minster, Winchester 25, 27
Old Rectory, The 67, 112, 133, 145, **146**, 160,
    162, **163**, 176
Old School House 85, 105, 175
Oppenheim, Nicholas 138
Opperman, Ernest 160–2
Opperman, Michael 161–2
Orchard House 165, 171
Ordinance of Labourers 55–6
Oswald, Saint 23
Oswald's Hill (*Oswaldes Berghe*) 12, 15,
    22–3
Ottersford 22, 24
Oxenwood 153

Pannage 51
Parish Council 111, 113, 167–8
Parish Meeting 111, 117, 120, 126–7, 150, 167
Partridge, Frances 129, 131, 133–4, **134**,
    148–51, 155–7, 180
Partridge, Ralph 128–9, 131–4, **133**, **134**,
    149–50, 155, 157, 159
Patagonia 109–10
Payne, Humphrey 89
Peasants' Revolt 56
Pembroke, Earl of 35–6
Pettit, Prudence 104
Pettits172
Pewsey, Vale of 12, 17
Philipps (family) 69
Philipps, Clare 165

Philipps, Jeremy 165
Philipps, Nicola (Nicky) 165
Philipps, Susie 165
Phillips, Mrs 171
Pidget Coppice 23
Pills Lane 15, 88, 139, 158–9, 167–8
Pinn, Herbert 125
Pinniger, Stanley 120, 129, 142
Pithouse, John 101
Pithouse, Mary 101
Plough (land measurement) 28
Polden 161
Polhampton family 37
Polhampton, Adam 38
Polhampton, Anne 38
Polhampton, Christian 37, 46
Polhampton, Edmund 33
Polhampton, Geoffrey 37, 46
Polhampton, John 37–8, 57–8
Polhampton, Margaret (de) 36–7, 49
Polhampton, Richard (de) 36–7, 58
Polhampton, Thomas 58
Polhampton, William 38
Pollhamptons (copyhold) 43
Pond Cottage 86, 138, **140**
Pondfeld, Johannes de 49
Pontentyne, William 57
Poole, Kate 126
Poor Fund 76–8
Poor Law Amendment Act 1834 99, 104
Poor of Ham Freehold Allotment 87–8,
    139
Porch Cottages 84, **122**, 138
Portland, Adam and Isabella 36
Prosperous Farm 25, 81
Prosperous Road 22
Punch 91, 112–4, 148
Pyddi's Gate 17, 22–3

Radele, William 46
Ralph of Hamme 46
Ramsbury Rural District Council 110, 111,
    128, 141, 144, 146, 154, 166
Randall 77
Reform Bill (Fourth) 1918 126
Reform Bill 1884 114
Reformation 60, 67
Reprieve Cottages 85, **122**, 139, 144, 154–5,
    172
Restriction of Ribbon Development Act
    1935 147
Richardson 77
Righe, John atte 33, 48–9
Rights of way 167
Rivar Copse 12, **16**, 23, 106, 180
Rivar Hill 24
Rodwell, Rev George 133
Rolfe 84, 96
Rolfe, John 77
Rolfe, Kate 157

Rolfe, Rupert 157, 171
Rolph, Edward 66
Roman roads 13, 14
Roman villa 14, 15, 17, **18**, 22, 180
Roque, Jean (map) 39
Rose Cottage 85, **122**, **142**, 158, **158**
Rose, William 77
Rothschild, The Hon Jacob and Serena
    171
Rumbold 84
Russell, Benjamin 90
Ryder, Rev Derek 156
Rye, William de la 49
Ryve, Robert 57

Sackville-West, Vita 148, 151
Sainty, Julian and Emma 171
Salisbury, Bishop of 112
Salt, John 96
Savernake Forest 28
Saxon Charter 14, 20–25, **21**, notes 8,
    11–13
Saxon(s) 16, 17, 19, 23
Scammell, William 126
SCAT (Società Ceirano Automobili
    Torino) 120
School, Village 101, **101**, 105, 114, **122**, 127,
    164, **174**, 175
Scots Guards 120, 125
Scudet, William 16–7, 32, 35, 136
Scutt, Norman 133, 139
Serf 28
Severalls, The 145, **146**, 155
Shalbourne 24, 29, 35, 43, 80, 92, 109, 140,
    148, 150, 158, 176
Shearman, Alexander 74, 80, 86
Shearman, Susannah 74
Sheppard, George 92
Shereborne – see Mulleward
Shuttle, Robert 73
Simes 77
Simms (severall) 94
Skynnere, John le 48
Slazenger, Magda 156
Smales (widow) 65
Smith 84
Smith (Doctor) 77
Somerset, Duke of 60
Sope, Daniel 90
South Fawley 37
South House 86, 165
Spanish Armada 10
Speenhamland System 92, 99
Spowage, Jim 145
Spray Road 17, **18**, 22, 24, 25, 29, 41, 139,
    144, **146**, 150, 166–7, 176
St Swithun's Priory 27, 45–6, 51–2, 56, 60
St Swithun's Priory Custumal 49–52
Staddlestones 172
Stan ceastla 14, 44

Stapeton, John 48
Staunford, Williamus de 45
Stevens, Reg and Brenda 173
Stileman, Brigadier Edward 157
Stockley, Alfred 149
Stockwell, Edith 82
Strachey, Lytton 128–30, 132–4, **133, 134,**
    144
Sumner Smith, Rev 92
Sunningdale 172
Sutton, James 82
Swenestyche 52
Symes, Robert 66

Tallage 50
Tarratt, Ivy 155
Taylor, Reginald 151
Thatcham 61
Three Swans Hotel, Hungerford 106
Tidcomb 84
Tidcomb's copyhold 94
Times, The 92–3, 108, 112
Torner, John 82
Town and Country Planning Act 1947 145
Town Farm 23, 170
Townshend, Viscount 81, 90
Tractors 148–9
Trained Bands 64
Treasure, Mr 139
Tubb, Robin 158
Tucker, Fred 120, 125
Tucker, Jean 158
Tucker, Stanley 141
Tudor Cottage 69, **70,** 71, 71, 85, 138, 158
Tull, Jethro 81, 90
Turner, Jim 152, 171

Underwood, Isaac 96
Upper Greensand 12
Upper Spray 148

Vale House 145, 168, **168**
Vanderplank, Rev Israel 82
Vaughan, Mr Baron 92–3
Venables, Bernard 170
Victoria, Queen 87, 117
Village Hall 138, 141, 167, 175
Villager 29

Virgate, Virgaters 49–51
Vivash, Charles 102
Vivash, Emma 102

Waite, William 96
Walbury Hill , 50, 180
Walkelin, Bishop 28, 60
Walter, Charles 97
Walter, Tom 147
Wan's Dyke End 144, **144,** 156, 170
Wandsyke Farms 32, 43, 94, 148, 151–2,
    165, 168–71
Wansdyke 10, 16, 17, 19, 22, 144
Wansdyke Cottages 144
Warrant, William 66
Wash Common 62, 65
Waters, Sidney 124
Watson, Ronnie 177
Watts, Elizabeth 35
Watts, Francis Richens 35, 39, 94, 96, 99
Watts, George 35
Watts, John 32
Watts, John Hunt 33–5, 39, 82, 90, 94, 96
Watts, Mary 33, 35
Watts, Richard 33–5
Watts, Thomas 39
Webb, Geoffrey 168
Webb, Quentin 169, 173
Well Cottage (see also Reprieve Cottages)
    85, **122,** 138, **139,** 144, 155, 160
Wescott, Dorothy 175
Weston 77
Whale, John 103
Whale, Sophie 101, 103
Whatton, Mrs 145, 150, 160
Wheedon, Harold 169
Wheeler, Rev Charles 152
Wheller, James 82
Whistler, Rev Hugh 68–9
White horse 106
White, William 133
Whitlock, Ted 169
Wiggin, Dick 144
William the Conqueror 20, 26–7, 35, 44
Williamus de Bedewynd 45
Williamus de Staunford 45
Willoby, Thomas 97
Willoughby, John 92

Willowes, Rev Richard 67
Wilmer, Rev John 67
Wilson Brothers 120
Wilson, Henry 119–20
Wiltshire County Council 126, 154
Wiltshire Emigration Association 109
Wiltshire Emigration Society 109
Wiltshire Militia 92
Wiltshire Yeomanry 90
Wiltshire, War Agriculture Committee
    124–5
Winchester Cathedral, Dean and Chapter
    40, 60, 65, **66,** 116
Winchester pipe rolls 54–5
Winchester, Bishop of 27, 45–6, 50, 54–5,
    68, 112
Windy Ridge 172
Wintermans, Anna 165
Wodin 17
Women's Land Army 148
Women's Timber Corps 148–9
Wood, Charlotte 159–60
Wood, Felicity 159
Wood, Flora 160
Wood, Humphrey 159–60, 167
Wood, Susanna 160
Woodman, Annie 120, 126, 132–3
Woodman, Henry 96
Woodman, Henry Deacon 39, 61, 98, 100,
    102, 105–6, 108–10, 117–20, **119,** 136,
    140, 151, 180
Woodman, Hugh 119, 159
Woodman, Lilla 111, 119
Woodman, Martha 97
Woodman, Mary 98, 111, 120
Woodman, Polly 120, 126, 132–3, 159
Woodman, William 92–3, 96–8, **98**
Woodman, William (Willie) 109–10
Woodmere 22, 24
Woodward 50
Wright, Charles 98, 106
Wulfgar 9, 20, 25, 28, 123, 180
Wyatt, T. H. 87
Wykeham, William of 46
Wynton 51

Yew Tree Cottage 86, 154